Illustrator:
José L. Tapia
Barb Lorseyedi
Larry Bauer

Editor:
Stephanie Avera, M.S.

Editorial Project Manager:
Ina Massler Levin, M.A.

Editor-in-Chief:
Sharon Coan, M.S. Ed.

Art Director:
Elayne Roberts

Cover Artist:
Keith Vasconcelles

Product Manager:
Phil Garcia

Imaging:
Alfred Lau
David Bennett

Early Childhood Assessment

Author
Grace Jasmine

Teacher Created Materials, Inc.
P.O. Box 1040
Huntington Beach, CA   92647
ISBN-1-55734-465-5

©1995 Teacher Created Materials, Inc.   Made in U.S.A.

Table of Contents

Introduction 4

Part One—All About Assessment 6

What is Assessment?

Assessment Circle—Observation—Record and Document—Diagnose and Prescribe—Report and Enlist—Action

Assessment Overview

Teacher/Team/Program Assessment—Parents Helping the Process—Children Beginning to Self-Assess—Assessment and Self-Esteem—Maslow in the Classroom/Safe Places to Learn—Anti-Bias Assessment—Inclusion and Assessment—Emergent Curriculum and Assessment

Part Two—Deciding Your Assessment Style 146

Assessment Style Quiz

Assessment Style Quiz Answers

Using the Rest of the Book — Suggestions

Part Three—Four Ways To Focus 155

Developmentally Appropriate Assessment

Assessment Checklist—What is it?—What Are the Specifics?—Assessed Activities Section (Activities and Assessment Tools)

Traditional Assessment

Assessment Checklist—What is it?—What Are the Specifics?—Assessed Activities Section (Activities and Assessment Tools)

Portfolio Assessment

Assessment Checklist—What is it?—What Are the Specifics?—Assessed Activities Section (Activities and Assessment Tools)

Alternative Assessment

Assessment Checklist—What is it?—What Are the Specifics?—Assessed Activities Section (Activities and Assessment Tools)

Bibliography 399

Acknowledgements 400

Part One

Table of Contents

Introduction

- Part One—All About Assessment

  - What is Assessment?

  - Assessment Circle

  - Observation

  - Record and Document

  - Diagnose and Prescribe

  - Report and Enlist

  - Action

Assessment Overview
  - Teacher/Team/Program Assessment

  - Parents Helping the Process

  - Children Beginning to Self-Assess

  - Assessment and Self-Esteem

  - Maslow in the Classroom/Safe Places to Learn

  - Anti-Bias Assessment

  - Inclusion and Assessment

  - Emergent Curriculum and Assessment

Introduction

Assessment Made Easy

Assessment—is it a complicated, highly confusing, and tedious addition to your classroom? Or is it a pleasant, rewarding, and beneficial part of your facility's commitment to its children? It is true, assessment can be either. Assessment should be as positive and possible for you as anything else you consider important for your early childhood classroom. So *Early Childhood Assessment* has been created to bring all the options to you in an easy-to-use and multi-dimensional resource.

Make a Molehill Out of a Mountain

The first thing that any busy teacher thinks when confronted with yet another mountain of paper work or yet another responsibility is "Why me? Don't I already give my heart and soul and all my weekends to this place?" Yes, and that is exactly why *Early Childhood Assessment* is for you. We all can use an easily organized and simple way to take the variety of assessment choices and capsulize them into usable options. Here is how *Early Childhood Assessment* will work for you.

All in One Place

The research has been done for you. Assessment today has a variety of options. The National Association for the Education of Young Children (NAEYC) calls assessment

> *the process of observing, recording and otherwise documenting work that children do and how they do it, as a basis for a variety of educational decisions that effect the child. (NAEYC AND NAECS\SDE 1991, p. 21)*

Within this one resource, you will find all the new and traditional ideas regarding assessment in a usable, easy-to-read-and-retrieve form. A simple format has been created in order to look carefully and knowledgeably at all of the assessment options in our profession today, to see exactly what is happening and why and how.

What is Right for You?

Next, you will find The Assessment Style Quiz. After reading the beginning of this book, simply take the quiz and find out what kind of assessment, you or your facility, lean toward. Certainly, it is possible to combine a variety of different assessment tools, but it is more than likely you and your team will lean in one direction. The idea is to find a comfortable way to start or a good way to add to what you already have in place.

Introduction *(cont.)*

Now What?

After deciding in what direction you would like to proceed, simply turn to the corresponding section in *Early Childhood Assessment*. In this section you will find everything you could possibly want to know, even if you do not know what to ask. This book is designed to relieve your headache, not create one. You will see exactly what kind of assessment you are considering, how to do it, what you will need, and what you need to know. You will learn how to set it up in your facility, and how to make it work. You will have at your disposal a complete section of sample curriculum and assessment tools designed to work with each activity, for you to use immediately to begin your program without waiting. You will have time-saving parent letters and forms in blackline masters, as well as information on creating places to store your assessment materials and student samples. Finally, you will find a teacher resource section giving you ideas about where you can get more information, including books, organizations, and other resources to keep you and your facility on the cutting edge of early childhood assessment.

Making It Easy

Assessment is a challenge. Each of us understands that effective assessment enhances the educational experience of the children we teach. Its importance from the very beginning of their educational experience is vast. This book is designed to give you more time to do what you love to do—empower the lives of the children you teach and let them leave you ready to face the world of their continuing education.

Pat Yourself on the Back

What teachers are doing is never an easy job, but if early childhood educators pay close attention to the developing needs of children and the best ways to address those needs, they can and do impact lives. Teachers all deserve a pat on the back!

What is Assessment?

The Basics

Assessment is defined by the National Association for the Education of Young Children as

> *the process of observing, recording and otherwise*
> *documenting the work children do and how they do*
> *it as a basis for a variety of educational decisions*
> *that effect the child.*
> —*NAEYC and NAECS\SDE, p. 21*

That means that everything children do from the time they enter your school or center, as well as what they do at home, makes up the total package of things that are assessed to best help these children reach their full potential.

Test Confusion

For years, and still in most places, people get assessment and testing confused. The general public has heard terrible things about how our schools are doing based on standardized testing without the benefit of knowing the parameters of the test or the population of students to which it was given.

While there certainly are times in life when regular tests are given, needed, and even appropriate, it is the general consensus of early childhood educators to lean toward developmentally appropriate assessment.

Three Ways to Focus

This book will focus on assessment in the following easy and useful ways:

1. Assessing children to plan the best curriculum for them to achieve their own best individual potentials.

2. Assessing children to determine if they have special needs and can benefit by early intervention (developmental screening; see Inclusion and Assessment, page 141).

3. Assessing programs to see how well they meet goals you intended them to meet.

There is a variety of ways to do these things, and there are many parts of the assessment puzzle. It is the intention of this book to provide a map to assessment—a place to start or continue, no matter where your team is today.

Definitions in a Changing World

One note before beginning that is important to remember: educational "buzzwords" are constantly changing. Everyone in early childhood education is aware of just how quickly words and theories come and go. Therefore, when using the definitions in this book, remember the main goal you and your team can achieve in assessment (and the corresponding curriculum) is to find consensus.

What is Assessment? *(cont.)*

In order to help your team "tailor" this book to suit its individual needs, there are—in each section where you find assessment tools—easy-to-use masters designed to help you adapt the forms you find here to your particular style or to create your own forms in any given area.

A Word Before Beginning

Many early childhood educators who have been working in the field for years will not need to spend much time thinking about what assessment is. For many, assessment is a given; the ways of making assessment work better in their own school is their focus. Others will use this section to assist their newer staff members or to help parents gain clarity about the subject of assessment. Remember, most people who are not in or around education think that assessment means tests. This section can be very useful in helping people who do not understand the rather complex workings of assessment to get a quick and easy overview without spending months researching countless books. There is no right or wrong way to use the material in this book. Pick and choose from what seems relevant and useful to you and your team.

Some Things Stay the Same

In any kind of assessment, whether you are assessing children in a day-to-day setting, determining if they could benefit from developmental screening, or assessing your program, the fundamental process remains the same. Notice the Assessment Circle model on page 9. At the top of the circle is the word Observation. That is followed by the next words going clockwise, Record and Document. Then you will see at the bottom right-hand corner, Diagnose and Prescribe. Next, continuing clockwise, is Report and Enlist. Finally, the word Action, leads back to the beginning. The Assessment Circle illustrates that assessment is really an ongoing process, beginning with the important skill of Observation.

Seems Simple Enough

Teachers of students pursuing certificates and degrees in early childhood education agree that observation is not as easy as it looks to the beginner. Most people have not learned to separate their judgements from their observations. While it is really true that when you assess a child, somewhere along the line you are going to make well-informed judgements, the first step of observation should be as neutral and unbiased as is humanly possible. It is important to be able to see what a child is doing without judging it good/bad, right/wrong, etc. Observation, in order to produce results that are accurate and valid, must be done over a long period of time.

While a one-time observation experience can be really interesting, it will not give you very much information. There is simply too much to see to make quick judgments. The idea is to observe without judgment. Then, over time, construct a pattern that gives you information, making sure that the pattern is actually true and not part of your own biases.

How Do You Prevent Biases?

Work and Commitment

Preventing biases takes work and commitment. Everyone, naturally, has some issues that involve biases. What we try to do as early childhood educators is to create diverse settings where children are celebrated and not condemned because of their differences. The dynamic of diversity is changing as we become more aware of it and as the world is changing. Yet, there are still places and people that assess children unfairly because of biases about languages and cultures, gender roles, cultural differences, or special needs.

Everyone is Special!

If we can see each child as whole and unique, developing according to an individual plan, and then look for norms based on the things we know after years of research, we will give children better opportunities to be treated without negative judgments and opinions.

Assessment Circle

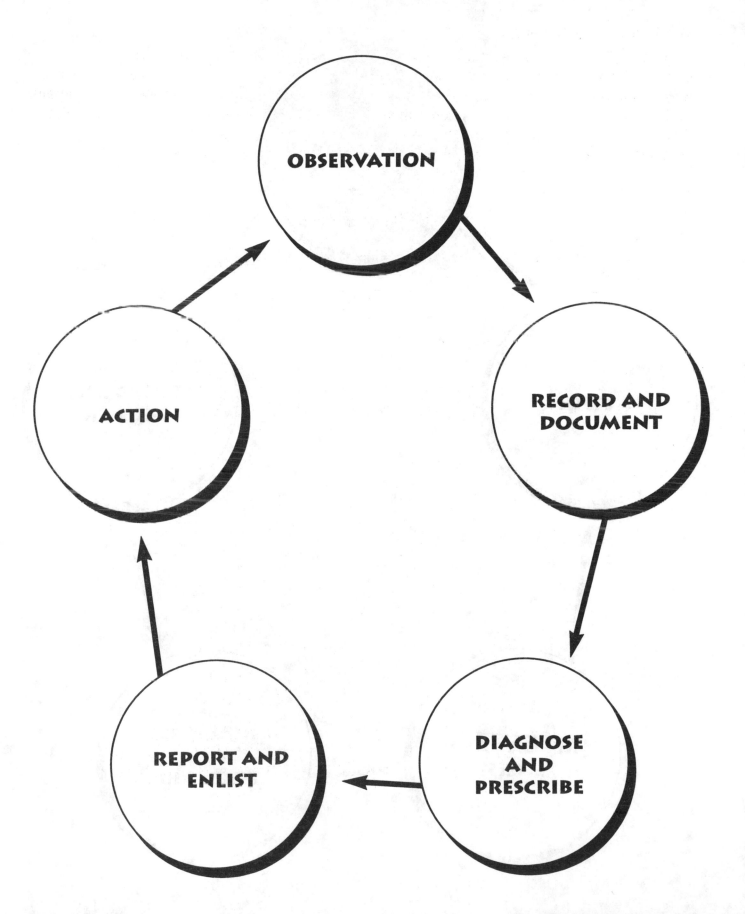

Assessment Circle

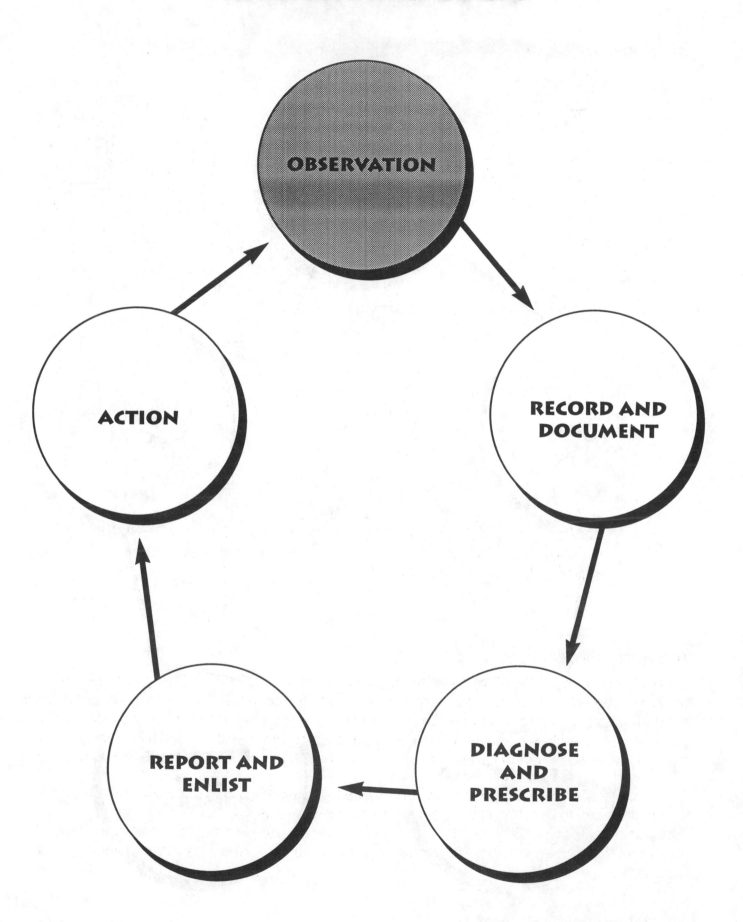

Learning to Observe

The Art of Observation

"Learn to observe? I have been observing children forever!" This may be true, however, whether you just walked into your center for the very first time this morning scared out of your mind, or you are planning your retirement party after 40 years in early childhood education, you can still benefit by occasionally checking and improving your assessment skills. It is like taking a driver's test every couple of years. It is amazing what we can forget or never knew.

The following pages contain some observation activities and games that you can use alone or with teammates to practice your observation skills. These activities will give you an opportunity to check where you are today with your own observation skills and notice any areas you might want to focus on in your day-to-day observations of children in your classroom.

Observation Games

Outdoor Observation Game

Purpose:

This game is designed for teachers to practice their observation skills in a setting that has nothing to do with children.

What You Need:

- Outdoor Observation Game log sheet

- Access to an outdoor view for at least 15 minutes (Any view will do; it does not have to be pretty or natural. A street will work as well as a meadow.)

- A chair or place to sit

What You Do:

The idea with this game is to record what you see with as little judgment as possible. Note as many of the activities as you can see around you. Give complete descriptions of actions as well as the scene. The idea is to describe the entire scene you see on as many levels as possible. Use these questions to help you.

1. What do I see?

2. Is anything moving?

3. What colors and shapes do I see?

4. What do I hear?

5. Describe as many things as possible without using value words.

The following are value words to watch out for.

pretty	ugly
stupid	ridiculous
odd	strange
nasty	mean
angry	happy
bad	good
funny	weird
nice	

Teamwork Step

Now compare your observation log with a teammate's log of the same place.

Note here the things that you saw that he/she did not see and vice versa.

Team Member One:

_____   _____

_____   _____

_____   _____

_____   _____

_____   _____

Team Member Two:

_____   _____

_____   _____

_____   _____

_____   _____

_____   _____

Were you mostly in agreement?

_____

How many differences in observation were there?

_____

How could these differences in perception affect the children you work with, both positively and negatively?

Positive:_____

Negative: _____

Outdoor Observation Log

Name: _____

Time of Day: _____

Partner's Name: _____

Describe Scene: _____

_____

_____

_____

_____

_____

_____

Describe Specifics:

_____

_____

_____

_____

_____

_____

_____

_____

_____

Observation Games

Aquarium Game

Week-Long Journal

Purpose:

This activity gives you the opportunity to do a long-term observation or a log or journal for five days, and then again for five more days with slightly different rules. Remember, these activities are designed to help you learn how to observe or refine your observation skills in a way where children are not the guinea pigs. (It is most likely true that if you assess a fish in your aquarium in a judgmental and biased fashion, it will not be emotionally damaged for life!)

What You Need:

- aquarium of fish to watch (a goldfish in a bowl will work too)

- Journal Master (Make as many copies as you need.)

- Personal Journal Follow-up form

What You Do:

Set aside 15 minutes every day to observe the aquarium (or fish bowl). Notice as much as possible on a daily basis, remembering to describe but not judge what you see as completely as possible.

Then, after a week's time, take a look at your entire log. See if you notice any patterns in what you saw. Summarize what you saw. Did you begin to notice new and different things about the fish everyday? If so, what were they? Did your written observations get longer in length, remain the same, or become shorter as the week progressed? All of these things can be important clues about keeping a journal or a log.

Now try the same observation for another five days, except note each time before you begin how you feel and how your day is going. Do you feel tired, hurried, or anxious? Angry, annoyed, or frustrated? Happy and positive? Whatever the emotion or kind of day you are having, make a note of it before you begin your observation.

At the end of the week, look again for patterns. Notice how possible it is to let human emotions affect one's observations. Share your results with a team member for feedback. Use these results to help you plan the best times to observe and to remain aware of how your own emotions can create a possible bias.

Journal Master—First Week

Day One _____

Date _____ **Time** _____

Observations: _____

_____

_____

Day Two _____

Date _____ **Time** _____

Observations: _____

_____

_____

Day Three _____

Date _____ **Time** _____

Observations: _____

_____

_____

Day Four _____

Date _____ **Time** _____

Observations: _____

_____

_____

Day Five _____

Date _____ **Time** _____

Observations: _____

_____

_____

Journal Master—Second Week

Day _____ _____

Date _____ **Time** _____

Personal Observations: _____

_____

_____

Observations: _____

_____

_____

_____

_____

Day _____ _____

Date _____ **Time** _____

Personal Observations: _____

_____

_____

Observations: _____

_____

_____

_____

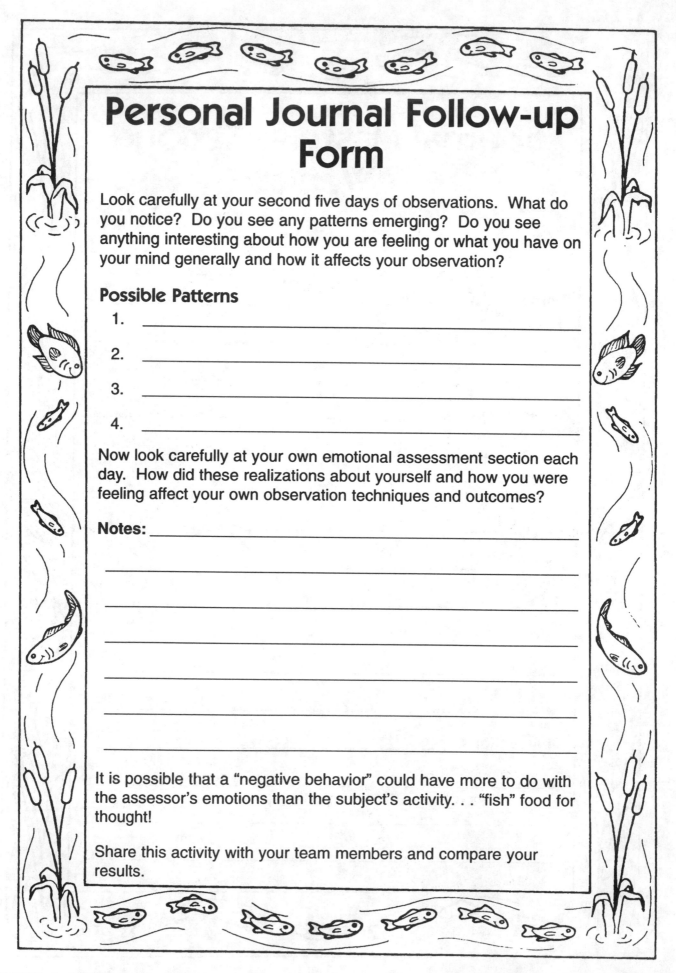

Personal Journal Follow-up Form

Look carefully at your second five days of observations. What do you notice? Do you see any patterns emerging? Do you see anything interesting about how you are feeling or what you have on your mind generally and how it affects your observation?

Possible Patterns

1. _____

2. _____

3. _____

4. _____

Now look carefully at your own emotional assessment section each day. How did these realizations about yourself and how you were feeling affect your own observation techniques and outcomes?

Notes: _____

_____

_____

_____

_____

_____

_____

It is possible that a "negative behavior" could have more to do with the assessor's emotions than the subject's activity. . . "fish" food for thought!

Share this activity with your team members and compare your results.

Assessment Circle

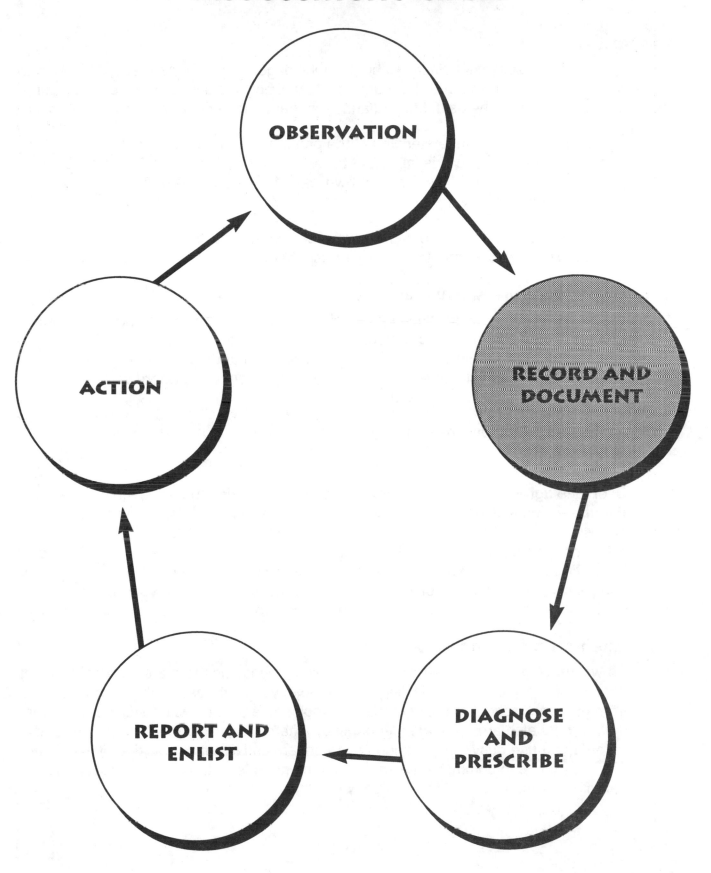

Record and Document

The Next Step

Look again at the assessment circle on the previous page. You will see that the highlighted part of the circle is now Record and Document. This simply means the process of keeping records in a way that will be useful to you and your team and best benefit your children.

In observing, from our own understanding of the process complemented by the activities in the previous chapter, we know it is important to remain neutral during the first part of the process and simply observe. This is so our own way of seeing things does not adversely affect the child we are observing.

Now, in Record and Document, the main focus is setting up a system, an easy-to-use way, to keep these records and documents so you can use them and so they make sense.

Early Childhood Professionals Say . . .

To best determine what early childhood professionals felt about the assessment they were already doing in their centers and classroom, we interviewed a number of them (reflecting a variety of different educational and philosophical viewpoints) to determine the common denominators of assessment. One recurring cry from teachers everywhere was "Keep it simple to use and simple to understand."

There are two important reasons for this:

Lack of Time

Everyone agrees that one of the major elements hindering the assessment program is that there simply is no time for implementation. Because of this, all the forms you choose, whether they are checklists, observation logs, anecdotal record forms, self-created forms, or any combination of these, should be easy to use. Nothing is more frustrating than tools that prevent you from doing what you need to do because of their complexity. So, when deciding which of the forms from this book your team will use, think about time—how much you have and when you can make regular time to assess.

Parents' Understanding of the Process

As we know, parents come from as many backgrounds as there are different kinds of people. In a typical day of dealing with parents, you might deal with educational levels from grammar school to post graduate school, and again, as with teachers, it seems that parents also are running short on time. Therefore, making the documents and records you use easy to read and easy to understand is not patronizing; it is helpful. This way you can communicate easily with the parents. Studies have proven that the parent/home connection is vital in early childhood education.

Record and Document *(cont.)*

Now What?

Therefore the best method is one that is simple and easy to understand. The reasons for this are so assessment can happen in all its steps and then communicate each child's needs to the parents and find a way to best help the child. How do we get these great and well-meaning ideas from paper to actually working as part of your program? The answer is this: Quick And Easy Organization.

Quick and Easy Organization

There are many ways to get organized, and certainly everyone has his or her own method. Often, many of us do not even have time to think about it. The following easy assessment organization plan is one way to start. Use this "as is" to start immediately, work with your team to pull from it the best ideas for you, or use it to compare to what you already have in place to determine any additions or missing pieces.

Finding Your Own Best Way

Remember, the main idea is to use these ideas to create a program that works best for you and your team based on your individual preferences and strengths.

Quick and Easy Assessment
Organization

Individual Plan

What You Need:

- one 1" (2.5 cm) binder for each child
- package of name stickers
- copies of assessment masters (Check each activity in each of the four "Assessed Activity Sections" of the book to decide which assessment tools will work for you.)
- a bookcase or some easy place to store the binders
- a three-hole punch
- a set of binder dividers for each child's binder

What You Do:

Look at the diagram on page 24. What you do is simple:

- Make a place to keep all the documentation for each part of the assessment circle in one place for each child. (Note: the left side of the diagram contains the assessment circles and the right side of the diagram contains the binder sections to which they correspond.)
- Use the binder divider labels on the next page; just cut them out and slip them into the binder dividers in each child's assessment binder.
- Use the label for the binding of the binder and write each child's name in bold print for easy access.
- Use the Child's Information Page on page 26 to write out important information for each child: name, address, phone number, picture, parents' work number(s), etc.

Put it all in the binder in the following order:

1. Child's information page
2. Observation records and document divider
3. Recommendations, evaluation records
4. Parent meeting records
5. Plan records

(Each binder will have five sections.)

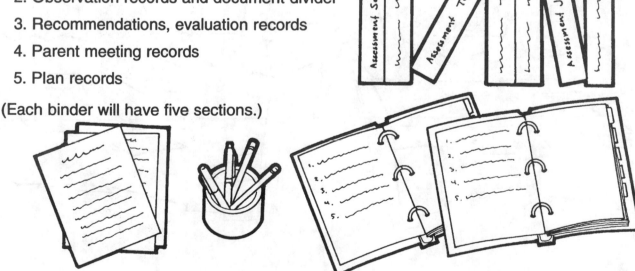

Printed Binder Section Labels

Simply cut out these binder section labels and insert in binder dividers. Also cut out side binding label and write child's name in bold print and tape on binding.

CHILD INFO RECORDS

OBSERVATION RECORDS

RECOMMENDATION RECORDS

PARENT MEETING RECORDS

ACTION PLAN RECORDS

Assessment FOR _____

How Does This All Work?

It is very easy. You have just created a place to store all your assessment materials and documentation for each child in your center or classroom. Each section in the binder you have created relates to the section of the assessment circle like this:

Assessment Circle

Assessment Organization Binder Sections

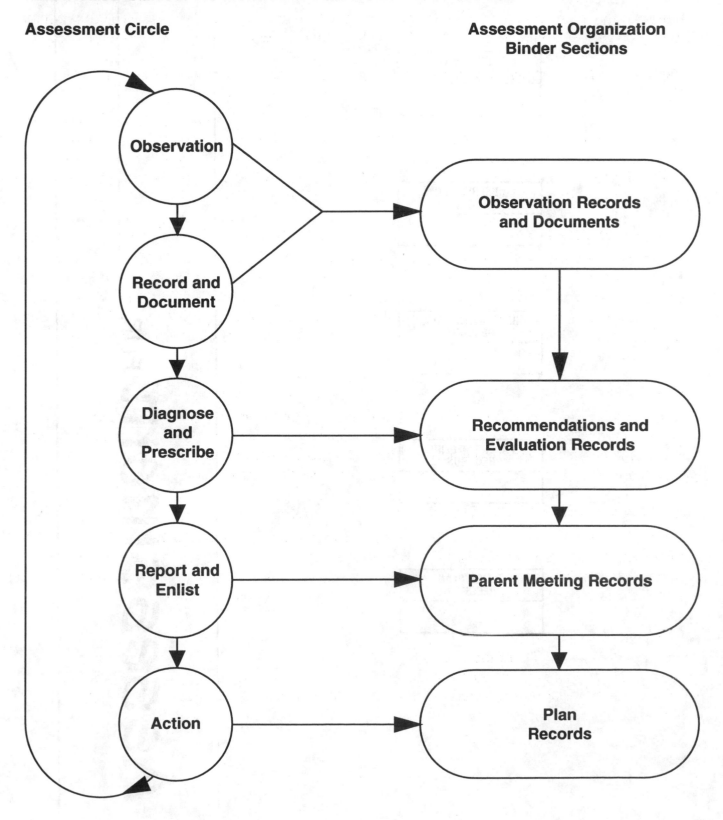

Record and Document *(cont.)*

Child Info Records

This section starts out with the Child Information Page on page 26. This form will immediately give you important information about any child, and you will know where it is if you need it in a hurry. In this section, put anything relevant to general information. This will vary from center to center and school to school, and will also be based on what you feel will work for you.

Observation Records (Assessment Circle sections **Observation** and **Record and Document**)

This is where to put all the records and documents you have kept for any child. Each of the forms in this book has been created to be copied, three-hole-punched, and inserted in a binder as soon as possible. You can also keep blank forms for observation in this section of the binder to be used as needed, and so you will know where they are. In fact, you may want to pull out the binder and use it when you are observing. That is up to you.

Recommendation Records (Assessment Circle section **Diagnose and Prescribe**)

This section is for all your records of your evaluations of each child. After the documentation step of the assessment circle, you have to look at all of your observations and figure out what is happening. Put your notes and actual recommendations in this section. Then, when you are meeting with a parent, you will be able to pull this out and have the observations and what you recommend based on what you and your team has observed. (See the section on "Diagnosis and Prescription" for more information.)

Parent Meeting Records (Assessment Circle section **Report and Enlist**)

In this section, keep notes about what happened in your parent meetings along with the Parent Meeting Scheduler form on page 27. This way you will know when you have set the meetings and what happened when you met. As assessment is an ongoing process, keeping records of what you have said and done in parent meetings is very important.

Action Plan Records (Assessment Circle section **Action**)

Use this section to make a note of all your plans and what happened. After you recommend something to a parent about his/her child, the next step is taking the action and seeing what happens. Use this section to make your plans for each child. Add follow-up about those plans and how they worked.

The On-Going Process

Remember the sections of the Assessment Organization Binder go right along with the Assessment Circle in an ongoing process. This is just one simple way to quickly and easily organize the documents involved in the process to best help you help the children you work with everyday.

Child's Information Page

Child's Name _____

Parent's Name _____

Parent's Name _____

Grandparent or childcare person's name

_____

Address _____

Phone _____

Work phone (Mom) _____

Work phone (Dad) _____

Emergency numbers: _____

_____

_____

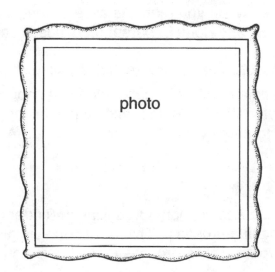

photo

Parent Meeting Scheduler

Meeting _____

Time _____

Date _____

Subject _____

Confirm _____

Meeting _____

Time _____

Date _____

Subject _____

Confirm _____

Meeting _____

Time _____

Date _____

Subject _____

Confirm _____

Meeting _____

Time _____

Date _____

Subject _____

Confirm _____

Assessment Circle

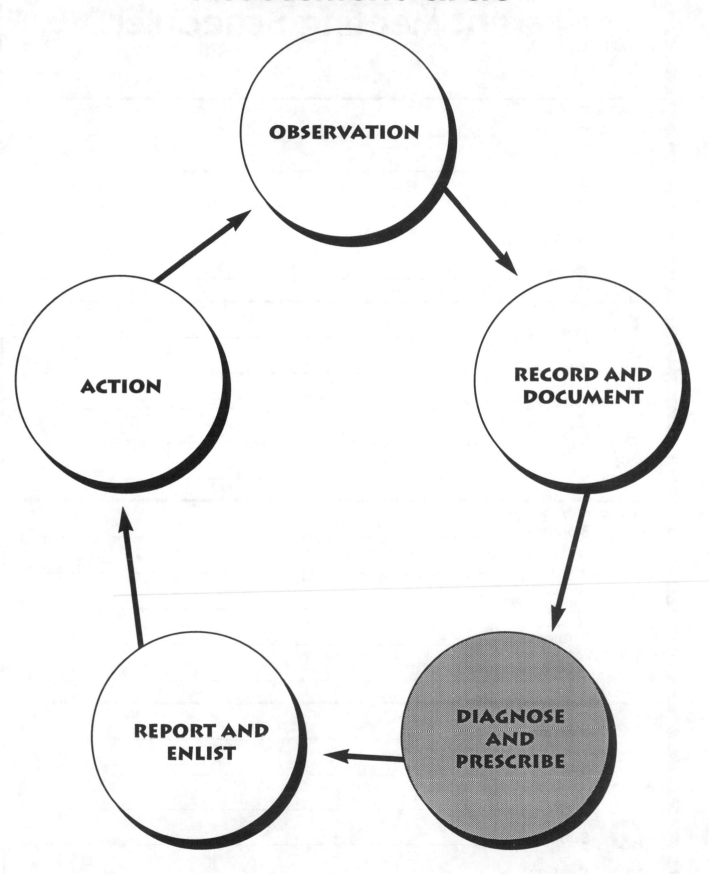

28

Diagnose and Prescribe

The Next Step

Now that you have set up the beginning of an organizational system, you are ready to think about the next step in the Assessment Circle. Notice on the preceding page that the section Diagnose and Prescribe is highlighted. This is the part of assessment where you and your team make educated judgments, evaluations, and decisions based on as much information as you can get.

In this section, it is important to follow the steps provided:
(Refer to the diagram on page 32 explained for you here.)

Communicate with Team

After you have gathered together all the observations you have for one child, your personal observations as well as those of other teachers, aides, and parents, then comes the time when you will want to talk to your team members about what you see. This can be as easy as casual conversation that happens everyday, or you might want to sit down over coffee and discuss matters that you feel are urgent or important.

Diagnosing and prescribing is the place in the assessment process where you have to be careful. This is the place where children get mislabeled and treated in ways that ultimately do them harm. This is the place where children's gifts may be ignored and where their problems may not be noticed. That is why having the feedback of your team (and parents) is very important.

Parents are becoming increasingly interested in being part of this step in the assessment process, and rightly so. Remember that parents' observations are very useful to you; after all, it is their child and they know him or her best. It is very important to consider both yourself and the parents as part of the team helping the child. This attitude will help you bond with parents and give parents the motivation to be involved with their child's educational process. It is their right to do so.

Consult

After you have reviewed and thought about your own observations and talked to your team members, and possibly had a casual conversation with parents, it comes time to get the advice of experts and professionals. If you are thinking that a child needs developmental screening or special assistance in any way, the work you do in this section of your diagnosis will point that out to you.

Consulting is really just gathering reputable and provable information. That might be difficult because it is an ever-changing part of assessment, but you and your team have some idea of what is developmentally appropriate for children and you use some kind of guidelines already. If you need more information, consult the bibliography at the back of this book or consult NAEYC and obtain a copy of their book list on developmentally appropriate practices.

Diagnose and Prescribe *(cont.)*

Consult *(cont.)*

This step is where you are constantly learning—about child development, about new theories about education, about anything that can help you figure out what is best for the child in question. The main thing here is to check and double check what you decide, and to keep an open mind about possibilities. This is what experts in early childhood education are always referring to when they talk about the need for assessment and diagnostic tools to be used so carefully.

Also, if you feel a child needs developmental screening for a potential special need, remember it is imperative to have parental permission regarding this before beginning. You will need to contact the parent(s) regarding this as soon as you know and certainly not bring in any professionals (such as those who provide diagnostic screening) without the written permission of the parent(s). (See more about this in Inclusion and Assessment on page 141.)

Confer

This is the step where you talk again about the information you have gathered from expert sources, NAEYC, developmental checklists, etc. with your team. At this point you need to sit down and diagnose what the situation is; that is, make an educated and informed evaluation, and come together with team members to see if you have agreement or if team members disagree about what a potential diagnosis is.

Remember, when presenting this information to parents in the next step of the process, that you can have more than one idea about what you need to address with their child. The main idea is to have clarity about all aspects of your diagnosis and what you think the prescription or the plan should be.

Construct Ideas

After you have gathered as much information as possible, talked with team members and consulted expert opinion (whether person to person or through classes or current educational books and materials), it is time to construct your ideas about how to best help this individual child.

The main thrust in developmentally appropriate education and assessment is dealing with individual children as individuals, so when you are thinking about what would help this child, think only of this particular child.

Guidelines for appropriate child development exist to help us, but we must use good judgment. Clearly, we should get diagnostic testing and help for children who are not developing the way they should. On the other hand, it is normal for a wide range of difference to exist at every stage of development, age, and learning. Pediatricians, for example will tell young parents that it is possible and normal for a child to walk before the age of one year. They will also say it is normal for a child to walk when closer to two years of age. Similarly, one child may talk fluently at two and a half; another may not use complete sentences until a year later. Both situations are normal.

Diagnose and Prescribe *(cont.)*

Remember, therefore, to construct ideas that keep the child's best interests and individuality in mind. Write down your ideas and think them through. Use the section of the child's assessment binder labeled Recommendation Records for everything you document in this section. Use the parent meeting plan on page 33 and the parent meeting outline on page 34 if you wish, or make your own notes in the way that is best for you.

Commit to Presentation and Potential Plan

Next, plan your parent meeting carefully. Know what your potential plan will be. Remember, in the next assessment step (Report and Enlist) your goal is to gain understanding and agreement with your parents, not to alienate and frighten them. The parent meeting needs to get across what you are seeing. Set it up so that anyone can see clearly what you are trying to say. Use anything you need to do this. The child assessment binder is a useful tool since it contains observations and documentation of all kinds for the parents to see. Also, use portfolios to show work examples over a period of real time. (See the Portfolio section, starting on page 271.)

Most important of all, remember not to act as if what you are going to do is etched in stone. What matters is not whether the parent thinks you are right; it is what is best for the child. And, ultimately, the parent(s) can veto your plan. Most of the time, parents are as anxious to help their child as you are, and often parent meetings are to report that everything is going along as planned, not that there are matters that need to be discussed.

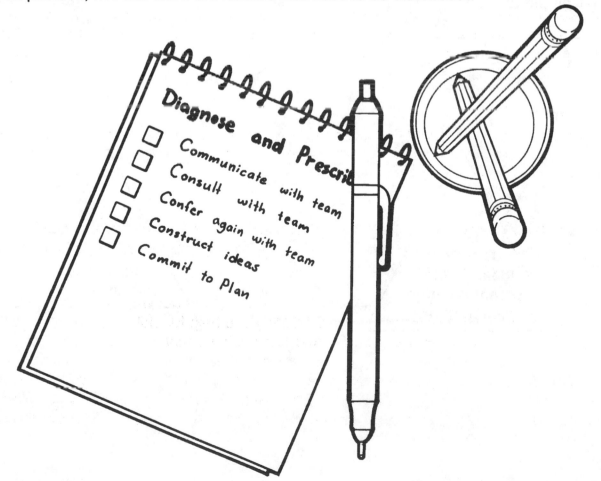

Diagnose and Prescribe *(cont.)*

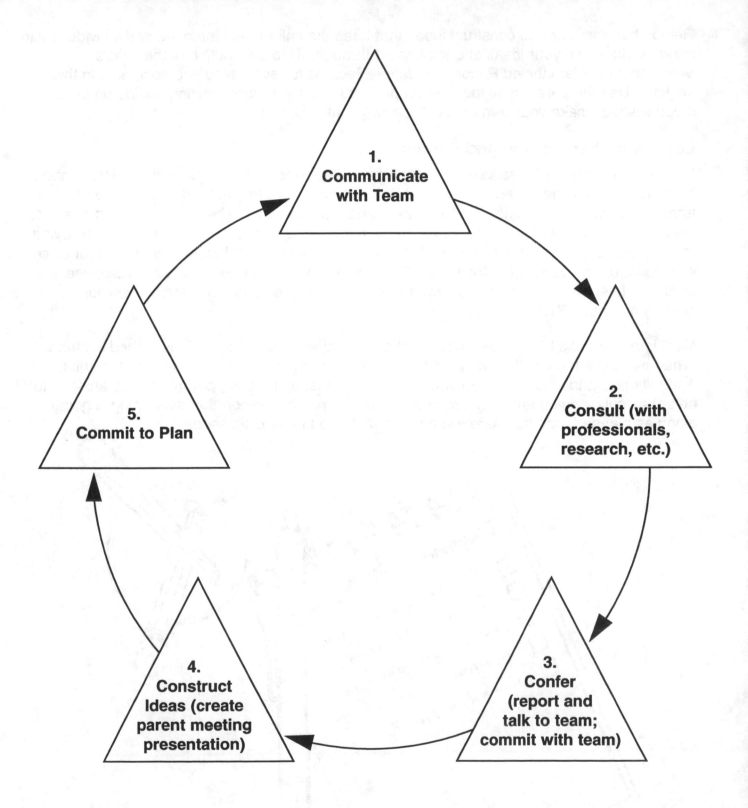

1. Communicate with Team

2. Consult (with professionals, research, etc.)

3. Confer (report and talk to team; commit with team)

4. Construct Ideas (create parent meeting presentation)

5. Commit to Plan

Parent Meeting Plan

Child's Name _____

Parent(s)' Name(s) _____

Date _____

Topic_____

_____

_____

Parent Meeting Agenda

    1. _____

    2. _____

    3. _____

Pre-Meeting Checklist

_____   Child Assessment Binder Prepared

_____   Director or Principal Notified

_____   Work Samples Prepared

_____   Meeting Outline Prepared

Notes:

_____

_____

_____

_____

_____

_____

Parent Meeting Outline

Child's Name _____

Parent(s)' Name(s) _____

Topic _____

   1. _____

      A. _____

      B. _____

      C. _____

Topic

   2. _____

      A. _____

      B. _____

      C. _____

Topic

   3. _____

      A. _____

      B. _____

      C. _____

Notes: _____

_____

_____

_____

_____

_____

Assessment Circle

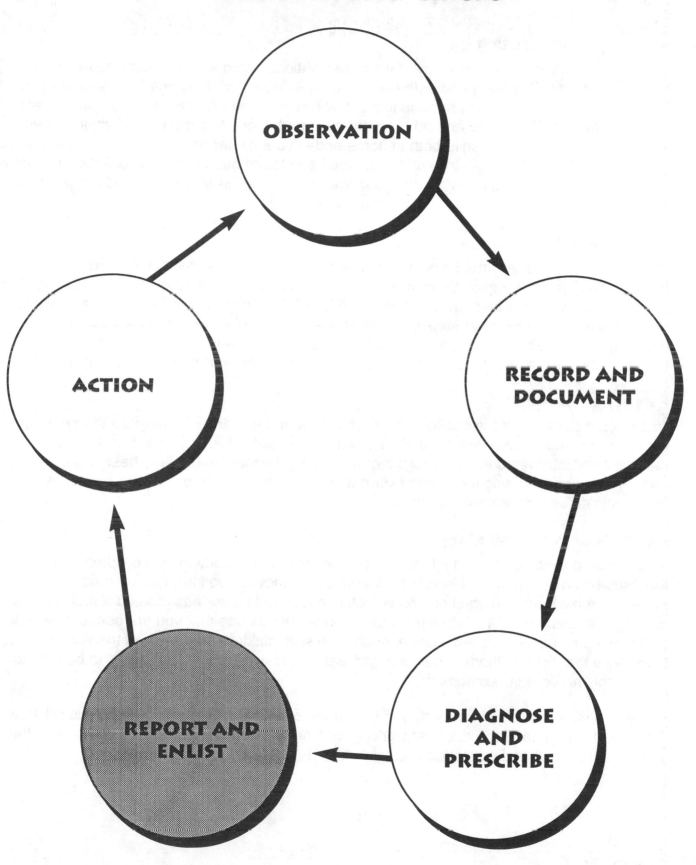

Report and Enlist

Reporting and Enlisting

Now that you have looked carefully at your observations and documentation regarding the child, talked with your team and gathered up-to-the-minute expert advice from sources you respect, it is time to bring the parents into a meeting with you. At this meeting you will report what you have found out so far and enlist their support in creating the kind of environment that will best support their child both at home and in your center or school. In short, the goal at this step of assessment is to report what you have found out, tell what you think it means, and get help from parents in whatever your plan is to make this individual child's experience more positive.

Parent Meetings

In this part of the assessment it is very positive to use the child's assessment binder that you have created and have everything you are going to share with the parents neatly put together. (See Record and Document on page 19.) At this point, your goal is to explain what you see, and talk about what the next step is with the parents. The communication in this part of assessment is to share what you have learned throughout the first three steps in a manner that is positive for everyone and then to reach a mutually desired plan of action for the child.

Parents as Partners

Parents are partners in their children's development and learning. Even more than partners, they are the decision makers about their children. As early childhood educators, we have a responsibility to parents to best assist their children. We may be the very best and most happily remembered teacher a child ever has, or we may not. Here is where our ability to communicate becomes very important.

All Kinds of Parent Meetings

What if you are not as good dealing with parents as you are working with children? Lots of teachers feel more comfortable around children than they do working with their parents. However, most parent interactions go smoothly once the teacher has created a technique for dealing with this part of the job— the interaction should be one that you are comfortable with and that works for you. It is difficult enough to assess children properly and then create curriculum that assists them to develop and learn. It is even more challenging to be able to explain this and create excitement.

However, once you explain (report) and create the excitement in others (enlist), you will have a group of concerned individuals all working together in the best interest of the child and that is what early childhood education is all about.

Report and Enlist *(cont.)*

What Do You Do in a Parent Meeting to Get Your Point Across?

The most important thing you can do in a parent meeting is have all of your facts straight and easy to understand—in short, it is crucial that you do your homework. Whichever method you decide will work for you in explaining the facts about their child's assessment to parents, a common theme remains: they must be able to understand what you are trying to show them and they must see tangible proof. Documentation and assessment tools must be there for them to look at, and it is helpful to have samples of the child's work using a portfolio or any other method you decide will work well.

What is the Best Way to Plan a Parent Meeting?

There are many ways to run a meeting. Some basics for parent meetings include these 10 points:

1. Have an agenda, know what you want to cover, and set a tentative time limit.

2. Give parents actual tangible documentation and examples they can look at, read, and touch.

3. If you are explaining a new program or a new kind of assessment, have literature and information available at the meeting.

4. Give parents plenty of time and opportunity to talk about their own concerns.

5. Be open to changing your meeting format in your own mind if you see the parents have concerns that need to be addressed regarding their child.

6. Set a follow-up meeting if necessary.

7. Give parents something written regarding the meeting to take with them.

8. Give parents something positive and happy about their child to take away from the meeting.

9. Give parents opportunities to become more involved in your center or school and their child's development and education.

10. Let your director or principal know what you are doing, so he or she can support you and remain informed.

Report and Enlist *(cont.)*

What About Intervening in a Problem Situation?

Meetings with parents in which you are reporting something potentially negative require all of your empathy and caring, as well as your best effort in having all the facts before you. If you are addressing a problem with a child, have solutions in mind. There are, however, some instances where you may not understand why a child is having a problem. In this case you may wish to approach the meeting as more of a fact-finding meeting.

If you are caught off guard or do not have an answer for something, never bluff. Simply say, "That is something I will need to find out about before I can answer intelligently." Or, "That is something we will both need to think over and talk about again." The key to good communication with anyone is your ability to listen, and to react calmly, and to look at the meeting as part of an on-going positive process to help the child.

Enlisting Support

Use the parent meeting as a place to enlist support from the parents about a specific way to help their child. In the previous step of assessment, you created a potential plan regarding an action step that would benefit the child. In this part of the meeting, explain the action and get agreement regarding the action. It can be as easy as suggesting the child have a larger breakfast or bring a midmorning snack to have before regular snack time or as serious as suggesting that a child be screened for a potential hearing loss or for vision problems. You can also enlist the parents' support in determining the problem, and you should—it is a joint venture.

Parents Helping at Home

One way to get parents involved productively in their children's education from a very early stage is by using the Helping at Home Kits included in this book. Use parent meetings to put this part of your curriculum follow-up and assessment at home into action. (See page 64 for Helping at Home Kit information.)

Parent Meeting Report

Date _____

Child's Name _____

Parent(s)' Name(s) _____

Teacher's Name_____

Subject of Meeting:_____

_____

_____

_____

Summary:

_____

_____

Teacher Recommendation:

_____

_____

Parent/Teacher Action Plan:

_____

_____

At School:

_____

_____

At Home:

_____

_____

Parent Teacher Meeting Record

Child's Name _____

Parent(s)' Name(s) _____

Meeting Date: _____

Discussed:

1. _____
2. _____
3. _____
4. _____
5. _____

Communication, Feedback, and Results

_____

_____

_____

_____

Action Steps

1. _____
2. _____
3. _____
4. _____
5. _____

New Meeting Scheduled for: _____

Screening Availability Letter

Dear Parents,

As part of our on-going commitment to help your child reach his/her full

potential, we are participating in pre-kindergarten screening, free of charge to

parents. We will have licensed professionals on site to conduct

_____ screening

tests for all children at your request and with your permission on

_____ at _____ o'clock.

Feel free to contact me regarding any questions you may have about this

screening. Please sign this form and return it to me no later than

_____ to enable your child to take part.

Your child will not be screened without your written permission.

Sincerely,

_____

for

_____

school

Post-Screening Letter

Dear Parents,

At your request your child _____

was screened in _____

as part of our school's free, routine developmental screening program.

Your child's results will be explained in detail at a parent/teacher meeting at your convenience. Please call the school to schedule a parent/teacher meeting that will fit in with your schedule.

Sincerely,

_____

for

_____

school

Assessment Circle

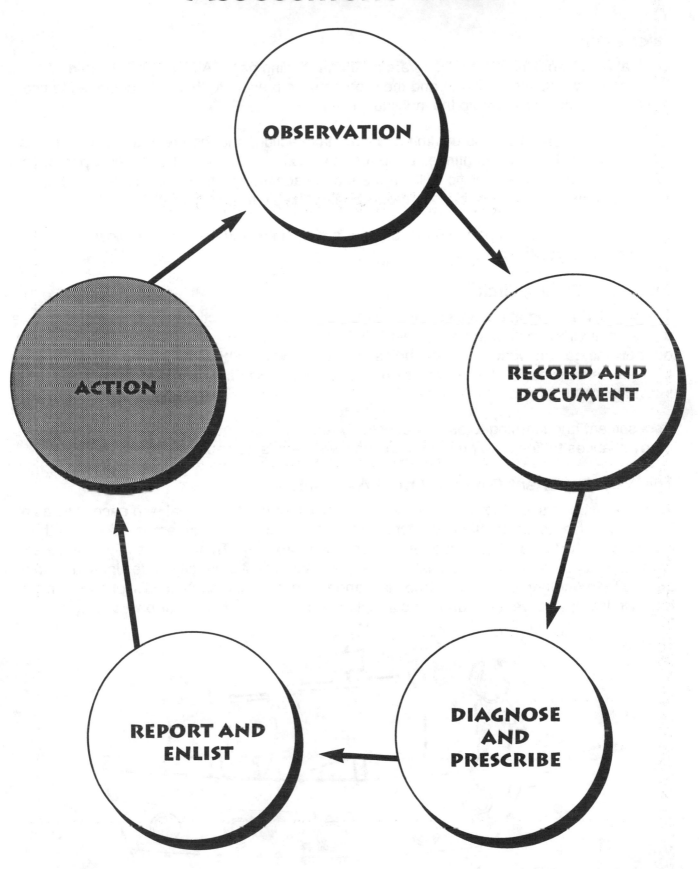

Action

Taking Action

Look at the Assessment Circle diagram on the preceding page: Action is highlighted. After all, the reasons we assess children and the programs we present to them are designed to find the best possible way to help the individual child.

The Action step is when you commit to a plan, take action, and then review the results. As you will notice, the circle continues to go around. As soon as you put some new part of your program into play for a specific child, you are once again beginning to observe what happens when the new part of the puzzle is introduced into the picture.

Use the Action Form on page 45 to plan your action steps and the Action Follow-Up Form (page 46) to evaluate them.

The Never Ending Circle

The wonderful thing about assessment is that, if it is done correctly, it gives us many chances to create environments that are consistently better for children. Assessment helps us figure out how things can work better and helps us think of ways to benefit children based on who they are as individuals. It is a process of fine tuning, all with the best interests of the individual child in mind.

Assessment and learning to assess effectively are ongoing processes as well. There are many chances to fine tune programs and see what works for each child.

The Most Important Concept About Assessment

There is just one secret to making assessment work for children. Deal with each child as an individual. Use assessments that best benefit the individual and, remember, like any other aspect of a child's development or education, it is a process. Think of it as navigating a ship. One plans a course and then adjusts and adjusts and adjusts. Finally, a destination is arrived at, and then another leg of the journey is planned. In this case each child's journey is his or her own learning adventure, and we can help each one to set his or her own course.

Action Form

Plan Your Action Steps

Child's Name _____

Parent(s)' Name(s) _____

Date _____

Observation Conclusion:

_____

_____

_____

_____

_____

_____

_____

Brainstorming Ideas:

_____

_____

_____

_____

_____

Possible Plans:

1. _____

2. _____

3. _____

Action Follow-Up Form

Evaluate Your Action Steps

Child's Name _____

Parent(s)' Name(s) _____

Date _____

Plan # _____

Action Taken: _____

_____

_____

Results:

_____

_____

Conclusion:

_____

_____

Additional Action Steps?

_____ Yes   _____ Not Needed

New Steps:

1. _____

2. _____

3. _____

Teacher/Team/Program Assessment

NAEYC Guidelines

In 1990 the National Association for the Education of Young Children combined with the National Association of Early Childhood Specialists in State Departments of Education to create guidelines for appropriate curriculum and assessment in programs serving children ages three through eight. They outlined in great detail how the aspects of curriculum and the corresponding assessment must meet the needs of the individual child and best help him/her to become a "healthy, sensitive, caring and fully contributing member of society." In any attempt we make at assessing children and creating the kinds of curriculum that will best benefit them, this quote should be our guide.

Your Team, Your Curriculum, and Your Assessment Procedures

It seems complicated, but it really is not. The main thing to keep in mind is that the curriculum we plan and the assessments we use to determine how children are doing are designed to benefit each child as an individual. We should also keep in mind that assessment is not only how we see children are doing as individuals. It also helps us to see how our curriculum is working, and if our curriculum goals are positive, and in keeping with what is appropriate for young children.

Excellent Resources

No matter what kind of assessment and curriculum your team favors, no matter what your approach, the NAEYC guidelines can benefit your program. These guidelines are widely endorsed and supported by a large number of highly reputable organizations. It is possible to get a variety of up-to-the minute materials and books from the National Association for the Education of Young Children that will give you an immediate sense of whether or not your program is meeting the needs of children in your center or school based on these guidelines.

The Teacher/Team/Program Assessment

Assessment can operate on all levels, and it does. In this book, you will have many resources to assess each part of your program. Assessment is far more than just observing children. It is seeing how children are doing and adjusting the curriculum to meet their individual needs. It is getting feedback from your observation and record keeping that can help you and your team create programs that will assist children to be the fully developed and fully participating members of society they deserve to be.

In this section of the book there are a number of assessment tools to help you assess your program, assess your own job, assess your work as a team, and tools for teachers to refine and redesign curriculum to meet the needs of the children in their centers.

Teacher/Team/Program Assessment *(cont.)*

Again, the main component is to make sure that the curriculum you are presenting benefits the children with whom you are working, respects them, allows them to develop as individuals, and does not label them, ignore them, or waste their time. The possible negative we are always facing is that a bad curriculum and assessment program gives children less than they deserve.

Tools You Can Use to Assess Your Curriculum, Your Team, Yourself, and Your Teachers

The following pages include a variety of planning tools you can use by yourself or with your team to assess your program and yourself. Working together as a group, you can find your own team's way of setting up and redefining curriculum and assessments that will best benefit your children. One excellent resource to assist with this process is a book called *Reaching Potentials: Appropriate Curriculum and Assessment for Young Children.* This book includes invaluable resources that will help your team make sure that your curriculum and assessments are in keeping with its developmentally appropriate guidelines.

Team Worksheets and Forms

The following section includes these helpful forms:

- **Teacher Self Assessment**
- **Curriculum Goals**
- **Director/Teacher Evaluation Assessment**
- **Teacher Evaluation Assessment Response**
- **Teacher/Program Feedback**
- **Form for Modifying the Curriculum Plan**

Each form available for you to use also includes a completed example form, so you can see how one team might use this form to benefit its own planning. Periodically use the forms again, set definite meeting times just as you would for children's assessments, to assess your own program. This way, you can be sure to keep the process of accurate and meaningful assessment happening in all aspects of your program.

Teacher Self Assessment— Example

Teaching situations in which I feel the most comfortable

1 _with children — in active play_

2 _circle time / Reading_

3 _interacting one-on-one_

Teaching situations in which I feel somewhat uncomfortable

1 _dramatic play_

2 _musical activities_ ←

3 _____ can't sing 😊

Teaching situations that I would like to explore for training

1 _we need some anti-bias information for parents_

2 _____

3 _____

Teaching situations in which I feel I have special ability or talents

1 _anything that has to do with story telling_

2 _____

3 _____

Special areas I would like to discuss with team

1 _We need to be more aware of keeping centers stocked_

2 _talk about doing more than one teacher observation_

3 _on same child_

Special areas I would like to discuss with director

1 _anti-bias training (I have workshop in mind)_

2 _____

3 _____

Additional Comments:

✳ _remember to copy workshop packet_

_____

_____

Teacher Self Assessment Form

Teaching situations in which I feel the most comfortable

1 _____

2 _____

3 _____

Teaching situations in which I feel somewhat uncomfortable

1 _____

2 _____

3 _____

Teaching situations that I would like to explore for training

1 _____

2 _____

3 _____

Teaching situations in which I feel I have special abilities or talents

1 _____

2 _____

3 _____

Special areas I would like to discuss with team

1 _____

2 _____

3 _____

Special areas I would like to discuss with director

1 _____

2 _____

3 _____

Additional Comments:

_____

_____

_____

Curriculum Goals—Example

Use this page with your team members to decide upon realistic goals you would like your curriculum to meet.

1. Creating self directed, center-intensive environment

2. Support individual child growth

3. respecting children

4. relevant activities that don't waste children's time

5. include Multiple Intelligence (This is an interesting idea = I HAVE NOTES ON THIS FROM WORKSHOP

6. letter and number activities)

7. thematic units —

8. NAEYC guidelines)
   LET'S GET & USE THESE!

9.

10.

Use this form first individually and then as a team to determine curriculum goals.

Curriculum Goals Form

Use this page with your team members to decide upon realistic goals you would like your curriculum to meet.

1. _____

   _____

2. _____

   _____

3. _____

   _____

4. _____

   _____

5. _____

   _____

6. _____

   _____

7. _____

   _____

8. _____

   _____

9. _____

   _____

10. _____

   _____

Use this form first individually and then as a team to determine curriculum goals.

Director/Teacher Evaluation Assessment Form—Example

Date 4/7/95

Teacher's Name Jan Alberto

Director's Name Marilyn Roberts

Relationship and Attitude Toward Children

General Evaluation:

Jan is very positive with the children. I really like the way she listens and treats each child with individual respect.

Suggestions:

Let children have more opportunity to move from center to center. Don't favor boys in sport activities! A must!

Attitude Toward Parents

General Evaluation:

Needs to keep in contact with parents a bit more—some parents have mentioned they have missed events.

Suggestions:

Once a month — check in calls

Director/Teacher Evaluation Assessment—Example Page Two

Curriculum Planning

General Evaluation: _I really like Jan's Multiple Intelligence activities her workshop experience in this new area is positive for the team._

Suggestions:

More parent involvement in activities a good way to communicate

Mastery of Early Childhood Concepts

General Evaluation:

good general knowledge
read about gender/anti-bias material

Suggestions:

▷ _get anti-bias material regarding gender from me._

Teacher Signature _Jan Alberts_ **Date** _4/7/95_

Director Signature _Marilyn Roberts_ **Date** _4/7/95_

Director/Teacher Evaluation Assessment Form

Date _____

Teacher's Name_____

Director's Name _____

Relationship and Attitude Toward Children

General Evaluation:

_____

_____

_____

Suggestions:

_____

_____

_____

Attitude Toward Parents

General Evaluation:

_____

_____

_____

Suggestions:

_____

_____

_____

Director/Teacher Evaluation
Assessment Form *(cont.)*

Curriculum Planning

General Evaluation:

_____

_____

_____

Suggestions:

_____

_____

_____

Mastery of Early Childhood Concepts

General Evaluation:

_____

_____

_____

Suggestions:

_____

_____

_____

Teacher Signature _____ **Date**_____

Director Signature _____ **Date**_____

Teacher Evaluation Assessment Response Form—Example

Date _4/10/95_

Teacher's Name _Jan Alberts_

Director's Name _Marilyn Roberts_

Relationship and Attitude Toward Children

Assessment Response:

_OK_

Relationship and Attitude Toward Parents

Assessment Response:

I NEED HELP WITH THIS— CAN YOU ASSIST WITH SOME PARENT COMMUNICATION INFO?

Curriculum Planning

Assessment Response:

WHAT ABOUT GETTING TEAM INVOLVED IN A SATURDAY WEBBING SESSION?

Mastery of Early Childhood Concepts

Assessment Response:

I AGREE ABOUT ANTI-BIAS

Additional Questions or Topics:

1. _SET MULTIPLE INTELLIGENCE MEETING_
2.
3.

Teacher Evaluation Assessment Response Form

Date _____

Teacher's Name_____

Director's Name _____

Relationship and Attitude Toward Children

Assessment Response:

_____

_____

Relationship and Attitude Toward Parents

Assessment Response:

_____

_____

Curriculum Planning

Assessment Response:

_____

_____

Mastery of Early Childhood Concepts

Assessment Response:

_____

_____

Additional Questions or Topics:

1. _____

2. _____

3. _____

Teacher/Program Feedback Form—Example

Name of activity _BUZZY BEE PARTY & PARADE_

How does this activity generally benefit the children participating?

GIVES CHILDREN TIME TO INTERACT POSITIVELY
WITH PARENTS IN THE CLASSROOM.

In what ways does this activity specifically benefit children?

Physically

1. _LARGE MUSCLE SKILLS — PARADE_
2. _COORDINATION (PARADE, MARCHING, USING INSTRUMENTS)_
3. _DANCE ⟶ LARGE & SMALL MUSCLE GROUPS_
4. _EYE HAND COORDINATION_

Emotionally

1. _POSITIVE FEELINGS ABOUT HAVING PARENT AT PARTY_
2. _LOTS OF SELF ESTEEM & AWARENESS OPPORTUNITIES_
3. _____
4. _____

Cognitively

1. _HELPING WITH CAKE_
2. _PARTY SET UP_
3. _MAKING DECISIONS ABOUT WHAT INSTRUMENTS & HOW THEY USE IT_
4. _DANCE — LEARNING DANCE COMBINES PHYSICAL & COGNITIVE_

Socially

1. _INTERACTING WITH CHILDREN_
2. _THEIR OWN PARENTS_
3. _OTHER PARENTS_
4. _PARTY MANNERS, SHARING COOPERATION_

What was your overall observation of the children participating in this activity?

Use the back of this page to write your observation

Teacher/Program Feedback Form

Name of activity _____

How does this activity generally benefit the children participating?

_____

_____

In what ways does this activity specifically benefit children?

Physically

1. _____

2. _____

3. _____

4. _____

Emotionally

1. _____

2. _____

3. _____

4. _____

Cognitively

1. _____

2. _____

3. _____

4. _____

Socially

1. _____

2. _____

3. _____

4. _____

What was your overall observation of the children participating in this activity?

Use the back of this page to write your observation

Form for Modifying the Curriculum Plan—Example

Use this page to recommend changes in curriculum based on observation/diagnosis and prescription of individual children.

Changes that would benefit individuals:

1. More outside activities
2. more movement
3. dramatic play —
4. more hands-on stuff
5. _____

Similarities in needs of children:

my kids all are less developed — Physically right now than cognitively — we have been doing lots of story stuff etc.

Differences in needs of children:

Several need more social activities

_____

Self-directed curriculum ideas:

1. Block center
2. Water table or sand box games —
3. Races outside? play ground equipment

Directed curriculum ideas:

1. Relay races? awards?!
2. do a play??
3. _____

Form for Modifying the Curriculum Plan

Use this page to recommend changes in curriculum based on observation/diagnosis and prescription of individual children.

Changes that would benefit individuals:

1. _____
2. _____
3. _____
4. _____
5. _____

Similarities in needs of children:

_____

_____

Differences in needs of children:

_____

_____

Self-directed curriculum ideas:

1. _____
2. _____
3. _____

Directed curriculum ideas:

1. _____
2. _____
3. _____

Parents Helping the Process

Teamwork Starts at Home

Early childhood assessment, like any other program in an early childhood classroom relies on many things. Remember that parents play a very important and constant role in the education of their children. Parents can be an excellent resource and support team for your classroom.

The First Learning

Even if parents have never spent a day in school as adults, they are the first teachers a child ever has. The way parents relate to their children, whether or not they speak with them (or read to them or interest them in the world, for that matter) makes an impact on the children you see enter your early childhood classroom on the first day. Because parents have such an important impact and because it is their responsibility and right to be part of their children's lives and education, they are definitely a part of your program.

Government Regulations

In some early childhood programs that are subsidized by the government, parent involvement is not chosen, but mandated. Programs like Head Start and others that fall under Title I regulation have definite requirements about parents' involvement in their children's program. If this is the case with your classroom, then parent involvement is not only a choice but a requirement. If Title I affects your school, you are probably already aware of the requirements of this law.

Early Childhood Choice

A large majority of early childhood programs make the choice about the kind of involvement and the way they would like parents to be involved in what happens in the classroom. Most early childhood programs have an open door policy for parents to visit at any time. This is a valuable policy. It insures parents that their children are being treated in a way that will not be changed based on the knowledge that they will be arriving to look, and it gives parents a feeling that the facility is not trying to hide anything. Security is a part of parents' concerns about their children and the place their children go every day. This is a realistic consideration.

Based on the fact that parents are so important to this process, the emphasis in this book will be to celebrate the parent/child connection. Parents can use a pat on the back just as early childhood educators can. Practically all parents are interested in helping their children. This combination can be used to make the experience in your early childhood classroom far more enriching for your children—right from the start.

How to Start

You are now ready to make parents an important part of your program. How do you start? The next few pages of this book will be devoted to helping you begin your parent helper program. This parent helper program will set the stage for the assessment programs in your classroom and carry them into the children's homes every day for additional reinforcement and acceptance.

Additionally, this parent helper program for assessment can be a part of your already existing parent program or help you create a program that encompasses all areas of your program. Since assessment is forever linked with all aspects of learning in your early childhood classroom, you really only need one program to make it work for you.

Many Ways to Make It Work

Here are some ideas that will help you begin including parents as an important part of your assessment team:

- Parent Helper Information Meeting

- Helping At Home On-Going Communication Meetings

- Helping At Home Assessment Kits

- Parent Helper Coffee Break

- Learning At Home Unit Activity Cards and Games
  (See individual **Assessed Activities Sections** starting on page 155.)

- Monthly Bulletins

An example idea, Parent Helper Information Meeting has been put together for you here, complete with all master forms. Included is a "generic" letter and "Helping At Home" form, so you can decide the level of your parent involvement.

Life as a teacher can be made far easier or infinitely worse based on parent input and opinion. Setting your program up for success is a good way to ensure that everyone gets started on the right foot.

Parent Helper Information Meeting

Materials Included in This Section
- Description (this page)
- Invitation master, page 68
- Reusable Meeting Agenda, page 69
- Parent Networking Form, page 70
- Helper Schedule, page 71

How to Start

Get together with your team and decide when the best time would be to host a parent information meeting. Because you will want to make parents an integral part of your learning and assessment process, you will want to schedule a regular meeting, but, for the first meeting, a more festive Welcome and Get Acquainted Meeting will help everyone get a feel for parental involvement.

Party Time

Use the parent information meeting introduction letter and invitation to invite parents to your first parent get-together function. You may wish to have this at night or have it on a Saturday, providing child care at your facility so parents do not have to make any special provisions for their children. There are many ways to do this, but a party makes people feel special and creates the kind of high energy and enthusiasm that a one-on-one meeting with a parent might not be able to accomplish.

The First Meeting

The first meeting is a time to get acquainted and a time to stress your program's commitment to its children. Many parents will be unfamiliar with the kinds of assessment that your program is using and many parents will have traditional ideas about assessment.

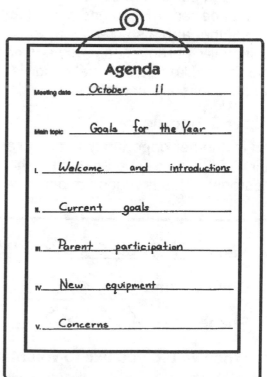

The Process

It will be important to give parents this information more than once and in several different ways. Use the first meeting to decide upon a time for subsequent meetings. A once-a-month information gathering will give parents a lot of current information and will also be an important process, the beginning of the exciting process of a child's learning all through school— not just in the preschool classroom.

Learning and Assessment

In this book there are several easy-to-use assessment information sections provided. Each of these sections gives you, or anyone who is interested, a quick overview of the type of assessment you are using and how it works.

Take-Home Information and Assessments

Each activity section features a "What Is It?" page, clearly describing the type of assessment. Then, there is also an optional "Parent Assessment Tool" to make parents part of the process whenever you feel necessary. You will want to decide which information is relevant to give to parents based on the kind of assessment process your team decides to use for your program. It is always easier to convey information when parents have an opportunity to hear about it, see it, and then hear about it again. The information gives parents something definitive to take with them and something to refer to when they need to clarify what was discussed at the meeting.

Easy-To-Use Master Forms

It is a good idea to use a meeting agenda to keep a meeting on schedule and give people a chance to know beforehand what will be discussed. Remember, when planning a parent meeting, that parents are often tired and busy on weekends. Keep it to the point, fun and short. The idea is to give them information that will help them to be part of their child's learning and assessment process without creating an additional burden in their lives. A 30 minute meeting with informal time afterwards is all that is necessary.

Parent Networking Form

Encourage parents to use the networking form. This form is to create a parent phone book that can be reproduced and given to all parents. This gives parents a chance to get to know one another and also creates a sense of community and excitement about your program. Additionally, parents can reach each other to car pool or for emergency pick-up reasons. Little things like this that make individuals feel part of something vital where their concerns and questions are important.

Helper Schedule

This is another opportunity to encourage parents to participate on site as well as at home with their child. Use the parent helper sheet to schedule times for parents to help in the classroom. This is a good experience for everyone.

Name _Sarah Turner_

Child's Name _Joel Turner_

Phone _371-5329_

When would you like to volunteer? _any time_

Do you have any special skills you would like to share with your child's class?

I can play the piano

Helping at Home

Dear Parent,

As part of our focus on  _____
Assessment, we are sending home a new Parent Assessment Tool. This tool will help you become part of the exciting process of observing your child's growth and development!

Please feel free to contact me with any questions or for more information. We will be holding our regular Parents' Helping At Home Meeting on _____.

Thank you again.

Sincerely,

_____
for

_____
school

Invitation

Dear Parents,

As part of our Learning At Home program, we want to provide you with as much up-to-the-minute information about your child's learning process as possible. We will be holding a parent helper information meeting on

_____ at _____.

Please feel free to bring your children for supervised play while you are attending this brief information meeting. This meeting will give you the new information about testing and assessment and give you hands-on information about how you can help your child explore learning in the most exciting and positive way possible.

We look forward to seeing you!

Sincerely,

_____
for

_____
school

Please feel free to call _____ with any questions or concerns.

Agenda

Meeting date _____

Main topic _____

    I. _____

   II. _____

  III. _____

  IV. _____

   V. _____

Parent Phone Book and Networking Form

○ Name _____
Child's Name _____
Address _____
Work Phone _____
Home Phone _____
Are you interested in car pooling? _____
Are you interested in volunteering? _____

Name _____
Child's Name _____
Address _____
Work Phone _____
Home Phone _____
Are you interested in car pooling? _____
Are you interested in volunteering? _____

○ Name _____
Child's Name _____
Address _____
Work Phone _____
Home Phone _____
Are you interested in car pooling? _____
Are you interested in volunteering? _____

Name _____
Child's Name _____
Address _____
Work Phone _____
Home Phone _____
Are you interested in car pooling? _____
Are you interested in volunteering? _____

Name _____
Child's Name _____
Address _____
Work Phone _____
Home Phone _____
○ Are you interested in car pooling? _____
Are you interested in volunteering? _____

Parent Helper Scheduling Sheet

○ Name _____

   Child's Name _____

   Phone _____

   When would you like to volunteer? _____

   Do you have any special skills you would like to share with your child's class?

   _____

   Name _____

   Child's Name _____

   Phone _____

   When would you like to volunteer? _____

   Do you have any special skills you would like to share with your child's class?

   _____

○ Name _____

   Child's Name _____

   Phone _____

   When would you like to volunteer? _____

   Do you have any special skills you would like to share with your child's class?

   _____

   Name _____

   Child's Name _____

   Phone _____

   When would you like to volunteer? _____

   Do you have any special skills you would like to share with your child's class?

   _____

○

Children Beginning to Self-Assess

When Does Self-Assessment Begin?

Children begin life looking at things from an egocentric point of view; that is, they see the world as it relates to them and then begin to de-center as they develop. There is a difference between seeing the world from an egocentric point of view and assessing oneself. Self-assessment is a skill that children acquire over time and is part of their development. The goal in teaching children to self-assess is to give them the kind of intrapersonal tools they will need to have an active part in their own education later and to be able to achieve the goals they plan for themselves. Additionally, children who learn to self-assess in a developmentally appropriate context have the benefit of the self-esteem that comes with being aware of their strengths and appreciating them.

Why Is Helping Children Self-Assess Useful?

Children who self-assess are aided in the formation of strong and healthy egos. They are able to think clearly about their capabilities, set, and attain goals for themselves later in life. And just as our goal is to help children to grow into thriving, sensitive, contributing adults, teaching them to assess themselves accurately is part of the process of teaching them to respect who they are and what gifts they bring to the world.

How Do You Encourage Children to Self-Assess?

Assessment that is developmentally appropriate builds self-esteem. It is not appropriate to let children criticize themselves or others in a damaging way. In fact, teaching the skill of self-assessment guards against that and fosters a sense of empathy and understanding not only for themselves but for their classmates.

Your attitude has a lot to do with how self-assessment will look in your center or classroom. It is important to remember that constructive criticism and guidance is always the order of the day. No one is stupid; no one gets to berate anyone including him/herself. Remember a child who is assessing himself or herself as stupid or dumb is sending you danger signals. This process of teaching children to self-assess also helps you as a teacher to gauge their emotional development and see to it that they have every opportunity to become happy, healthy, active learners.

Using Children's Self-Assessment Tools in This Book

In this book, after every activity in the second section, there is, a tool for child self-assessment. Each tool is designed for young children and is a developmentally appropriate way of understanding how children feel about themselves in the context of an activity. Each assessment respects the child and encourages his or her own self-respect.

Assessment and Self-Esteem

Self-Esteem and Effective Assessment

Assessment is a challenging process no matter what the situation. Self-esteem is a crucial issue in performance whether it is the performance of our teams, ourselves, or our students. Researchers have been telling us for years that how people feel about themselves directly relates to the kind of work they do, their achievements, and their abilities. Good early childhood educators are very aware of the care we must take with children's self-esteem in order to create an environment of mutual respect and happiness where children can begin the learning that will take them through their lives.

Setting the Assessment Stage

Assessment and self-esteem are so closely linked; therefore, in this book is provided a detailed hands-on section for you to boost the self-esteem of everyone around you at your school or center—your whole team, yourself, and the children you work with. In four mini-sections you will find the following hands-on self-esteem tools:

Section One	Section Two
• Team Self-Esteem Checklist • Team Self-Esteem Boosters	• Teacher Self-Esteem Checklist • Teacher Self-Esteem Boosters
Section Three	**Section Four**
• Children Self-Esteem Checklist • Children Self-Esteem Boosters	• Parents' and Children's Self-Esteem Checklist • Self-Esteem at Home

Assessment and Self-Esteem *(cont.)*

Check the Checklist!

Use the checklist portion of each section to see where you, your team, or your children are today. Get parents involved in the all-important task of supporting their children using Section Four. Ask them to complete the checklist to see how they are doing as well.

How About a Boost?

After using the checklist portion of the section, choose a booster activity that will give you a boost in the area needed. It is that simple to have a quick mental and emotional pick-me-up for anyone who needs it! You will find that frequent attention to self-esteem issues will result in a better, happier, and more accurate environment for assessment of any kind.

Easy Ideas

- Use the team checklist and booster section for your team's monthly meetings. You will find it is a pleasant way to get everyone into the attitude needed to discuss curriculum activities or other tasks at hand.

- Having a down day? Use the teacher checklist to notice what is going on and then help yourself to a self-esteem booster. When you are at your best and feeling good, your children benefit as well as you.

- Make your classroom an emotionally safe place for your children. Use the child self-esteem checklist as part of each child's individual assessment. Then use the boosters according to what is appropriate for each child. You will find that children who feel good about themselves develop faster and learn easier with better results.

- Parents need a boost too! Parenthood, like teaching, is often a thankless job. Use these self-esteem tools as a gift you can give to the parents of your children. It will be a gift for them that will help them give to their children.

Self-Esteem Success

Use all of these sections at once to best benefit everyone. Remember, that happy, comfortable, emotionally healthy children have the best chance for optimum development and learning. The foundation that you can provide for them today will last them all their lives.

Achievement and Self-Esteem

Assessment with positive and constructive results is an important part of building self-esteem. Children and adults alike have been proven to dramatically improve their feelings of self-worth based on feeling the effect of completing a task, large or small, successfully. The final section in this part of the book will help you and your team use assessment to build rather than defeat children's self-esteem.

What Is Self-Esteem?

Everybody Always Talks About It

Self-esteem is talked about all the time. You cannot pick up a magazine or self-improvement book without being asked if you are happy, healthy, and the proud possessor of great self-esteem. Schools talk about it; newspapers report that the lack of it contributes to gang violence and other crimes. People look at each other and say, "Hmmm, that person must have low self-esteem."

What exactly is it? Is it just how we feel about ourselves? No. It is more than that. It is how we feel about ourselves, if we feel competent and in control, if we feel as if we are part of a group, as well as somebody who has his or her own individual identity. Self-esteem has something to do with our values and notion of right and wrong and how well we are living up to those values as we see them. Self-esteem has something to do with whether or not we see existence as worthwhile and what we do everyday as meaningful. Self-esteem has something to do with how we view other people's opinions of us and how we see the world. Self-esteem is also about real achievements, and the things we have accomplished both successfully and without success.

What is Self-Esteem? *(cont.)*

More Than Just Saying "You Are Wonderful"

Self-Esteem is more than just saying you are wonderful, or your team is wonderful, or the children in your class are wonderful. It is about experiences and reality and what happens every day as well as what we do and think and say, and how we feel about all that.

It will not work to rush into class every day and tell everyone we meet that they are great and wonderful and perfect in every way. In fact, the negative talk about self-esteem these days is about just that. It does not make sense to tell children they are great and wonderful when they are doing something mean. It does not make sense to tell a child he can do something he can not do. Children are the first ones to sense lies.

It does make sense to tell children that you expect a certain set of behaviors, and that they need to treat their friends and classmates according to the rules. It makes sense to tell a child who does not know how to do something that he or she can try it and practice. You can also give children both a realistic view of the world and a positive view of themselves in the world. If you have a negative or unrealistic view of yourself or the world around you, it will affect the children you teach. It is easy to see how important your own self-esteem is to the whole picture.

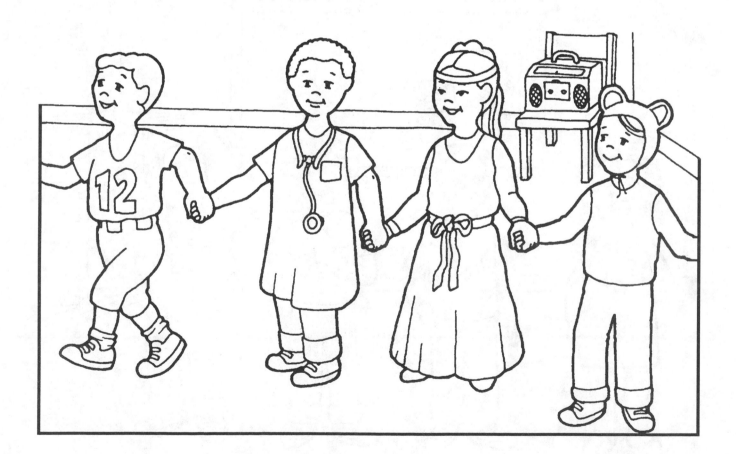

What is Self-Esteem? *(cont.)*

What Parts Add Up to a Whole?

In this book are a few aspects of self-esteem that are easy to look at and work on for your team, yourself, your children, and their parents. In the sections that follow, you can easily decide out of these six areas what aspect of self-esteem could be "boosted" for teams, teachers, children, or parents. Self-esteem is a personal matter. While you can decide as a team, or by yourself, what would be good for certain children and use those specific activities, you might want to let parents discover for themselves what they would like to work on regarding their own self-esteem. Just as you would not like to be told "what is wrong with you," remember these activities are about making everyone feel better, not making a new problem to add to their already long lists.

The six areas each section will focus on are these:

Strengths

(competence)

Values

(ethics, right and wrong)

Worthwhile Feelings

(life having meaning and purpose)

Feeling Connected

(belonging, interacting, understanding, compassion)

Specialness

(uniqueness, individuality, autonomy)

Being Realistic

(who I really am, what I really can do, how the world really is)

Team Self-Esteem Assessment— Checklist

Use this checklist as a team to determine in which aspects of self-esteem your team can benefit from a boost!

Team Self-Esteem Includes:

Check all of those that apply. The areas with the least number of check marks are the areas in which your team can use a boost!

Strengths (competence)

Strengths, in a team environment include:

_____ Your team does things together easily and well.

_____ Your team succeeds at group projects.

_____ Your team enjoys working together.

_____ Your team uses the individual strengths of each member to best advantage.

Values (ethics, right and wrong)

Values, as they relate to your team include:

_____ Your team has a shared vision.

_____ Your team agrees about policies toward children, parents, and each other.

_____ Your team is aware of both your agreement and disagreement regarding teaching philosophies.

_____ Your team deals easily with differences in personal values.

Worthwhile Feelings (life having meaning and purpose)

_____ Your team has good feelings about your school.

_____ Your team has good feelings about your program.

_____ Your team has good feelings about each other.

_____ Your team feels what you are doing every day is valuable.

Feeling Connected (belonging, interacting, understanding, compassion)

_____ Your team feels close to each other.

_____ Your team is a support system.

_____ Your team can discuss problems easily.

_____ Your team deals well with the emotions of its members.

Specialness (uniqueness, individuality, autonomy)

_____ Your team is making a unique difference in the lives of the children you teach.

_____ Your team is creative.

_____ Your team supports individuals.

_____ Your team allows its members to be themselves.

Being Realistic (who I really am, what I really can do, how the world really is)

_____ Your team knows the areas it needs to work on.

_____ Your team handles conflict well.

_____ Your team has straightforward discussions.

_____ Your team changes when it needs to.

Team Self-Esteem Boosters

Strengths (competence)

Activity: Strength Circle

What You Need: one Strength Circle master for each person (page 82)

What You Do:

This activity helps team members become clear about their own strengths and the strengths of the members of their team. Begin with partners. Each person writes strengths they recognize about his/her partner on the paper outside of the circle. Each person should do this for his or her partner, thinking of as many varied strengths as possible. Next, partners trade back circle masters, and look at what his/her partner sees as his/her strengths. Then, each person fills in the circle with strengths that he or she recognizes but were not mentioned by partners. Partners then talk about the activity, and how they see themselves versus how others see them. Meet as a whole team to review this process and let each person share his or her strengths. **Note:** The last step is very important, because team members need to recognize each others' strengths. Finish the activity by making copies for everyone of all the Strength Circles.

Values (ethics, right and wrong)

Activity: My Way, Your Way, Our Way

What You Need: Problem Master and pen for each team member (page 84)

What You Do:

This activity helps your team to determine your group ethics regarding children and what you see as right or wrong. To begin, have each team member write down an actual or pretend situation with a child (determine this beforehand) and what they did to solve or deal with the problem. Then, in a group, each person shares his/her situation and response. Decide if everyone agrees with their action and why or why not. Remember, this is about positive ways of dealing with situations. The idea is to get your team to look at the values of each individual and come to agreement about how you might all work together on these various issues. Just as you want your children to treat each others' ideas with respect, remember that this is important for adults too. Using the My Way, Your Way, Our Way grid, your team must find a compromise that makes everyone happy for each situation. If your team can do this one successfully, you can be sure you are presenting a united and positive organization to your children, parents, and community. Congratulations!

Team Self-Esteem Boosters *(cont.)*

Worthwhile Feelings (work having meaning and purpose)

Activity: Team Vision Table Maps

What You Need: Team Vision Circle master (one copy for each group), Ladder master (one copy for each person), Team Vision Table Map Directions (pages 85–87)

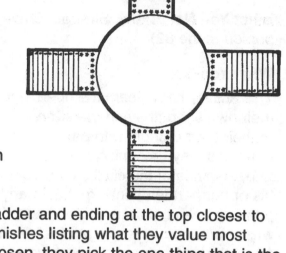

What You Do:

Team members sit around a table with the team vision circle in the middle. Each team member uses their own ladder to list the ten most important things about his/her job step by step starting at the bottom of the ladder and ending at the top closest to the circle (see diagram). When each team member finishes listing what they value most about their job, then out of the 10 things they have chosen, they pick the one thing that is the most important to them. When all team members have chosen the thing that is most important to them, teams discuss the important things that each member has chosen, and out of them they all craft a team "Vision"; that is, the single community value that is the most important thing to all of them about their jobs. This activity is great for starting a discussion about what your team values, and learning about what is important to each of you, and coming together about what is important about your school.

Feeling Connected (belonging, interacting, understanding, compassion)

Activity: Secret Power Pal

What You Need: Secret Power Pal Note masters (page 88)

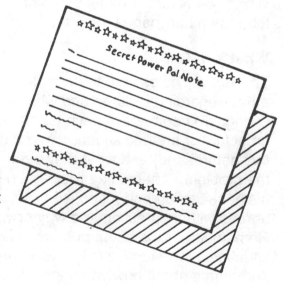

What You Do:

Draw names of team members from a hat. Each Secret Power Pal writes little positive notes to make his or her pal feel good, to acknowledge performance or qualities, or just a little friendly word for no reason at all. You decide with your team the length of time you would like to do this activity. A good team idea is to end this activity with a party where Power Pals give each other small gifts and reveal themselves. Have each "Pal" read her favorite Power Pal note and team energy will soar!

It is also possible to use this team activity as an on-going activity or for special occasions like holidays or the beginning or ending of a school year. This activity will build happy feelings

Team Self-Esteem Boosters *(cont.)*

Specialness (uniqueness, individuality, autonomy)

Activity: Feel Good Fortune Cookie Jars

What You Need: fortune cookie strips, jars or coffee cans, art supplies

What You Do:

Each member of your group puts his/her name in a hat. Team members select a secret name. Each team member then creates a jar full of affirmations for their secret person. An affirmation is a positive statement that gives the person reading it a boost—like a positive fortune cookie. They can be uplifting, humorous, or supportive. Focus on the issues that are meaningful to the team member you have selected. Some affirmations examples are:

- You are great!

- No matter how hard the day is, you have a friend.

- Take life a little easier!

- Smile—it makes people wonder what you are up to!

- Dream big dreams; the world is your rainbow!

Being Realistic (who I really am, what I really can do, how the world really is)

Activity: Good News!

What You Need: daily newspaper

What You Do:

Each member of your team shares Good News. Find a place in the teachers' room or break room to post good news stories that will brighten everyone's outlook, instead of the grim front page headlines we are all used to. It is true and realistic that there are many good things that happen in the world every day, and we owe it to children to focus on the good, as well as everything else in the world.

Strength Circle

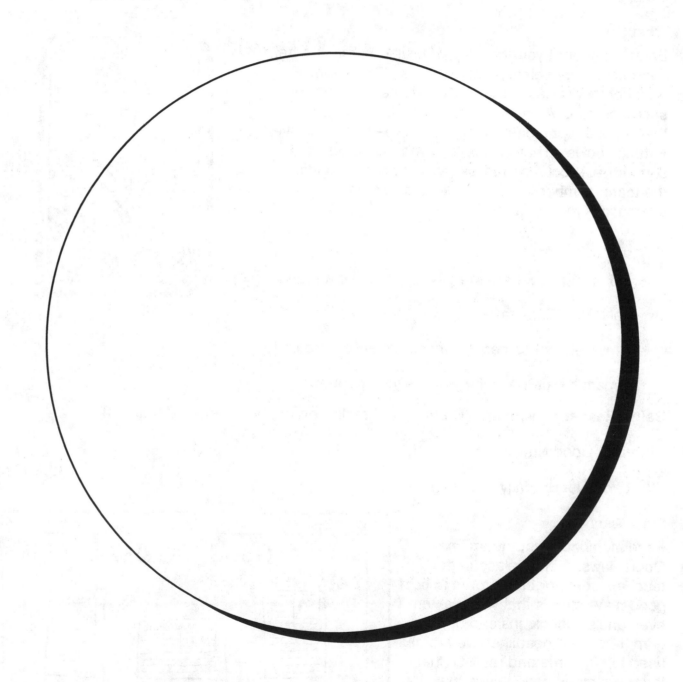

Strength Circle—Example

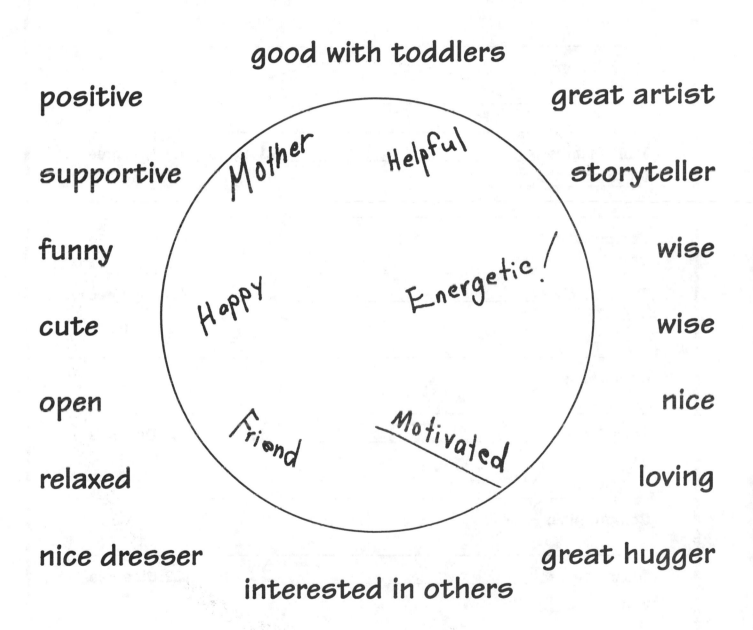

good with toddlers

positive   great artist

supportive   storyteller

funny   wise

cute   wise

open   nice

relaxed   loving

nice dresser   great hugger

interested in others

Mother   Helpful   Happy   Energetic!   Friend   Motivated

My Way, Your Way, Our Way

Problem:

_____

_____

My Solution:

_____

_____

Team Member _____ ❑ **Agree** ❑ **Disagree**

Why:

_____

Compromise:

_____

Team Member _____ ❑ **Agree** ❑ **Disagree**

Why:

_____

Compromise:

_____

Team Member _____ ❑ **Agree** ❑ **Disagree**

Why:

_____

Compromise:

_____

Team Member _____ ❑ **Agree** ❑ **Disagree**

Why:

_____

Compromise:

_____

Vision Circle

attach ladder here

TEAM VISION

TEAM VISION

TEAM VISION

TEAM VISION

attach ladder here

attach ladder here

attach ladder here

Ladder

10.

9.

8.

7.

6.

5.

4.

3.

2.

1.

Team Vision Table Map Directions

Use a large piece of butcher or construction paper to mount your team vision table map like this:

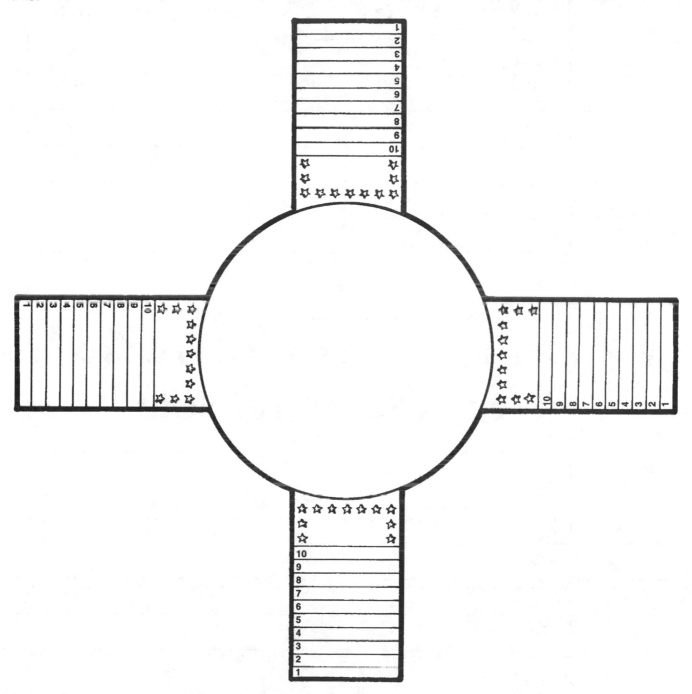

Have each member sit at a ladder and list the 10 things they value the most about their job.

Next, have each member decide the most important thing out of the 10 they listed and place that in the starred box.

Finally, talk about your teams' individual visions and out of those create a team vision. Write team vision in the center of the circle.

☆★☆★☆★☆★☆★☆★☆★☆★☆★☆★☆

Secret Power Pal Note

Dear_____

_____

_____

_____

_____

Have a Powerful Day!

Signed,

_____

☆★☆★☆★☆★☆★☆★☆★☆★☆★☆★☆

Secret Power Pal Note

Dear_____

_____

_____

_____

_____

Have a Powerful Day!

Signed,

_____

☆★☆★☆★☆★☆★☆★☆★☆★☆★☆★☆

Fortune Cookie Form

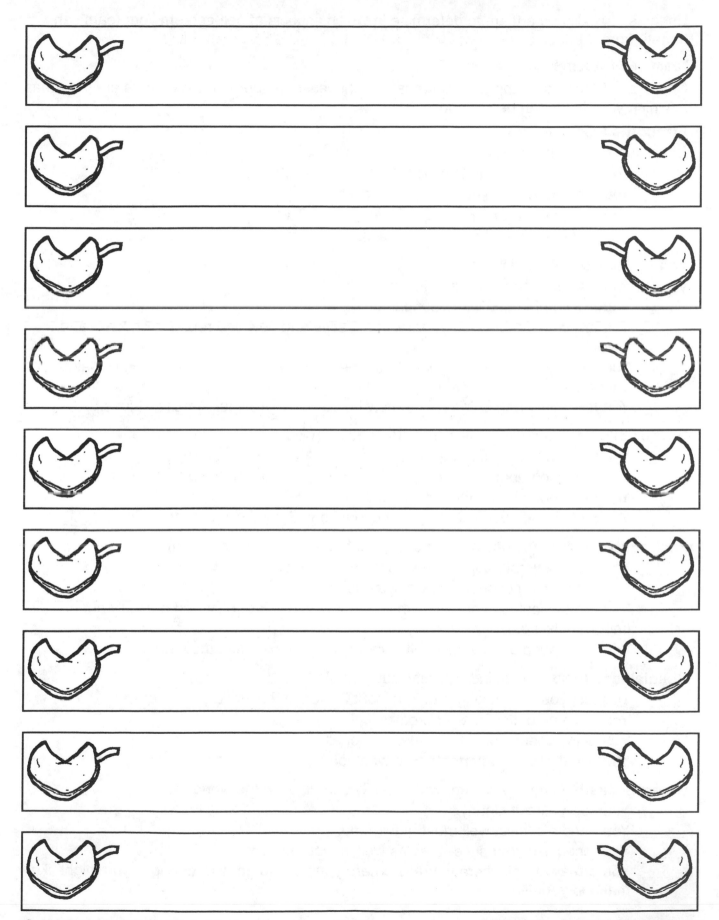

Teacher Self-Esteem Assessment Checklist

Use this checklist as a team to determine in which aspects of self-esteem your team can benefit from a boost.

Team Self-Esteem Includes:

Check all of those that apply. The areas with the least number of check marks are the areas in which your team can use a "boost."

Strengths (competence)

Strengths, in a team environment, include:

_____ You feel you do things you want to do easily and well.

_____ You are happy with your level of success.

_____ You recognize your special qualities.

_____ You feel confident about your abilities.

Values (ethics, right and wrong)

Values, as they relate to your team, include:

_____ You are comfortable with your values.

_____ You are comfortable with your teaching style and how you relate to children and parents.

_____ You can agree or disagree with team members without feeling guilty, intimidated, or angry.

_____ You feel comfortable around others who do not share your specific values.

Worthwhile Feelings (life having meaning and purpose)

_____ You feel your life has a purpose.

_____ You feel good about yourself generally.

_____ You feel good about others generally.

_____ You feel you are valuable to your school, to your family, and to yourself.

Feeling Connected (belonging, interacting, understanding, compassion)

_____ You have several people you would count as friends.

_____ You have an emotional support system.

_____ You have people in your life with whom you can talk openly and honestly about important issues.

_____ You have people in your life with whom you can express emotion.

Specialness (uniqueness, individuality, autonomy)

_____ You feel you are making a unique contribution in the world.

_____ You have an outlet for your creativity.

_____ You enjoy spending time alone occasionally.

_____ You usually feel comfortable with who you are.

Being Realistic (who I really am, what I really can do, how the world really is)

_____ You see yourself clearly.

_____ You handle conflict well most of the time.

_____ You recognize your successes as well as your failures.

_____ You are aware of where you are, where you want to go, and changes you might like to make in your life.

Teacher Self-Esteem Boosters

Strengths (competence)

Activity: Assessing Your Strength

What You Need: Assessing Your Personal Quality List form (page 94)

What You Do:

This activity gives you an opportunity to think about all your good qualities. Most people feel uncomfortable listing their own good qualities but could easily tell you 25 things they love about their own best friend. For this activity, pretend you are telling your best friend about his/her good qualities. Except, you are actually talking about yourself! Do not stop at five or ten or even fifteen qualities. Use this list over a month's time and think of 100 qualities you like about yourself. Start small and work your way up. Being aware of your good qualities is a useful tool when you are dealing with your boss or your spouse or your children. Remember, it is easier to help others with their own good feelings about themselves if you have had the experience of recognizing and thinking about your own good qualities.

Values (ethics, right and wrong)

Activity: Assess for Success Teacher Self-Assessment

What You Need: Teacher Self-Esteem Assessment, Success Journal masters, three-ring binder (page 95)

What You Do:

This journal is an opportunity for you to look at your own day. It allows you to think about your successes with children and how they are reminders of what you value about teaching and what is important to you. Spend five to ten minutes at the end and perhaps the beginning of every day and use the forms in your journal to write quickly about stand-out moments with children and what they mean to you. This is handy in helping you to be aware of your own teaching style and to notice potential problems with children so that you can deal with them before they happen.

Teacher Self-Esteem Boosters *(cont.)*

Worthwhile Feelings (life having meaning and purpose)

Activity: Assessing Your Happiness—Happiness Collage

What You Need: old magazines, large piece of poster board, glue, scissors

What You Do:

Often when teachers' lives get hectic, they seem to end up pleasing everyone but themselves. Teachers are givers, and often at the end of the day they have nothing left to give themselves. In this activity, assess your happiness, not only whether or not you are happy, but what it is that makes you happy. Look through old magazines with the idea in mind that you are looking for pictures or words that represent the things that make you happy. Clip words and pictures and make your own Happiness Collage. The idea is to give yourself time to ponder the things that are important to you and where they are in your life today. Do you love to garden? Then your collage may be filled with flowers. Are you gardening now? Do you live in a place where you can use your green thumb? Do you allow yourself time for the pleasure that this activity brings you? Why or why not? Besides reminding yourself of what you love, this activity will give you an opportunity to remember "lost loves" and think about new things you would like to add to your life but have not yet. Place your collage somewhere at home where you can look at it every day.

Feeling Connected (belonging, interacting, understanding, compassion)

Activity: Assessing Your Relationships—Building a Network

What You Need: Personal Network Map (page 96)

What You Do:

Having a support network of friends and loved ones is a very important part of the world for everyone. In this activity, you will have a chance to think about who your support network is and look carefully at the group of people you have in your life who appreciate you the most. This is very helpful not only to realize these special people exist but to be able to call on them and let them make your life more positive and connected. Begin this activity by enlarging the network master to 11"x 14"(28cm x 36cm). Then fill in the circles until you have thought of everyone in your life. See how you feel about your network. Do you need more close friends? Do you have more friends than you can keep up with? Is there anyone important to you whom you have not seen or talked to in a long time? Which of these people are there for you whenever you need them? Which of these people would brighten your day if you called them? Use this support network to make your life happier and to be part of an important network for them as well as for you.

Teacher Self-Esteem Boosters *(cont.)*

Specialness (uniqueness, individuality, autonomy)

Activity: Assessing Your Past Successes

What You Need: Assessing Your Past Successes master (page 98)

What You Do:

Take some time and think about all the wonderful past "wins" you have had. This list is about anything you are proud of that you have succeeded at in the past. Remember when building this list, anything goes. Most people, often especially teachers, have a tendency to play down their own successes and are rather humble. However, it is really important to be able to assess yourself accurately and give yourself mental pats on the back for excellent performance in the past too.

Being Realistic (who I really am, what I really can do, how the world really is)

Activity: Assessing Your Stress—Being Realistic About Your Life

What You Need: What's Bugging You? Assessing Your stress worksheet (page 99)

What You Do:

Everyone has stress in his/her life; it is part of everyday living. But sometimes stress can start to wear you out. Use this activity to assess your own stress and think of better ways to react to situations and minimize your stress. Begin by using the What's Bugging You? worksheet. Think about the work- or home-related situations that bug you, how you react to them, and why. Then, think about ways you could react differently, either by actions or attitudes. Reduce your stress by changing your reaction. Use this activity to deal with whatever is bugging you and find new ways to become happier and more relaxed.

Assessing Your Personal Qualities List

Use this page to make a running list of your worthwhile and wonderful qualities. Think of it as describing the qualities of a good friend.

_____   _____   _____

_____   _____   _____

_____   _____   _____

_____   _____   _____

_____   _____   _____

_____   _____   _____

_____   _____   _____

_____   _____   _____

_____   _____   _____

_____   _____   _____

_____   _____   _____

_____   _____   _____

_____   _____   _____

_____   _____   _____

_____   _____   _____

Teacher Self-Esteem
Assessment—Success Journal

Date _____

Success Situation:

_____

What happened?

_____

_____

_____

How did you feel?

_____

_____

_____

How did this experience affect your:

    own feelings? _____

    _____

    others' feelings?

    _____

    _____

Who did you tell about this experience?

_____

_____

Personal Network Map

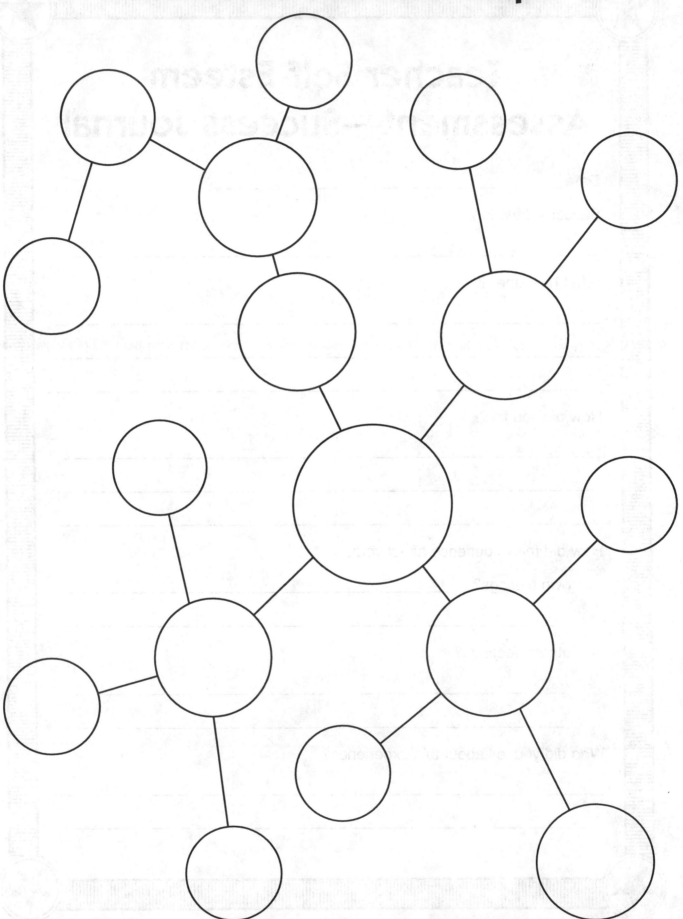

Personal Network Map—Example

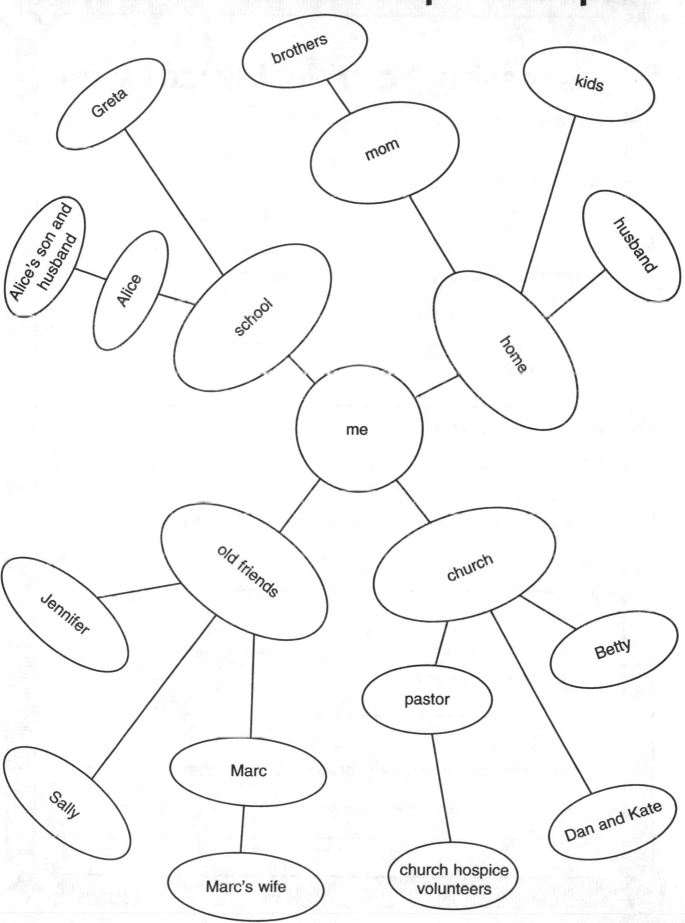

Assessing Your Past Successes

Success in the past:

_____

How this affects me today:

_____

_____

Because of this experience, I am confident about my ability to. . .

_____

_____

Success in the past:

_____

How this affects me today:

_____

_____

Because of this experience, I am confident about my ability to. . .

_____

_____

Success in the past:

_____

How this affects me today:

_____

_____

Because of this experience, I am confident about my ability to. . .

_____

_____

Assess Your Stress

What's Bugging You?

What is bugging me:

_____

_____

_____

_____

When this happens, I react like:

_____

_____

I react this way because I am feeling:

_____

What could I do so I would have a different outcome?

_____

How could I change the situation?

_____

How could I change my reaction?

_____

How could I change my attitudes or feelings about this?

_____

(Notice when the same stress situation happens again. Refer to these notes and see how you react in the future.)

Children's Self-Esteem Checklist

Use this checklist to determine in which aspects of self-esteem your students can benefit from a boost.

Children's Self-Esteem Includes:

Check all of those that apply. The areas with the least number of check marks are the areas in which your students can use a "boost."

Strengths (competence)

_____ Your students are often comfortable with parallel play and have begun to play cooperatively.

_____ Your students usually enjoy listening to stories in a group.

_____ Your students often take part in sharing activities.

_____ Your students are proud of their skills most of the time.

Values (ethics, right and wrong)

_____ Your students usually know your classroom rules.

_____ Your students often know the difference between being polite and being rude.

_____ Your students can take turns with toys most of the time.

_____ Your students can usually tell you the best way to act in a given situation.

Worthwhile Feelings (life having meaning and purpose)

_____ Your students know what things make them happy most of the time.

_____ Your students usually know what to do to make other children happy.

_____ Your students often enjoy doing jobs to help each other.

_____ Your students often enjoy doing jobs to help teacher(s).

Feeling Connected (belonging, interacting, understanding, compassion)

_____ Your students are usually caring if another child is sad or angry.

_____ Your students often try to help one another.

_____ Your students act as if they like each other most of the time.

_____ Your students sometimes inquire about students who are absent.

Specialness (uniqueness, individuality, autonomy)

_____ Your students are usually creative with art materials.

_____ Your students are usually creative with games.

_____ Your students often try to do things for themselves.

_____ Your students allow others to do things for themselves most of the time.

Being Realistic (who I really am, what I really can do, how the world really is)

_____ Your students sometimes use manipulatives.

_____ Your students often practice using crayons, paints, and other tools.

_____ Your students are usually interested in the work adults do.

_____ Your students sometimes talk about what they will do when they grow up.

Children's Self-Esteem Boosters

Strengths (competence)

Activity: Look What I Can Do—Sharing

What You Need: will vary based on child

What You Do:

Building self-esteem in children requires more than saying, "Aren't you wonderful!" Children feel increasingly confident when they have mastery over age and developmentally appropriate tasks.

This activity can be done both formally and informally to build children's feelings of competence in themselves. In a regular sharing time, you can ask children to demonstrate for the other children something they know how to do. Taking it a step further, you can ask a child to teach another child how to do something that he or she already knows how to do. You might want to make this part of your regular sharing or circle time based on the level and ages of your children.

Another way to build children's awareness of their strengths is to do this informally. When a child has mastered something new, comment on it at that moment and ask them to show you again. Then congratulate the child and ask someone else to watch. This way a child has a feeling of real accomplishment. Real accomplishments build children's self-esteem.

A possible script might look like this (noticing Sara tying her shoe for the first time).

"Wow, Sara, I see you are tying your own shoe. That is really neat. Can you do it again and show me? Hey, Bobby, look how Sara can tie her own shoe. Good for you, Sara!"

It is that simple, but done consistently this will reinforce young children's feelings of competence and awareness of their own strengths.

Values (ethics, right and wrong)

Activity: Positive Puppets

What You Need: any puppets will work for this; you will need two

What You Do:

Children, like adults, gain self-esteem from knowing what their own values are and acting in ways that do not go against those values. While this seems complicated, it is really just about right and wrong. Children need to learn basic appropriate behavior to survive in the world and be healthy and happy children and then adults. You know in your own center what the rules are. By using puppets to help children think of constructive ways to work out problems they have with following the rules, you can give yourself and them an alternative to a traditional time-out. This approach is one that respects them as human beings and gives them an opportunity to begin to reason about rules, which will later be the way they come to understand their own values.

Children's Self-Esteem Boosters (cont.)

Worthwhile Feelings (life having meaning and purpose)

Activity: What I Like Pictures

What You Need: art supplies, old magazines, large pieces of paper or poster board, paste or non-toxic glue

What You Do:

Just like adults, children know what kinds of things make them happy and feel good. Use old magazines for children to find pictures of things they like or things that make them feel happy. Have children use scissors to cut out the pictures, or cut a variety of pictures ahead of time for students who are not ready to use scissors.

Have children select things that make them happy for their collages and then glue them on to the paper. Talk with each individual child about his/her collage, not only to communicate and reinforce with them about the things that make them happy and the things that they like, but also for your own information, to get to know each child better.

Feeling Connected (belonging, interacting, understanding, compassion)

Activity: Everyday Valentines

What You Need: Valentine masters (page 108)

What You Do:

A big part of children feeling good about themselves is knowing they are loved and liked and also knowing that they have caring feelings towards others. Use the Everyday Valentines on pages 108-109 for children to have opportunities to give and receive valentines.

You can easily set up a self-directed part of your art table with a variety of these valentines printed on different colored paper, and you can use glitter and other different kinds of exciting materials to make them special.

Also, use these valentines as a way of saying "I like you!" to children on a daily basis. Take the time every day to give several of the children in your class a boost from you with a personalized everyday valentine.

Children's Self-Esteem Boosters *(cont.)*

Specialness (uniqueness, individuality, autonomy)

Activity: Special Kid Day, Week, and Party

What You Need: Kid Crown master (page 105), Good Notes master (page 104), and party supplies (party optional)

What You Do:

Feeling special does not always have to have a reason. Sometimes the best happy events are the ones that are unexpected. Use the Special Kid Crown master on page 105 to make several crowns for your class. You and your team can decide when "special kids" get to wear the crowns and what the reasons will be. Next, use the Good Notes on page 104 to add a wonderful finish to your "special kids' day."

It is also possible to expand on this theme and make a Special Kid Party once a month, or whenever you feel like all your children need a boost. A party can be as simple as a bag of cookies and some party hats, or make crowns and decorate them for each child in your class to wear at your Special Kid Party!

Being Realistic (who I really am, what I really can do, how the world really is)

Activity: Someday Stories

What You Need: large sheets of paper, drawing and painting supplies

What You Do:

During circle time or during individual time with children, talk about what they would like to do someday that they do not know how to do now, or what they would like to do when they grow up, etc. You can approach this self-esteem builder either way, but for best results, get children to focus on tangible real things they will be able to do soon and that they will enjoy having mastered. Additionally, if a child has a certain goal he/she wants to achieve, you can help him/her meet that goal if you are aware of it.

Have children draw or paint pictures on a large piece of paper that is labeled "Someday I want to. . ." Then let children dictate stories to you about what they are doing in the picture. Talk with them about their goals and how they might achieve them. Try to devise ways they can practice toward their goals, and encourage children to think about things realistically. It is good to have dreams that are far away, but one of the best ways to help children feel good about themselves is to help them do what they want to do now, comfortably and successfully. Keep these pictures and label them with the date, and then label them with the date the child achieves his or her goal.

Good Notes

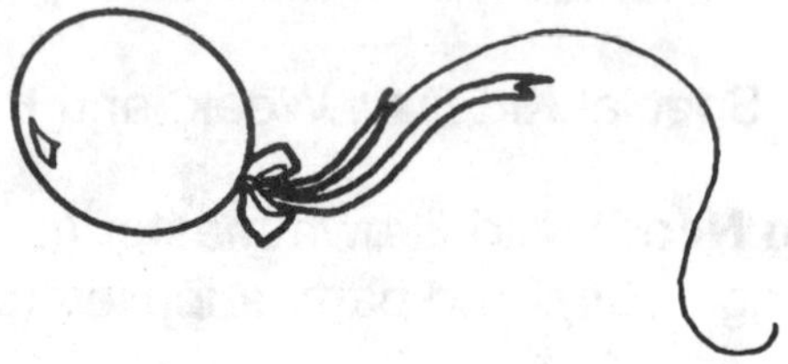

Dear _____,

Your child _____

was awarded the **Special Kid Of The Day Award** for

_____

_____

_____

We are very proud and knew you would be too!

Sincerely,

_____

at _____

_____

school

Attach string here to tie.

Crown

IS A SPECIAL KID!

Attach string here to tie.

I Can Do Something New Buttons

I
can
do
something new!

Ask Me!

I can do
something new!

Ask Me!

I
can do
something new!

Ask Me!

I
can do
something
new!

Ask Me!

Who I Like Happy Face

I like

_____

I Love Heart

I love

_____

Who Loves Me Heart

_____

s

me!

Who Likes Me Happy Face

I like

_____

Special Kid Award

is a special kid

Date

Teacher

Special Kid Badges

Self-Esteem At Home

Parent and Child Activities

Activity: Kid Art Gallery

What You Need: wall space or refrigerator door, letter masters to make at home art gallery, example page for ideas (page 114), construction paper, tape, various art supplies

What You Do:

Children appreciate compliments. What better way to compliment them than to encourage parents to make an at-home art gallery where they can display their children's paintings and drawings. Parents can acknowledge their children's work in a way that will make them happy and build their self-confidence.

Use the Art Gallery masters and send home directions. In minutes, parents will have a designated place where children can display their art. Each time they add a drawing or painting, they will know their parents think their work is special.

Encourage parents to take the time, each time a child brings home a picture or creates one at home, to add it to the "art gallery" together!

Art Gallery—Example

Kid Art Gallery

Art Gallery Sign

Kid Art Gallery (cont.)

Name Tag

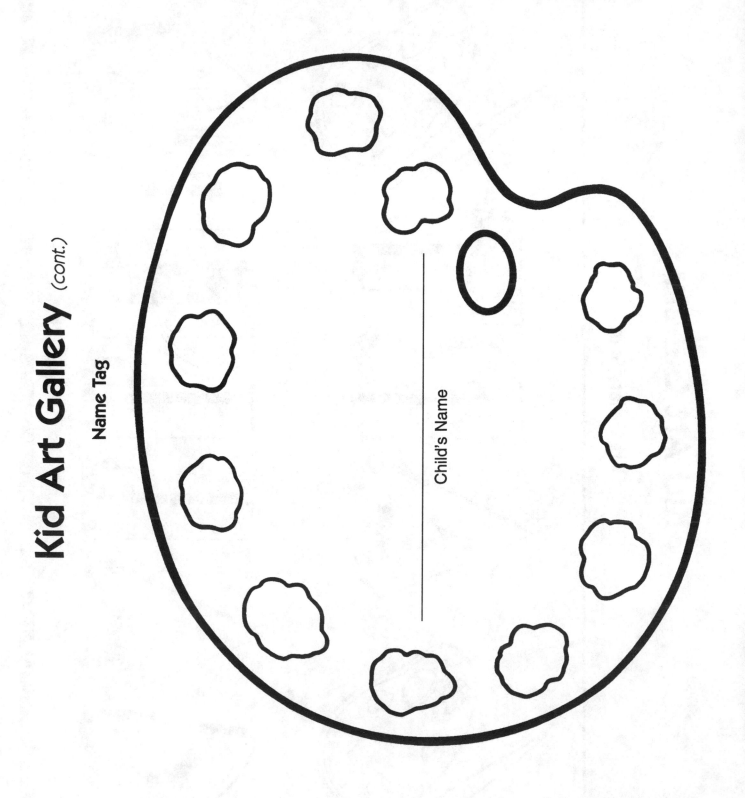

Child's Name

Parent Communication Letter

Dear Parent(s),

As part of our assessment program we are focusing on self-esteem. Studies show that how children feel about themselves dramatically affects their performance. Because of this we are sending you a "Self-Esteem at Home" package. In it are these helpful tools:

- Children's Self-Esteem Checklist

- Children's Self-Esteem Booster Page

- Art Gallery Ideas

- Reward Chart

- Love Notes

Included in your Self-Esteem at Home package are all the ingredients you need to give your child a self-esteem boost!

Please call me with any question you might have about how to use this material. You are always welcome to volunteer at school, and we would love to have you come, either to take part or to observe any of our programs. Please call ( ) ___-____ with questions. Thank you again, and we hope you and your child find this activity helpful, fun, and positive!

_____

Sincerely,

_____

for

_____

school

Reward Chart

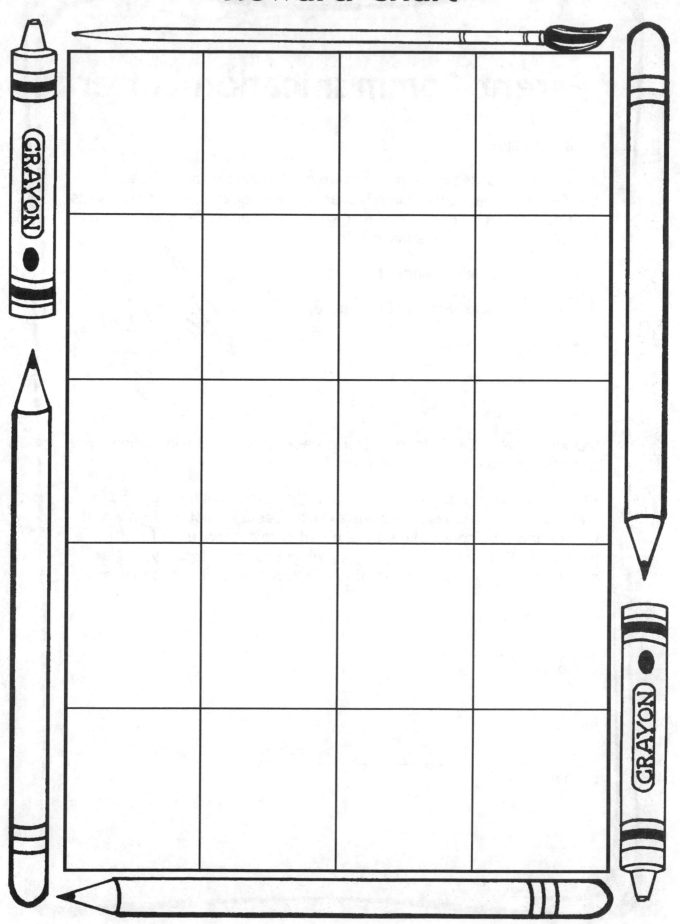

Parent/Child Love Note

Dear _____,

This is how I feel about you today:

Here is why:

1. _____

2. _____

3. _____

Love,

_____

Maslow in the Classroom

Safe Places to Learn

Setting the Stage for Assessment

Look below at this familiar model. You have probably seen it before. Teachers at sometime or another hear about Abraham Maslow. He was a psychologist who felt that people were basically good and that they could change based on their own choices. He created a model that works very well in the early childhood classroom, explaining issues that sensitive teachers already have feelings about, some knowing without knowing, when they think about making a great environment for young children.

How Is This Related to Assessment?

In order to have an environment where your assessments will be accurate and even possible to do, certainly the bottom levels of this triangle are necessary. To have an environment that produces and nurtures happy, healthy, appropriately developed children, all the areas of the hierarchy need to be kept in mind.

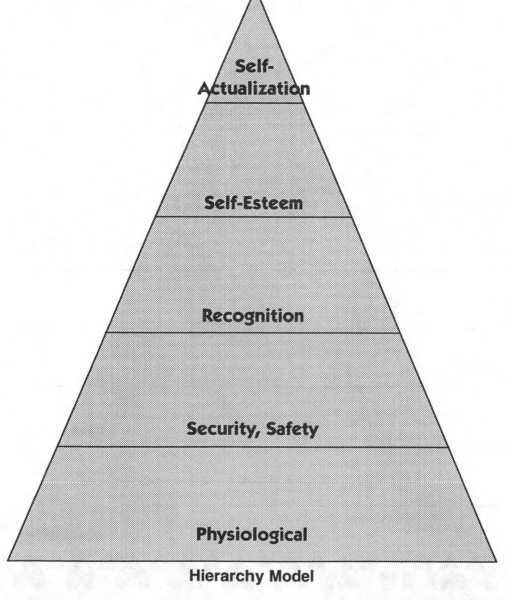

Hierarchy Model

Maslow in the Classroom *(cont.)*

A Safe Place for Children to Be

What did Maslow know about making an early childhood classroom safe for children, emotionally and physically, that we do not know? Maybe nothing. However, his hierarchy of needs makes an easy-to-look-at model that helps us as teachers look at what we feel is happening in our classroom environments as well as in the individual lives of children. Experts say that, without at least the bottom level of these needs consistently met, children cannot develop at all.

On the following pages you will have an easy-to-read description of Maslow's hierarchy of needs, and a way to use his model to assess the environment of your classroom, as well as a plan to build a model to assess your children in another interesting and helpful way.

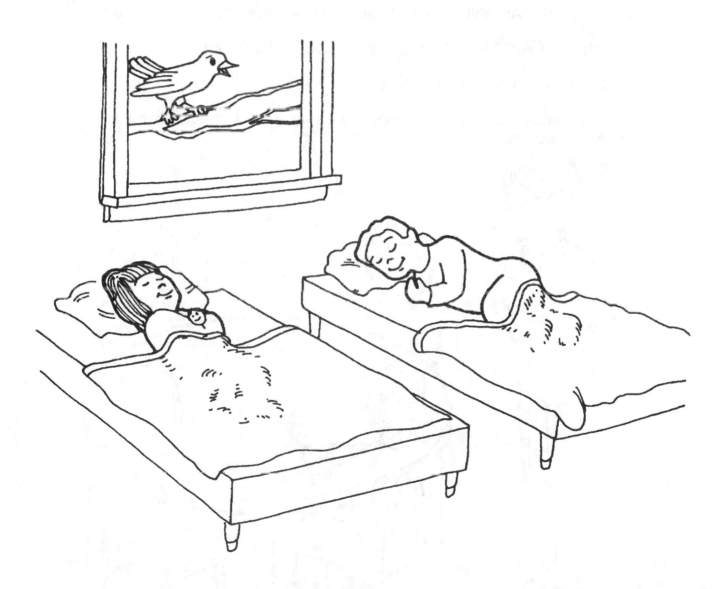

Maslow in the Classroom *(cont.)*

Quick and Easy

The following is a quick and easy description of the basics of Maslow's hierarchy and how it relates to all of us in our early childhood classrooms. As you read it, think about where your classroom is today. Is any part of the hierarchy missing or weak? Are there children who have parts of their own hierarchy missing at home because of poverty, family problems, or neglect. We can create a setting in which children can develop appropriately and then learn, with every possible advantage, to reach their own individual potential. Refer to the numbers in each level of this hierarchy for a description.

1. **Physiological**—Basic Survival Issues: Do children have adequate food, water, and shelter?

2. **Security, Safety:** Are children out of danger; is the physical environment safe?

3. **Recognition:** Are children loved, cared for, liked, and nurtured?

4. **Self-Esteem:** Children like, care for, and love themselves.

5. **Self-Actualization:** Children are happy, confident, and self-directed and enjoy school. They feel successful.

Hierarchy Blank

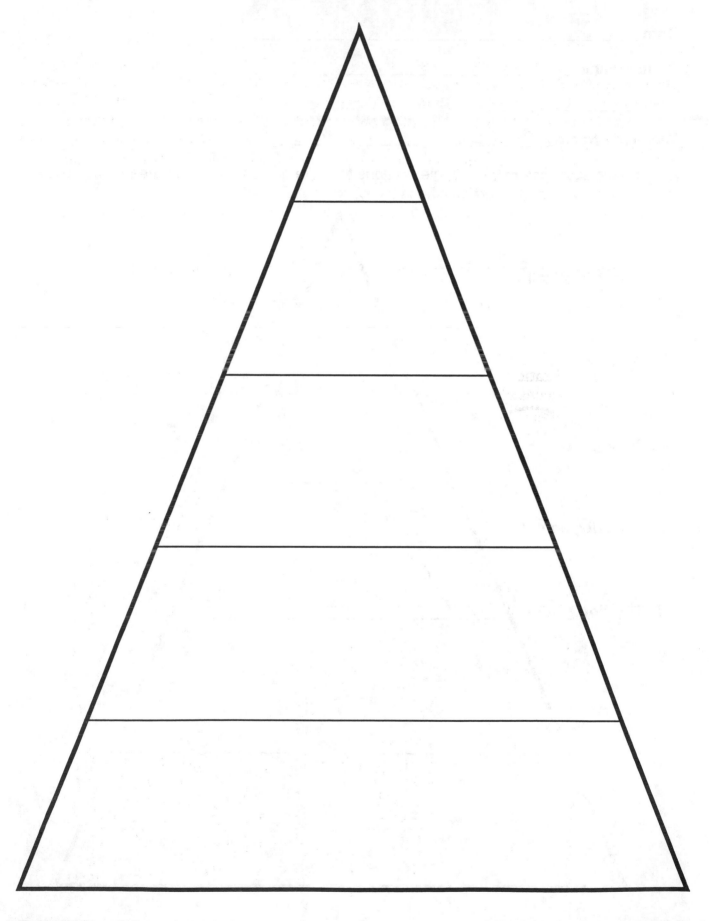

Child Assessment Form

Date_____

Child's Name _____

Age_____

Teacher's Name_____

Use the blank spaces in the triangle sections to make notes about each area of the child's life in your classroom and where he/she is today.

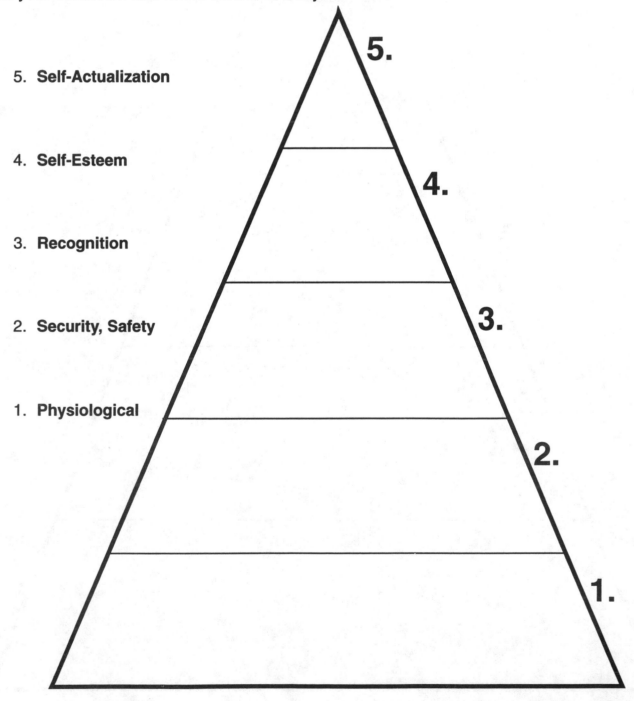

5. **Self-Actualization**

4. **Self-Esteem**

3. **Recognition**

2. **Security, Safety**

1. **Physiological**

Child Assessment Form—Example

Date _1 – 17_

Child's Name _Jason   Montes_

Age _4_

Teacher's Name _Mrs. Vai_

Use the blank spaces in the triangle sections to make notes about each area of the child's life in your classroom and where he/she is today.

5. **Self-Actualization**

4. **Self-Esteem**

3. **Recognition**

2. **Security, Safety**

1. **Physiological**

5. N/A such a sweet kid— normally smiles

4. Been calling himself stupid & dummy lately— talked w/him about this.

3. Has one good friend, Jamie who has been gone. I made Jason "Special Kid" last week.

2. He seems unusually scared lately, cries about everything.

1. Jason always seems tired even when he gets here in the morning.

Classroom Assessment Form

Date_____

Teacher's Name_____

Use the blank spaces in the triangle section to make notes about life in your classroom and where it is today.

5. **Self-Actualization**

4. **Self-Esteem**

3. **Recognition**

2. **Security, Safety**

1. **Physiological**

5.

4.

3.

2.

1.

Classroom Assessment Form— Example

Date _1 - 23_

Teacher's Name _Mrs. Chandah_

Use the blank spaces in the triangle section to make notes about life in your classroom and where it is today.

5. **Self-Actualization**

4. **Self-Esteem**

3. **Recognition**

2. **Security, Safety**

1. **Physiological**

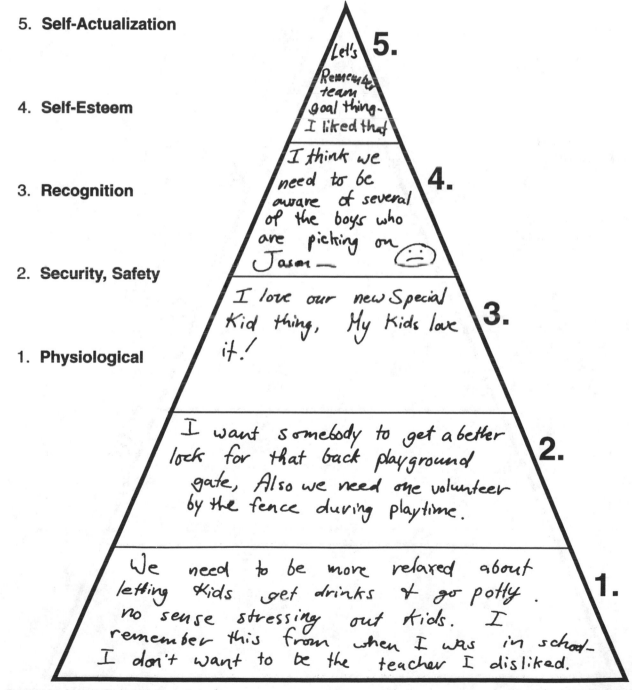

5. Let's Remember team goal thing- I liked that

4. I think we need to be aware of several of the boys who are picking on Jason —

3. I love our new Special Kid thing, My Kids love it!

2. I want somebody to get a better lock for that back playground gate, Also we need one volunteer by the fence during playtime.

1. We need to be more relaxed about letting Kids get drinks + go potty. no sense stressing out Kids. I remember this from when I was in school- I don't want to be the teacher I disliked.

Create Your Own Assessment Form

Date_____

Teacher's Name_____

Assessment of_____

Use the blank spaces in the triangle sections to make notes.

5. **Self-Actualization**

4. **Self-Esteem**

3. **Recognition**

2. **Security, Safety**

1. **Physiological**

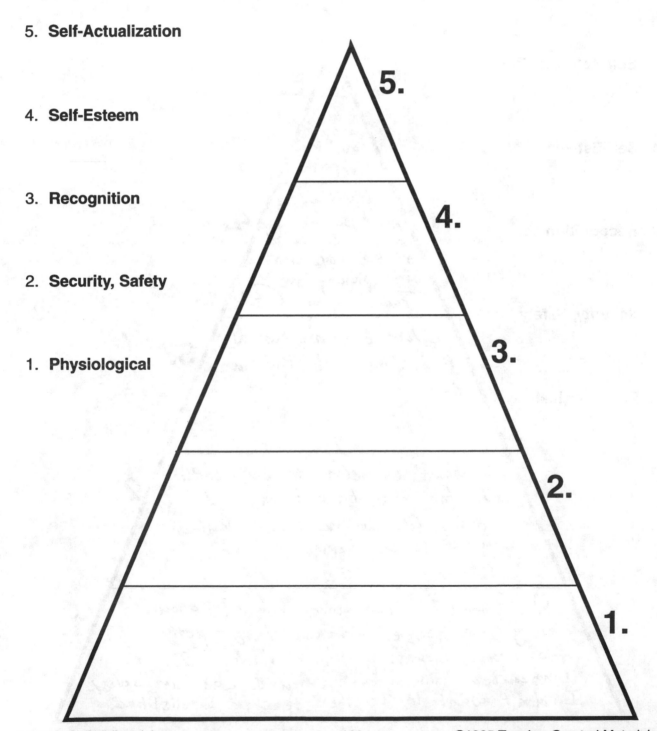

Safe Places to Learn

Team Activity

Purpose:

This team activity will help you and your team become aware of the idea behind Maslow's hierarchy and how it can help you assess your shared attitudes about dealing with and assessing young children.

What You Need:

- several large pieces of butcher paper for every team of four
- hierarchy explanation masters, page 122, one for each team
- individual hierarchy blanks
- large marking pens, as well as regular pens
- masking tape

What You Do:

Begin by creating a poster-size blank triangle divided with five levels like the example of Maslow's hierarchy on page 122. Draw a triangle with ample space to write a variety of things in each section. Mount this on an easy-to-reach wall space.

Next, with your team go over the levels of the hierarchy and make sure that everyone is clear about the meaning of each level and what it includes. Now each team member uses a small blank triangle form and writes down all the things they can think of about your school or center in each of these five areas. (These areas are listed here in order of necessity or from the bottom or base of the triangle first, to the smallest part of the triangle last.):

1. physiological
2. security, safety
3. recognition
4. self-esteem
5. self-actualization

To best assess how your program and school policies are working in this area, decide with your team what questions you will keep in mind while filling out the blanks in the hierarchy triangle individually. Choose from questions like the following, but remember to set these parameters with every member of your group before beginning.

- What are the things that you are doing individually or as a team in these areas that you are very comfortable with?
- What are the things that you are doing in these areas that you are undecided about?
- What are the things you are doing in these areas that you are uncomfortable with?

You might wish to have individuals answer these questions after the fact; that is, think of everything that relates to each section of the hierarchy without judgment. Then ask the participants to circle the things they feel they are very comfortable with, underline the things they are uncomfortable with, and leave the things about which they are undecided blank.

Webbing Form

Team Members

Hierarchy Level

Use this form to web all the ideas you can think of that relate to your main idea in the center of the circle. Do one web for each of the five areas of the hierarchy.

Webbing Form—Example for Security Safety, 2.

non skid stickers on bathroom floor toddler area

call that service that checks everything

make entire facility safer

lock on gate

new first aid kit

we could also have an extra person there at playtime

check plugs/outlets

buy extra outlet covers

locksmith—extra keys

do activity for kindergarten kids regarding first aid

we need to step up the parent volunteers

let's get new CPR training!

Webbing Results Action Plan

Team Member(s) _____

Concern	Action	Result
_____	_____	_____

Notes:

_____

_____

_____

_____

_____

_____

_____

_____

Director Approval _____

Team Member(s) _____

Concern	Action	Result
_____	_____	_____

Notes:

_____

_____

_____

Director Approval _____

Webbing Results Action Plan— Example

Team Member(s) _JAN SMITH & JULIE ROGERS_ (TODDLERS— 1 & 2 YR OLDS)

Concern	Action	Result
FIRST AID FOR KIDS	CPR CLASS & CERTIFICATION	All TEACHERS CERTIFIED! ☺

Notes:

7-15 WE NEED TO MAKE SURE EVERYONE IS TRAINED IN INFANT/TODDLER CPR.

8-15 HAVE SET UP ON-SITE CPR CERTIFICATION CLASS 9-1-9 4 PM—(SATURDAY)

9-1 CLASS WAS GREAT SUCCESS!

Director Approval _Mary Johnson_

Team Member(s) _MAC EVANS_

Concern	Action	Result
OUTLET COVERS	CHECK!	ALL OUTLETS COVERED PROPERLY

Notes:

3-1 — CHECKED All OUTLET COVERS 1 DAMAGED 2 MISSING

3-1 — REPLACED, ORDERED EXTRAS

Director Approval _Mary Johnson_

Anti-Bias Assessment

What Is Anti-Bias?

Anti-bias means insuring that your classroom or center operates in a way that brings curriculum and assessment to it that do not discriminate based on culture, religion, race, or gender differences or special needs and physical ability. In today's centers and classrooms we are all very interested in providing children with an opportunity to explore and celebrate their differences. We want to bring the necessary information for dealing appropriately with the different customs and lifestyles and learning styles and behaviors into our curriculum and the assessment of children.

How Do We Do It?

There are many ways to address the subject of anti-bias, that is to create a center or school environment that does not condone or operate with bias toward children. The main idea is to give all children every opportunity to grow into healthy individuals who are not hindered by prejudice, sexism, racism, handicap-ism, ageism, size-ism, or by any stereotyping. There are many ways to guard against bias in your classroom or center and to respect the differences of others.

Multicultural and Anti-Bias

Multicultural as it applies to both curriculum choices and assessment means to bring an appreciation of different cultures into our programs in a variety of ways. It means to include all cultures as part of what we do and learn about and share in our classrooms and centers. However, in *Anti-Bias Curriculum, Tools for Empowering Young Children,* Derman-Sparks discusses the need to watch out for what she calls "Tourist Curriculum." She defines this as a tourist approach to looking at different cultures in a way that highlights their "exoticness" rather than highlighting the needs for acceptance and understanding of all of us as unique kinds of people, living and working and learning together. She further feels that a standardized approach of exploring cultural differences in the manner of a "tourist" does not allow for the vital relationship that people of all cultures, genders, races, and physical abilities need to construct to make the world a better, more enlightened place. Therefore, the idea is to include all different kinds of people as special and not highlight different cultures or races in a spectacle approach.

This does not mean you cannot celebrate Chinese New Year if you want to, but if tourist trips into other lands through your curriculum are all that happens as far as creating an anti-bias classroom or center, you will be missing the thrust of what we understand about this issue now.

The Assessment Connection

Creating an anti-bias approach in your assessing of children is vital if you are to allow each child equal opportunities and chances to reach his or her own special individual potential in your classroom. The following pages highlight some excellent ways both to bring an anti-bias attitude into your classroom or center and to assure you that you are assessing with an anti-bias attitude as well.

Anti-Bias Images Checklist

Use this checklist to see how your classroom or center's visual materials meet these anti-bias ideas and suggestions.

_____ Your center has a variety of pictures of all different kinds of ethnic and cultural groups.

_____ Your center or school guards against representing a kind of people, race, or minority as a token representation.

_____ Your center or school has visual images of different genders doing a variety of things that cross lines of traditional gender roles.

_____ Your center has pictures of a variety of children and adults that have disabilities.

_____ Your center has many opportunities for children to create and share pictures of their own families.

_____ Your center has pictures of people who are all different shapes and sizes and ages.

_____ Pictures of people with disabilities are shown in a variety of activities and not as cared-for or dependent.

_____ Images of the elderly in vital situations and interacting with a variety of different ages are displayed.

_____ Images of different family mixtures show a variety of family possibilities.

_____ Actual photographs of children and staff are displayed.

_____ Your center has images of parents sharing family responsibilities.

_____ Images of children from inner city, rural, and suburban environments are displayed.

_____ Images are displayed that are positive to minorities and "majorities"; be aware of reverse racism as well as racism.

Anti-Bias Toys and Hands-On Materials Checklist

Use this checklist to see how your classroom or center's materials meet these anti-bias ideas and suggestions.

_____ You have books that reflect different cultures and customs and more than one book depicting a specific culture.

_____ You have books that highlight everyday activities of people in different kinds of family groups and different living situations.

_____ You have books that depict different incomes and living spaces.

_____ You have books that depict the use of different languages, including those languages used in your classroom or center, and books using American Sign Language and Braille.

_____ You have books with positive and various nontraditional gender role models.

_____ You have books showing different ages of people as vital in society.

_____ You have books that do not assume the reader is necessarily Christian.

_____ You have books that show one-parent families.

_____ You have dolls that are diverse; there is a variety of different kinds available or make your own; these should reflect a large possibility of skin tones, not simply black and white.

_____ You have dramatic play equipment that highlights diversity, costumes and cooking equipment from other cultures, and supplies such as a wheelchair or canes and crutches.

_____ You have art materials in different skin tones, including paper, paints, crayons, and clay.

_____ You do not have toys that promote cultural stereotypes like "cowboy and Indian" sets.

_____ You have materials for creating your own anti-bias manipulatives, like paper doll blanks in different skin tones, video and recording equipment for making musical and dramatic presentations and tapes, and Polaroid cameras for adding to anti-bias images, etc.

Anti-Bias Activities Checklist

Use this checklist to see how your classroom or center's activities meet these anti-bias ideas and suggestions.

_____ Activities that allow children to share about their own home lives.

_____ Activities that allow children to share tangible things from their own homes.

_____ Activities that support empathy, understanding, and tolerance.

_____ Activities that explore cultural holidays and festivals that are relevant to your children specifically.

_____ Activities that include awareness of all kinds of holidays and religions, not just one or a few.

_____ Activities that allow children's parents and family members to share their cultural gifts.

_____ Activities that let children touch, see, hear, and feel hands-on materials that are different from what they would experience in their own home environments.

_____ Activities that do not promote gender stereotyping.

_____ Equal emphasis on physical activities for both boys and girls.

_____ Activities structured to include the children with disabilities in your classroom.

_____ A wide variety of activity choices for self-directed activity times.

_____ Activities that encourage children to deal with real-life diversity situations in a positive and anti-bias manner.

_____ Activities that explore the diversity of your own neighborhood.

_____ Activities that expose children to cultures they are not familiar with and life styles they are not familiar with.

Anti-Bias Attitudes Checklist

Use this checklist to see how your classroom or center's attitudes meet these anti-bias ideas and suggestions.

_____ Teachers respect the cultural differences of different groups in their classrooms.

_____ Teachers are sensitive to the different holidays and customs of the children in their classrooms.

_____ Teachers are accepting of boys who may cry or become emotional.

_____ Teachers give children of both sexes equal access and time to engage in physical activities.

_____ Teachers give children of both sexes equal access and time to use "playhouse and homemaking" activities.

_____ Teachers address children's questions about race, gender, or religion with respect and with honest communication.

_____ Teachers do not allow any form of intolerance in their classrooms.

_____ Teachers act against personal stereotyping, acting as a role model for their children of both genders.

_____ Teachers respect the various learning styles of the children in their classrooms.

_____ Teachers provide many different activities and ways to learn for the children in their classrooms.

_____ Teachers are aware of their possible biases and work to not contaminate their students with these potential prejudices.

_____ Teachers respect the individual children in their classrooms, their rights and their potentials.

_____ Teachers provide many ways for specially-abled children to be active participants in classroom activities.

_____ Teachers do not "baby" or over-protect specially-abled children.

Anti-Bias Assessment Checklist

Use this checklist to see how your classroom or center's assessment practices meet these anti-bias ideas and suggestions.

_____ Teachers' observations do not include biased language or attitudes.

_____ Teachers work with teammates to insure they are observing in an anti-bias manner.

_____ Teachers check curriculum and activity choices regularly to prevent bias material from being presented.

_____ Teachers learn about the cultures and life-styles of their children and their parents and determine how each child can best learn based on those differences.

_____ Teachers provide assessment materials in translated form if necessary.

_____ Teachers arrange for interpreters at parent-teacher meetings if possible.

_____ Teachers pay special attention to developmental screening to best determine if a child needs special diagnostic testing.

_____ Teachers interact with parents promptly regarding developmental screening issues.

_____ Teachers provide appropriate assessment for specially-abled children.

_____ Teachers work with government and state agencies in compliance with legislation for the specially-abled.

_____ Teachers educate parents regarding anti-bias issues in parent meetings if needed.

_____ Assessment and screening materials are used that respect cultural differences.

Anti-Bias Assessment Form

Date _____

Child's Name _____

Situation:

_____

_____

Potential Bias Situation:

_____

_____

Remedy Ideas:

1. _____

2. _____

3. _____

4. _____

Parent Contact Results:

_____

_____

_____

_____

_____

_____

Inclusion and Assessment

What Is Full Inclusion?

Full inclusion is the term for including children with special needs into the regular classroom or early childhood setting. This practice is becoming more and more common today, and it is something that every early childhood educator should know about. We need to know how to deal effectively and in an anti-bias manner with children with special needs in our classrooms. We also need to know how to notice through our regular assessment procedures which children need to have developmental screening. Through this screening, we can determine if the student needs more thorough diagnostic assessment regarding a potential special need.

What Is Developmental Screening?

Developmental screening is a limited screening procedure to determine if a child should have a diagnostic assessment. It is the first step in seeing if there is a potential problem that might require a child to have his or her needs met in a special way. This can be as simple as thinking a child might need glasses and contacting the parents regarding having the child take part in a free on-site vision test (which would be part of developmental screening). Or it can be as complicated as suspecting a variety of learning problems and getting the child the necessary developmental screening to determine if diagnostic assessment (the second and more intensive step) is needed.

What Is Diagnostic Assessment?

Diagnostic assessment is the testing that determines a child's specific area of special needs. Through this testing, the best way of assisting this child through the use of special services and in compliance with legislation is determined.

What Steps Do I Take If I Think a Child Has Special Needs?

Most centers take part in or refer students to a pre-kindergarten screening process of some kind. These developmental screening tests can test hearing and vision, motor skills, and a variety of other things. Find out what your center or school's procedure is in this area. Here is a list of steps that you will need to take:

- Determine through your regular assessment if you think a child might need to be screened for potential special needs.

- Contact parents regarding screening availability at your school or referral sources.

- Do not have a child screened in any way without the written permission of the parent(s).

- Remember that tests are not cast in stone; different screening tools can produce different results. The goal is to provide children with the best opportunity to learn and develop properly, not to label or exclude them in any way.

- Find out what screening tools your center or school is using and make sure that these tools are reputable and proven.

Inclusion and Assessment *(cont.)*

Readiness Testing and Developmental Screening

Readiness testing determines what a child already knows in relation to what he is going to learn in the grade level he will be entering. Developmental screening explores the child's potential to learn rather than what he or she knows. You and your team need to be well-versed in what kinds of testing you do, what testing tools you use, and what referral sources you can call on.

The Goal

The idea behind developmental screening is to give each individual child the resources he or she needs to be able to achieve full developmental and learning potential. Testing of any kind requires that those responsible for it be extremely diligent about making sure that children are screened more than once using different tools and that no one is misdiagnosed and hurt because of the process.

More Information

There is a variety of good books and information available on the subject. Contact your local chapter of whatever educational organization your school or center belongs to for more information regarding appropriate practices in this area.

Forms in This Book

Included in this book are several forms to help you put your own developmental screening program to work in your center or school. These include:

- Parent screening availability letter

- Parent post-screening letter and meeting schedule

Screening Availability Letter

Dear Parents,

As part of our ongoing commitment to help your child reach his/ her full potential, we are participating in pre-kindergarten screening, free of charge to parents. We will have licensed professionals on site to conduct

_____

screening tests for all children. We will test your child at your request and with your permission on _____ at _____ o'clock.

Feel free to contact me regarding any questions you may have about this screening. Please return this form signed to me no later than _____ to enable your child to take part.

Your child will not be screened without your written permission.

Sincerely,

_____

for _____

_____

school

Post-Screening Letter

Dear Parents,

At your request your child _____

was screened in _____

as part of our school's free, routine developmental screening program.

Your child's results will be explained in detail at a parent/ teacher meeting

at your convenience. Please call the school at _____ to

schedule a parent/teacher meeting that will fit in with your schedule.

Sincerely,

_____
for

_____
school

144

Emergent Curriculum and Assessment

What Is Emergent Curriculum?

Emergent curriculum is a method of curriculum planning that enables teams to create curriculum through an ongoing, vital, and changing process. It highlights self-directed teaching because it lends itself to focus on the interests of children at the moment, but it is not controlled by children. In other words, in emergent curriculum, teachers are very much facilitating and masterminding the planning of curriculum, but it is a kind of curriculum that has a vital and ever-changing thrust. It highlights teachers' ability to work in groups, to brainstorm, to web, to change direction, and to listen to and react to the developmental needs of children.

Constantly Changing

As early childhood educators believe children learn by playing, there is an element of play in the process of creating emergent curriculum. It is a kind of group creativity. Centered often around the process of brainstorming in many forms, it is a way of teams focusing on a wide variety of ideas that they can shape into a kind of ever-changing curriculum. It is almost a living thing growing with the interests of the children and the values and experiences of the staff that is planning it.

How Can It Impact Assessment in My Classroom or Center?

If you and your team are trying to use some aspect of emergent curriculum in your classroom or center, you can apply this same kind of open-ended, changing, and vital philosophy to the kinds of assessment tools you use and create in your center or school. You can use the theory behind emergent curriculum to create an assessment style for your center or school that is based on the individual needs of students and explores different ways to assess those needs.

This idea can lead you and your group into your own brand of alternative assessment based on the specific "culture" your school or facility has and its everyday changes and discoveries.

Part Two

Table of Contents
Deciding Your Assessment Style

- Assessment Style Quiz

- Assessment Style Quiz Answers

- Using the Rest of the Book — Suggestions

Deciding Your Assessment Style

What Are My Choices?

Assessment, like curriculum, allows in many choices. In this book there are four main areas to give you a chance to try assessments from all of them or to focus on the area you feel is the most relevant to you and your team. While assessment and the research about assessing children has changed over time, and there are constantly new ways of looking at things in early childhood education, research has narrowed philosophies down to four main areas.

These are the following:

Developmental

Traditional or Academic

Portfolio

Alternative

For the purposes of this book, all of the activities (to which the assessment choices correspond) are developmentally appropriate. That way, even if you would like a more traditional approach you will still be developmentally appropriate. And if you stress developmentally appropriate curriculum, you will still be able to add some of the basics of an academic curriculum without altering your personal philosophy and what you know is right for young children.

In the alternative section you will find we have chosen to highlight the area of multiple intelligences, with a variety of developmentally appropriate activities in each area of intelligence as theorized by Howard Gardner. Certainly, this is not the only kind of alternative assessment of learning; it is just one interesting way to look at learning and development in young children.

Taking the Assessment Style Quiz

On the next few pages you will find a quiz that will help you and your team gain a sense of where you fall as far as assessment (and corresponding curriculum). Remember, there is no right way to do this, you can use all of the activities in this book and be comfortable with the fact that they have been designed with the current knowledge about young children that is important today, and with great respect and attention paid to what is developmentally appropriate according to the guidelines set forth by the NAEYC as well as a host of other notable and respected sources.

Take the quiz in four different areas:

Children

Teachers

Activities/Curriculum

School or Center Philosophy

Deciding Your Assessment Style *(cont.)*

What Will the Quiz Tell Me?

The quiz will give you information about how you see yourself, your classroom or center, and your attitudes about planning and philosophy. It will also point you toward one of four assessment choices. Then, you will be able to get a sense for which section of activities and their corresponding assessments would be interesting for you to try and experiment within your own center or classroom.

You might find that you lean toward more than one kind—that is a perfect opportunity for you to blend two or more kinds of assessment in your classroom and take a look at how a possible combination approach might work for you. Any way you approach it, each activity in each section has three assessment tools for you to use immediately.

Where Do I Go from Here?

Just like any other part of your job as a teacher, you know you have to try things out, experiment and see what works for you, talk to your team and director or principal, and whatever else you do in your personal decision-making process. Remember, there is no right way to use this book. You can follow the directions to the letter, or let the book fall open and say "that looks interesting!" Each way works; it is all based on who you are as a teacher and what your preferences are.

You Are Part of the Process

One wonderful thing about teaching young children is that we are all part of the process of discovery. New ways that have not been thought of yet that will change the way we look at children and their development and learning are right around the corner—perhaps some of the new ideas and discoveries will be your own.

Children

Choose the child description that sounds most like the kind of child you encounter.

#A

Brian is an adventurous child. He has a lot of curiosity and has an ability to create his own activity out of nothing, or at least it seems like that to an unaware observer. He has a lot of interest in a number of things. He has the ability to play with his peers or by himself and is beginning to show signs of enjoying cooperative play. He has been at the preschool two years, enjoys using the various centers, and is interested in the changes in the centers and also returning to his favorites. He is bright, interested, and has made several good friends among the other children.

#B

Meet Tiana. Tiana loves to look at picture books and spends a lot of time at the center using crayons and pretending to write and make "grown up" writing. Tiana is a pleasure at circle time; she loves to listen to stories and her mother tells us she often reads to her at home. Tiana came to the center already able to count to 20. She is very verbal, talks in paragraphs and has a good ability in recalling number sequences and the alphabet. She can recite simple nursery rhymes and loves hearing them read to her as well as looking at the nursery rhyme big books in the center.

#C

Lu's parents are both professors at a local university and she has had the benefit of being part of a university experimental preschool. She shows a real ability in music and is currently studying the violin. Her father is a mathematics professor who plays violin in chamber music recitals and often Lu has the opportunity to attend concerts and other musical events. Lu can pick out a tune on a piano by ear at five years old.

#D

Timmy is a very considerate and organized child. He has a spotless and attractive cubby. He likes to watch videos and take part in sharing. He has an interest in history and what is said during circle and sharing time. He likes to do things for the teachers at the center and enjoys making choices. He has responded well to the various responsibilities given him in the center— and he currently is the guinea pig monitor, a job he loves.

Teachers

Choose the teacher that sounds most like you.

#A

Ms. Sharron majored in English in college. She loves the idea of children in her center being exposed to books and is always watching *Reading Rainbow* to get ideas about what book might be appropriate for her group of four-year-olds. She recites poetry to her class, something they seem to enjoy, and she has a talent for making up rhymes which the children like. She thinks that it is very important for her to give her class as much ability in reading readiness as possible. She has attended a variety of math workshops over the last couple of years to bring math and science concepts into her pre-kindergarten classroom in a relevant way.

#B

Shyanne, works at a Native American reservation day school in New Mexico founded by a husband and wife Harvard graduate team. She has just returned from an all day conference that highlighted webbing and emergent curriculum. She is very excited about sharing the ideas with her open minded and positive team members. As she walks through the door, children run to greet her and a harried, happy colleague says, "I hope you brought us lots of great new stuff!"

#C

Dan Garcia is a graduate student working full time at a university preschool. He is thinking about writing his thesis on the relationships among teachers recognize and respecting each other's differences and the impact that respect has on how they treat children. He has created a new center idea called a nature art center, and he is currently trying out new materials from nature as part of those that he will keep on hand for impromptu art projects. He has checked all of his materials with a nursery to make sure all are non-toxic. Right now he is observing an impromptu dramatic play situation that is taking place at the water table with several dolls getting ready for a vacation.

#D

Sue Smith is determined to get organized this year. She has a hard time dealing with parents because she is fairly new in town as well as in her school. She is brainstorming ideas after school about how she can make her parent/teacher conferences for her kindergarten class go better this year. She loves having things easy to explain and is trying to find a style of writing with parents that is more streamlined.

Activities

Choose the activity that appeals to you the most.

#A

This activity package looks like a lot of fun. It highlights a big book with adorable alphabet letters that children can use again and again. It also has a tape of the story that children can listen to. There are also master pages the teacher can copy easily to use for children to see the letter and trace it in the sand or for older children to try writing the letters. This activity can be used by individual children or working quietly together as well.

#B

This activity is called, "Putting on a Show." It gives children an opportunity to act out a fairy tale and for teachers to take a video of it to keep and show parents. The activity suggests taping the play several different times for each child and has some nice organizational forms that come with it.

#C

This activity is really interesting—it is a circus theme with a variety of circus booths you set up. Children have a chance to do art, dance, listen to music, and learn about animals. There will be a lot going on at once in this activity, and the possibilities seem endless. This could get a little confusing, but it looks like a great one.

#D

This activity calls for setting up a movement center that has a lot of different hands on manipulatives that children ages three, four, and five years old can all use according to their different abilities and at their own speeds. It can remain as part of the room after the children have tried it, and they may use it whenever they want.

Philosophy

Choose the philosophy that most closely matches your center or school.

#A

The director of your center or school principal likes to maintain good relations with both the parents and the community. She is a person that likes you to prove what you are saying and back up your ideas with tangible examples in meetings. She likes her staff to be well-organized. Your center or school plans changes in curriculum based on what happened before and teachers keep records from year to year.

#B

The director of your center is getting her doctorate. The entire staff are always being whisked off to another conference; you never know what new invention is going to greet you at teachers' meetings. The parents of the children you teach are open minded and positive, and you have a lot of volunteers. You are near a university and you share ideas with a few other schools at regular monthly meetings. One of your staff writes for an educational magazine, and you have met a few people that have come to study your school for their books.

#C

Your school principal comes from a conservative background and the parents at your school are very worried about how children are going to do in the later grades. Many parents have purchased phonics sets for their children and do a lot of reading to them at home. Lots of parents are interested in what you are doing, and are anxious for their children to read. The area is conservative and the principal likes you to make definite lesson plans.

#D

The director of your center is also a teacher at the junior college level in early childhood education. She is innovative and a bit of an activist for children's' rights. She is always saying, "Don't waste the children's time; plan activities that show children you respect the way they think and their individuality." Your team is undergoing a NAEYC accreditation again, its time, and everyone is getting together this Saturday for a webbing meeting.

How to Score Your Quiz

Give each answer the following points, add up your total points, and chart them on graph.

Children (page 149)	Teachers (page 150)	Activities (page 151)	Philosophy (page 152)
A. 7	A. 12	A. 16	A. 9
B. 5	B. 15	B. 17	B. 11
C. 8	C. 14	C. 19	C. 8
D. 6	D. 13	D. 18	D. 10

Numbers Used as a Way of Clarifying

To score the assessment style quiz, there are assigned number equivalents to each possibility in each section. Notice the line graph to see where your combined numerical score falls. The sections are not clearly divided because assessment can not be decided upon in black and white; there are, indeed, grey areas based on human individuality, both in the children you are assessing and in you.

Additional Ways to Look at Your Assessment Type

In each section of the assessed activity portion of the book, there is a detailed checklist with descriptions about each point about the particular kind of assessment. After taking the quiz, check the section you feel you are leaning toward and see if it fits. If it is not close enough, then you are someone who needs to blend assessment styles (most people fall in this category).

Look at the other section checklists and descriptions and then the activities and the assessments that go with them. Use these following pages to plan with your team and to plan individually your activity and assessment choices and how they will fit into the rest of your regular planning.

Charting Your Quiz Score

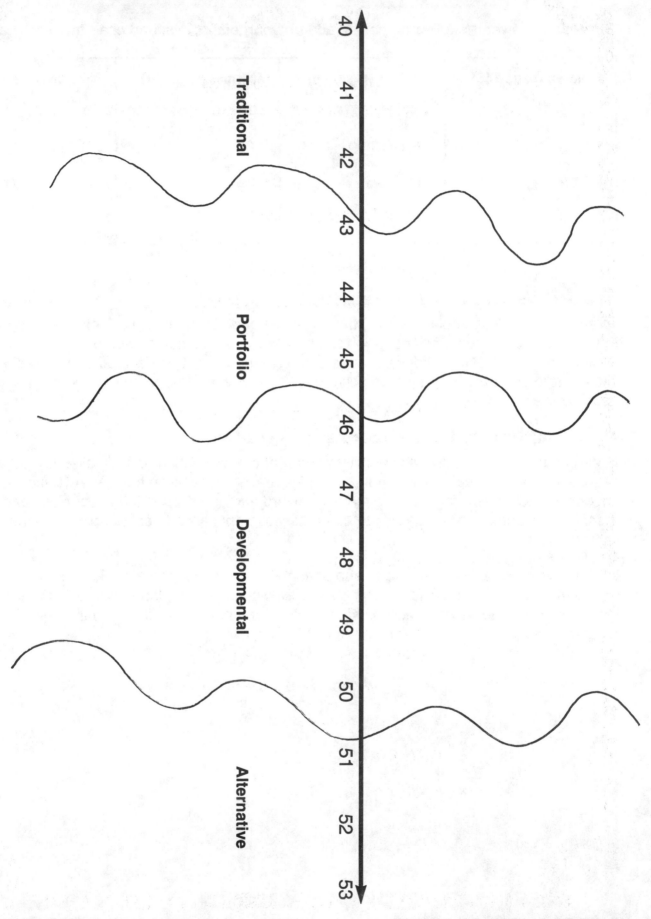

Part Three

Table of Contents

Developmental Appropriate Assessment

- Assessment Checklist

- What Is It?

- What Are the Specifics?

- Assessed Activities Section
  (Activities and Assessment Tools)

Traditional Assessment

- Assessment Checklist

- What Is It?

- What Are the Specifics?

- Assessed Activities
  Section (Activities and Assessment Tools)

Portfolio Assessment

- Assessment Checklist

- What Is It?

- What Are the Specifics?

- Assessed Activities Section
  (Activities and Assessment Tools)

Alternative Assessment

- Assessment Checklist

- What Is It?

- What Are the Specifics?

- Assessed Activities Section
  (Activities and Assessment Tools)

Four Ways to Focus

- **Developmental Focus**

- **Traditional Focus**

- **Portfolio Focus**

- **Alternative (Multiple Intelligence) Focus**

Four Ways to Focus

In the next major section of the book, you will find four different ways of teaching and assessing activities. These activities have been divided into four main headings to correspond with the kind of assessment style you and your team determine works best for you and the children you are assessing. You can determine which set of activities will best fit your team's philosophy by taking the individual or team test on pages 149-154.

Before Beginning

While each of these activity sections corresponds to a special kind of assessment, the activities, even the ones with a traditional or academic focus, have been written so you may use them no matter what your teaching philosophy is. They simply have a focus, you may alter the activity and choose to use whatever assessment tools in the book you wish. You do not have to use them together or in any particular order. We have presented them in four different ways so that you choose whatever section works best for you.

An Example

All of the activities in every section have been written to be used as developmentally appropriate tools in your classroom or center. For example, in the Traditional section, you will find ABC Mouse Hole. This activity features a master book that can be copied and distributed to each child for a take home book to read with parents as part of a Parent Helping at Home Kit. Each master gives children a space to write the letter of the alphabet, and the corresponding word that goes with the alphabet story in the book. You may wish to use this activity as is, or you may not want to present a "reading readiness" activity. Then all you do is cut the master page at the page divider and simply create a developmentally appropriate book for any age, or any level of development. As you can see, it is up to you!

The Four Sections

Each of the four sections thoroughly explains the kind of assessment used in the section and gives any information needed to get started using a particular section right away. Each section features three assessment tools after every activity, one for teachers, one for children to self assess, and one for parents to help assess at home, or on site. Use these assessment tools in any way that seems relevant to you. Each activity features reproducible masters and detailed directions for any part of the activity you create. One special feature is several useable books, one alphabet book, one reusable picture book in which children can create their own stories again and again, and one book that highlights the issues of specially-abled individuals, and anti-bias.

Four Ways to Focus *(cont.)*

Something for Everyone

Feel free to combine these activities in anyway you choose. You can print and reprint the book sections and give them to children to take home to use again and again. The idea is to give instant resources for a variety of teaching and assessment styles all in one place.

The four sections are as follows:

Developmental Focus—Activities and Assessment

These activities are developmentally appropriate and feature a large self-directed activity section that allows children the opportunity to explore the concept in a self-directed and solitary play manner. Each activity also has a directed teaching focus. It is possible for teachers who prefer to use the activities in this manner to have an opportunity to do so. This section features dramatic role playing, a Bee Parade, fun with dinosaurs, and opportunities for children to have hands-on fun with cooking!

Traditional Focus—Activities and Assessment

These developmentally appropriate activities feature a traditional or academic focus that might be termed readiness activities and the appropriate assessment to go with them. They also feature directions to lessen the academic or traditional focus in a relevant way.

This section features a full-length picture alphabet book that children and parents will love! A simple number-recognition puzzle works as a reproducible and reusable puzzle for children to take home. Both the book and reusable activity will be loved by children and parents alike!

Portfolio Focus—Activities and Assessment

This section highlights a different kind of portfolio to store children's work, art, and your observations with each activity. One favorite that you can also give children as a gift is the Doll House Portfolio that will make your center look inviting to everyone who sees it and will double as a real doll house for every child. The directions are easy and completely detailed.

Alternative Focus—Activities and Assessment

This section highlights a different activity for every area of the seven areas of multiple intelligence. Children will have a chance to explore the many ways they are intelligent in activities that respect their individuality and their differences as people and as learners. This section features a full-length reproducible book called *Benny's Wheels* that celebrates the uniqueness of all of us and carries the relevant topics of anti-bias and full inclusion into your classroom in a positive way.

How the Book Works

Example Activity With Explanations of Each Section

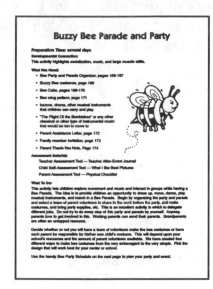

Buzzy Bee Parade and Party

Preparation Time: several days

Developmental Connection:
This activity highlights socialization, music, and large muscle skills.

What You Need:
• Bee Party and Parade Organizer, pages 166-167
• Buzzy Bee costumes, page 168
• Bee Cake, pages 169-170
• Bee wing pattern, page 171
• kazoos, drums, other musical instruments that children can carry and play
• "The Flight Of the Bumblebee" or any other classical or other type of instrumental music that would be fun to move to
• Parent Assistance Letter, page 172
• Family member invitation, page 173
• Parent Thank-You Note, Page 174

Assessment Materials
Teacher Assessment Tool — Teacher After-Event Journal
Child Self-Assessment Tool — What I like Best Pictures
Parent Assessment Tool — Physical Checklist

What To Do:
This activity lets children explore movement and music and interact in groups while having a Bee Parade. The idea is to provide children an opportunity to dress up, move, dance, play musical instruments, and march in a Bee Parade. Begin by organizing the party and parade and select a team of parent volunteers to share in the work before the party, and make costumes, and bring party supplies, etc. This is an excellent activity in which to delegate different jobs. Do not try to do every step of this party and parade by yourself. Anyway, parents love to get involved in this. Working parents can send their parents. Grandparents are often an untapped resource.

Decide whether or not you will have a team of volunteers make the bee costumes or have each parent be responsible for his/her own child's costume. This will depend upon your school's resources and the amount of parent volunteers available. We have created four different ways to make bee costumes from the very extravagant to the very simple. Pick the design that will work best for your center or school.

Use the handy Bee Party Schedule on the next page to plan your party and event.

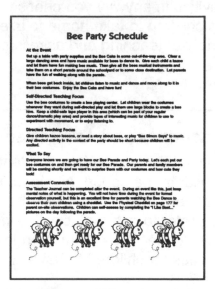

Bee Party Schedule

At the Event
Set up a table with party supplies and the Bee Cake in some out-of-the-way area. Clear a large dancing area and have music available for bees to dance to. Give each child a kazoo and let them have fun making bee music. Then give all the bees musical instruments and take them on a short parade around the schoolyard or to some close destination. Let parents have the fun of walking along with the parade.

When bees get back inside, let children listen to music and dance and move along to it in their bee costumes. Enjoy the Bee Cake and have fun!

Self-Directed Teaching Focus
Use the bee costumes to create a bee playing center. Let children wear the costumes whenever they want during self-directed play and let them use large blocks to create a bee hive. Keep a child-safe tape player in this area (which can be part of your regular demonstramatic play area) and provide types of interesting music for children to use to experiment with movement, or to enjoy listening to.

Directed Teaching Focus
Give children kazoo lessons, or read a story about bees, or play "Bee Simon Says" to music. Any directed activity in the context of the party should be short because children will be excited.

What To Say
Everyone knows we are going to have our Bee Parade and Party today. Let's each put on our bee costumes on and then get ready for our Bee Parade. Our parents and family members will be coming shortly and we want to surprise them with our costumes and how cute they look!

Assessment Connection
The Teacher Journal can be completed after the event. During an event like this, just keep mental notes of what is happening. You will not have time during the event for formal observation yourself, but this is an excellent time for parents watching the Bee Dance to observe their own children using a checklist. Use the Physical Checklist on page 177 for parent on-site observations. Children can self-assess by completing the "I Like Best..." pictures on the day following the parade.

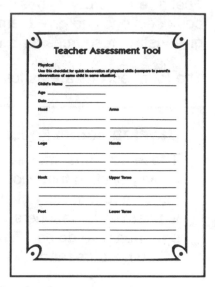

Teacher Assessment Tool

Physical
Use this checklist for quick observation of physical skills (compare to parent's observations of same child in same situation).

Child's Name _____

Age _____

Date _____

Head _____   Arms _____

Legs _____   Hands _____

Neck _____   Upper Torso _____

Feet _____   Lower Torso _____

As you can see in the example pages printed above, each activity includes these mini-sections:

- Preparation Time
- Self-Directed Teacher Focus
- Concept
- Directed Teacher Focus

- Materials/Assessment Materials
- What To Say
- What To Do
- Assessment Connection

Detailed explanations of the above sections follow.

Preparation Time: Each activity is clearly labeled with the time it takes to prepare. This way, it is possible to skim the book and find an activity that fits into your schedule.

Concept: Each section has an at-a-glance concept explained briefly with no guesswork.

Materials: The materials are listed with page references to other sections, if needed; nothing is left to chance.

Assessment Materials: Each activity features three assessment tools: Teacher Assessment Tool, Child's Self-Assessment, and Parent Assessment Tool.

What To Do: This section includes simple preparation and presentation directions.

Teaching Focus: The teacher focus section includes directions for self-directed and directed emphasis to best suit your individual needs.

What To Say: This includes a simple script that will give you an idea of how to direct the activity. Some teachers may wish to actually use the script; others will read it for review.

Assessment Connection: This is handy information on how to make the assessment tools provided work to your best advantage.

Checklist for Developmentally Appropriate Assessment

Check off those items that you recognize as part of your current assessment.

Developmentally appropriate assessment. . .

- ☐ 1. is about exploration.
- ☐ 2. is about discovery.
- ☐ 3. is about potential.
- ☐ 4. is about change.
- ☐ 5. is sometimes loud.
- ☐ 6. is sometimes disorderly.
- ☐ 7. requires the teacher to change objectives at times midstream.
- ☐ 8. is based on observation.
- ☐ 9. is creative.
- ☐ 10. is based on loosely structured criteria.
- ☐ 11. does not classify students as "smart" or "dumb."
- ☐ 12. explores a variety of intelligences.
- ☐ 13. allows for a variety of theories and practices to work at once.
- ☐ 14. lets children develop as individuals with different aptitudes.
- ☐ 15. works with full-inclusion, as well as gifted, students.
- ☐ 16. is exciting.
- ☐ 17. is empowering for children and teachers.
- ☐ 18. is informal.
- ☐ 19. relies on children to learn self-discipline.
- ☐ 20. "scares" the community.

Developmentally Appropriate Assessment

What Is It?

Assessment that is developmentally appropriate bases itself on the individual child, rather than the curriculum. The idea that children are individuals who develop according to their own appropriate speed and readiness is key to developmental assessment.

In this book, the following three sections of assessment activities stress the developmental approach. Developmental assessment of children between two and eight years of age allows them to be assessed in a way that does not limit or improperly "brand" them with any label about their intelligence or their ability.

Benefits Children

Developmental assessment is good for children. It goes hand in hand with the kind of program and curriculum that stresses the individual, encourages young children to explore their surroundings, and allows them to be led by their own natural intelligence and creativity.

Observation

Developmental assessment is based on observation. In fact, learning how to observe without bias and then later using this assessment to make observations is the foundation of this kind of assessment. Observing children according to what is considered developmentally appropriate for them is a skill that has to be learned and must be constantly practiced to be effective.

NAEYC

The National Association for the Education of Young Children has developed a variety of guidelines for what is appropriate for children between the ages of two and eight developmentally and what they can be expected to learn generally. These guidelines celebrate the differences of children. If used correctly as part of a program, these guidelines create a positive happy learning environment.

Developmentally Appropriate Assessment *(cont.)*

Is About Exploration

Developmentally appropriate assessment is based on the fact that children are creative, natural creatures who love to explore their environment in a naturally curious and excited way.

Is About Discovery

Children are interested in the world around them and do not necessarily want to spend a lot of time on one thing. Children may move from activity to activity rapidly, or they may devote themselves specifically to one thing. This will be based on individual preferences and taste.

Is About Potential

Assessing children in a developmentally appropriate way does not label the child in any negative way. A child is not numbered and categorized but is seen as a vital, changing, and special young person.

Is About Change

Assessing children in a developmental context is as ever changing as the needs and desires of the children. It is a creative process that is never static or boring or consistent. It requires that the teacher be flexible and relax rigid standards that one would find in a more traditional learning and assessment setting.

Is Sometimes Disorderly

When children are moving in a self-directed way, there will be confusion. A self-directed classroom does not have the quiet, sitting-in-one's-seat look that a traditional classroom has. Children move about, exploring their environment.

Requires the Teacher to Change Objectives, at Times Midstream

When a teacher learns how to use a self-directed environment to everyone's benefit, he or she "goes with the flow" in some cases. If an activity about cloud shapes shifts focus suddenly to airplanes, a good facilitator lets the focus change from his or her preplanned cloud activity to things in the sky, what a child's natural curiosity has brought to the activity.

Is Based on Observation

Assessment is done by looking carefully at a child's actions in real classroom activities rather than contrived ones over a period of time. Learning to observe well may be the most important aspect of assessing developmentally.

Is Creative

Developmentally appropriate assessment gives teachers and teams a chance to work together and explore the outcomes of their observations and use all of their pooled resources to best benefit the children they are assessing. This kind of assessment relies on people being able to take in many new ideas as well as have their own and being able to communicate those ideas about assessment, as well as use them.

Developmentally Appropriate
Assessment *(cont.)*

Is Based on Loosely Structured Criteria

Developmentally appropriate assessment can change daily if you want it to. In fact, it changes along with the process of discovering what a group of children or an individual child is interested in and drawn to. Many early childhood teachers and teams create their own adaptations of assessment tools based on important theorists like Piaget and Gardner.

Does Not Classify a Child as "Smart" or "Dumb"

Because developmental assessment looks at the whole child and the child as an individual there is no such thing as "smart" or "dumb." There are children at all different levels of development in every early childhood classroom, and developmental assessment seeks out the best way to enhance the experience of the individual child based on what is important in his/her own particular growth pattern of development.

Explores a Variety of Intelligences

Work like that by Howard Gardner who has determined that there are at least seven kinds of intelligences lends itself to the open-minded attitude found in developmental assessment. In this kind of assessment, one is always looking for new and better ways to assess children; therefore, the door for advancement and discovery is always open.

Allows for a Variety of Theories and Practices to Work at Once

Because theory is an open-idea policy in a developmental setting, teams and individuals can look at assessment in a variety of ways all at once. It is possible to use portions of Piaget's theories, aspects of Montessori, as well as Howard Gardner's work to make up a great package of assessment tools.

Lets Children Develop as Individuals with Different Aptitudes

Developmentally appropriate assessment focuses on the whole child and realizes and acknowledges that all children are different even though there may be a great many similarities in development; each is unique and needs to be viewed as such. This is why theories that celebrate diversity are very welcome in a classroom that uses developmentally appropriate assessment.

Works with Full-Inclusion as Well as Gifted Students

Because children are recognized and celebrated for being different and unique, this kind of assessment lends itself to include everyone. It is possible to plan curriculum based on the assessments derived in a developmentally appropriate setting. These assessments will best benefit every child, because everyone has special needs whether they are classed as gifted or part of a full-inclusion program.

Developmentally Appropriate
Assessment *(cont.)*

Is Exciting

Developmentally appropriate assessment is exciting because it is always new. Just as small children spend each day in discovery, teachers using developmentally appropriate assessment spend each day discovering the children they work with as well as many things about themselves, their team, and their world. The environment of this kind of setting lends itself to the discovery, and in such a setting, everyone is excited.

Makes Children and Teachers Feel Competent and Positive About Their Results

When the emphasis on right and wrong is removed, children feel free to explore. Naturally, this does not mean there are not right and wrong behaviors or right and wrong answers, but that there are many ways of getting to the same destination and the way, rather than the destination, is more intensely part of the focus. The result is that there are many ways to do a good job, to be competent, and to be a great teacher too. Both children and teachers do not have to fit tightly into a preformed role.

Is Informal

The order of the day in a developmentally appropriate classroom can alter quickly; therefore, a teacher assessing might find himself or herself setting aside one idea down to learn about another idea. The rules are not rigid and the informal attitude leans toward developing assessment, rather than completing assessment tasks.

Relies on Children to Learn Self-Discipline

Developmentally appropriate assessment is part of an environment where children are increasingly responsible for their own behavior. That means they are given more responsibility for their own actions early in life. They must learn the rules and abide by them because they want to, ultimately. Even small children begin to think logically about their own part in making this kind of environment work.

"Scares" Community

The "community," this being a generalized term, is afraid of things that they do not have first-hand knowledge about. Developmentally appropriate assessment and the curriculum it depends upon is one of those things that your average American does not understand. The most important task of the early childhood educators to make the community of parents, as well as the community at large, aware of the benefits in this kind of assessment, as well as this kind of classroom setting. It is important that there is constant communication between parent and teacher, teacher and team, and school and community.

Buzzy Bee Parade and Party

Preparation Time: several days

Developmental Connection:

This activity highlights socialization, music, and large muscle skills.

What You Need:

- Bee Party and Parade Organizer, pages 166-167

- Buzzy Bee costumes, page 168

- Bee Cake, pages 169-170

- Bee wing pattern, page 171

- kazoos, drums, other musical instruments that children can carry and play

- "The Flight of the Bumblebee" or any other classical or other type of instrumental music that would be fun to move to

- Parent Assistance Letter, page 172

- Family member invitation, page 173

- Parent Thank-You Note, page 174

Assessment Materials

Teacher Assessment Tool — Teacher After-Event Journal

Child Self-Assessment Tool — What I Like Best Pictures

Parent Assessment Tool — Physical Checklist

What to Do:

This activity lets children explore movement and music and interact in groups while having a Bee Parade. The idea is to provide children an opportunity to dress up, move, dance, play musical instruments, and march in a Bee Parade. Begin by organizing the party and parade, selecting a team of parent volunteers to share in the work before the party, making costumes, and bringing party supplies, etc. This is an excellent activity in which to delegate different jobs. Do not try to do every step of this party and parade by yourself. Anyway, parents love to get involved in this. Working parents can send their parents. Grandparents are often an untapped resource.

Decide whether or not you will have a team of volunteers make the bee costumes or have each parent be responsible for his/her own child's costume. This will depend upon your school's resources and the number of parent volunteers available. We have created four different ways to make bee costumes, from the very extravagant to the very simple. Pick the design that will work best for your center or school.

Use the handy Bee Party Schedule on the next page to plan your party and event.

Bee Party Schedule

At the Event

Set up a table with party supplies and the Bee Cake in some out-of-the-way area. Clear a large dancing area and have music available for bees to dance to. Give children kazoos and let them have fun making bee music. Then give all the bees musical instruments and take them on a short parade around the schoolyard or to some close destination. Let parents have the fun of walking along with the parade.

When the bees get back inside, let the children listen to music, dance, and move along to it in their bee costumes. Enjoy the Bee Cake and have fun!

Self-Directed Teaching Focus

Use the bee costumes to create a bee playing center. Let children wear the costumes whenever they want during self-directed play and let them use large blocks to create a bee hive. Keep a child-safe tape player in this area (which can be part of your regular dance/dramatic play area) and provide tapes of interesting music for children to use to experiment with movement, or to enjoy listening to.

Directed Teaching Focus

Give children kazoo lessons, or read a story about bees, or play "Bee Simon Says" to music. Any directed activity in the context of the party should be short because children will be excited.

What to Say

Everyone knows we are going to have our Bee Parade and Party today. Let's each put our bee costumes on and then get ready for our Bee Parade. Our parents and family members will be coming shortly and we want to surprise them with our costumes and how cute they look!

Assessment Connection

The Teacher Journal can be completed after the event. During an event like this, just keep mental notes of what is happening. You will not have time during the event for formal observation yourself, but this is an excellent time for parents watching the Bee Dance to observe their own children using a checklist. Use the Parent Assessment Tool on page 177 for parent on-site observations. Children can self-assess by completing the "I Liked Best..." pictures, page 176, on the day following the parade.

Bee Parade and Party Organizer

Three Weeks Ahead

❑ **Set Event Date**

❑ **Send Parent Assistance Letters**

❑ **Choose Volunteer Team**

1. _____
2. _____
3. _____
4. _____
5. _____

❑ **Supplies**

Costume Supplies   **Name**

1. _____   _____
2. _____   _____
3. _____   _____
4. _____   _____
5. _____   _____

Music Supplies   **Name**

1. _____   _____
2. _____   _____
3. _____   _____
4. _____   _____
5. _____   _____

Party Supplies   **Name**

1. _____   _____
2. _____   _____
3. _____   _____
4. _____   _____
5. _____   _____

Bee Parade and Party Organizer *(cont.)*

Two Weeks Ahead

❑ Have parent volunteer group come in several days to make costumes.

Costume Makers

1. _____

2. _____

3. _____

4. _____

5. _____

❑ Ask a parent to make the Bee Cake. (directions on page 170)

❑ Send Parent/Family Member Invitations

One Week Ahead

❑ Costumes Completed

❑ Music Ready

❑ Party Supplies Ready

❑ Parent Invitations Sent

❑ Parade Route Decided Upon

❑ Event Volunteers Decided On

Event!

After Event

❑ Send Thank You Notes (see page 174)

❑ Create Bee Play Center

Bee Costume Directions

Buzzy Bee costumes can be done quickly and easily in a variety of ways. Here are four simple ideas. (Each set of directions is to make one costume.)

Pillow Case Method

What You Need:

- one pillow case
- yellow dye
- black fabric paint or material and fabric glue

What You Do:

1. Buy a yellow pillow case or dye a white one.
2. Glue or sew on black stripes.
3. Have child wear yellow or black tights or pants.

T-Shirt Method

What You Need:

- one yellow or black T-shirt
- yellow or black pants
- yellow or black material (remember material and shirt must not be same color)

What You Do:

1. Sew or glue material stripes on yellow or black t-shirt.
2. Have child wear yellow or black pants.

Leotard Method

What You Need:

- yellow or black leotard
- yellow or black material or fabric paint
- yellow or black tights

What You Do:

1. Sew or paint yellow or black stripes on leotard.
2. Have child wear yellow or black tights.

Bee Head Dress

What You Need:

- one child-size plastic hair band—black or yellow
- two pipe cleaners
- black spray paint
- two small Styrofoam balls

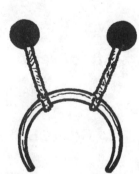

What You Do:

1. Spray Styrofoam balls black; let them dry.
2. Poke pipe cleaner ends into balls and attach them to hair band.

Bee Cake Picture

Bee Cake Directions

What You Need:
- prepared chocolate or white cake mix
- two round layer cake pans
- yellow/lemon frosting
- brown/chocolate frosting
- large package of M & M's ®
- two yellow Fruit Roll Ups ®
- large cake plate or tray covered with foil
- frosting tube and attachments

Directions:

Step One

Mix and bake two round layer cakes according to package directions; cool thoroughly.

Step Two

Cut layer cake into bee shapes and place on large flat cake plate or tray (see cutting diagrams).

Step Three

Frost cake with yellow frosting; add detail with brown frosting using frosting tube and attachments.

Step Four

Add M & M's candy decoration on bee stripes.

Step Five

Add Fruit Roll Up wings last; see pattern page 171.

Step Six

Enjoy!

Bee Cake Wing

Place on Fruit Roll Up.

Trim around edges with sharp knife.

Keep knife away from children.

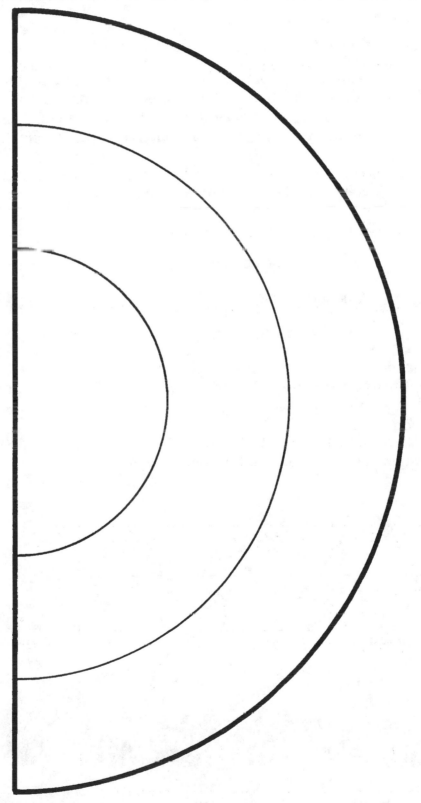

Parent Assistance Letter

Dear Parent,

We will be having a Buzzy Bee Parade and Party as part of our developmentally appropriate learning unit. We are going to need a variety of volunteers to help with a lot of enjoyable tasks. Here are a number of ways you can become involved. (Check any that interest you.)

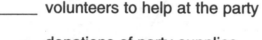 volunteers to make bee costumes

_____ volunteers to bake cakes

_____ volunteers to help at the party

_____ donations of party supplies

_____ donations of materials and costume supplies

Please contact me if you would like to help and do not see anything listed here you can do. Everyone is invited to our special Buzzy Bee Parade and Party! Your invitation will be following soon.

Thank you again for your help and interest.

Sincerely,

_____

for

_____

School

Invitation

You Are Invited
to a
Buzzy Bee
Parade and Party

Where _____

When _____

Come join the fun!

Have a happy time with Buzzy Bees and friends.

We are going to have a Bee Parade, Bee Music, and Bee Cake!

So bring your camera, for there will be beeeee-youtiful pictures you can take!

RSVP _____

Parent Thank-You Note

Dear _____,

Thank you very much for your help with our Buzzy Bee Parade and Party! We could not have done it without your special talents. We really appreciate your extra effort in helping us to make your child's experience a positive one.

Again, thank you very much!

Sincerely,

_____
For

_____
School

Teacher Assessment Tool

Physical

Use this checklist for quick observation of physical skills (compare to parent's observations of same child in same situation).

Child's Name _____

Age _____

Date _____

Head	Arms
_____	_____
_____	_____
_____	_____

Legs	Hands
_____	_____
_____	_____
_____	_____

Neck	Upper Torso
_____	_____
_____	_____
_____	_____

Feet	Lower Torso
_____	_____
_____	_____
_____	_____

Child Self-Assessment

I Liked Best . . .

Child's Name _____

Additional Notes:

_____

_____

_____

Parent Assessment Tool

Buzzy Bee Parade and Party

Take a moment and observe your child's physical development as he/she dances, moves and marches. Note your observations here of how he/she moves the following parts of his/her body. Leave this observation with the teacher before you go. Thank you!

Child's Name _____

Age _____

Date _____

Head

_____

_____

_____

Arms

_____

_____

_____

Legs

_____

_____

_____

Hands

_____

_____

_____

Neck

_____

_____

_____

Upper Torso

_____

_____

_____

Feet

_____

_____

Lower Torso

_____

_____

Soap Boat Races

Preparation Time: one hour

Developmental Connection:

This activity highlights curiosity and allows children to explore water, making models, the concepts of cause and effect, and thinking skills that will all later be related to science exploration.

What You Need:

- Ivory soap bars (because they float), one for each boat

- sails, see page 180

- craft sticks or child's plastic suction cup darts to act as mast for sailboats

- water table center or small wading pool

- sailor Hat, page 181

- boats (stick boats for puppet play), pages 182-184

- Sailor Ribbon Award, page 185

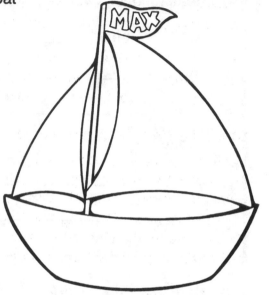

Assessment Materials:

- Teacher Assessment

- Child Self-Assessment

- Parent Assess-At-Home

What To Do:

This activity gives children an opportunity to explore the water table and all its interesting pre-science topics. Children will float Ivory soap boats, make and attach simple sails, and find out what makes them go slower or faster, using air, pushing them along in the water, etc. Finally, they will have a sailboat race for added fun!

Before beginning this activity, make enough copies of the sail master so that you will have one boat sail for each boat you are making. Each boat consists of a bar of Ivory soap (which floats) and a sail. Sails are easy to make. Simply attach a paper sail to a craft stick and stick in a bar of Ivory soap. If you don't care to use craft sticks with the children in your center or school, you can also fashion a child-safe sail by using a child's plastic dart with a suction cup end. See the sail page master for further directions.

Prepare the water table area and set out pre-made boats with sails attached, because very young children will be anxious to begin. The older the child, the more he or she will want to experiment with changing or altering a boat, looking at the sail, etc. Depending on the ages of the children in your group, you will either want to have everything prepared or give some children the opportunity to attach the sail, etc.

Soap Boat Races *(cont.)*

Begin this activity by talking about boats and ships with your students. Use boat pictures on pages 182-184, which show simple kinds of boats that children may already have some familiarity with. These boats can be made into stick puppets, as well as copied larger for a bulletin board, etc. (You can also use the boats in your already existing puppet theater to add a funny water dimension to dramatic puppet play.)

Explain to children that they will be having boat races and show them the water table area.

Show children the soap boats and model the activity. Explain that they will all get a chance to sail and race boats. Give each child a soap boat to race and watch the fun begin!

(**Note:** Remember to make sure this activity is highly staffed by members of your team or parent volunteers. Water, even in small amounts, can be dangerous to toddlers and other small children. Water tables must be supervised, even if the play is self-directed.)

Self-Directed Teaching Focus

Let children experiment on their own in parallel play situations at the water table with a variety of boats and water equipment. Provide objects that sink and float and let them come to their own conclusions. Talk about what happens informally with children and let them talk with you about what they are doing and what they find out while they are experimenting at the water table. Use boat pictures to make easy-to-use boat puppets, to be added to your puppet theater so puppets can have water adventures!

Directed Teaching Focus

Hold races. Say "Ready, set, go!" and let children blow on their sails and see whose boat can go the fastest. Talk about what might make the boats go faster. Open a window for wind, fan the boats, ask the children for ideas. Give children sailor hats to wear during races. End the day by giving everyone a sailor ribbon (page 185).

What to Say

Today we are going to learn about boats and then sail some boats at our own water table. Let's look at these boats that we can use at our puppet theater. Who can tell me about these boats? Has anyone here ever been on a boat? Great! (Teacher discusses boats with children during circle time and moves activity to water table.) Now, let's try our boats and have boat races!

Assessment Connection

The teacher can assess cognitive development with the problem-solving observation form. Use the parent/child conversation observation form with parents to look at cognitive skills, such as memory and information and event recall. Help children to self-assess using the "What Happened Yesterday?" sequence form.

Sails

Cut out and attach these sails to craft sticks and stick into soap boats.

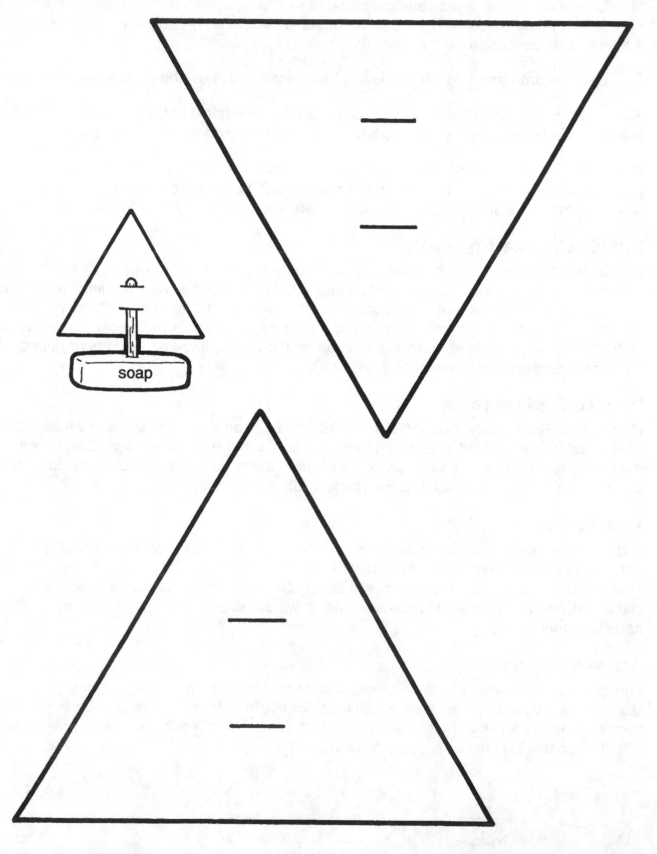

Sailor Hat

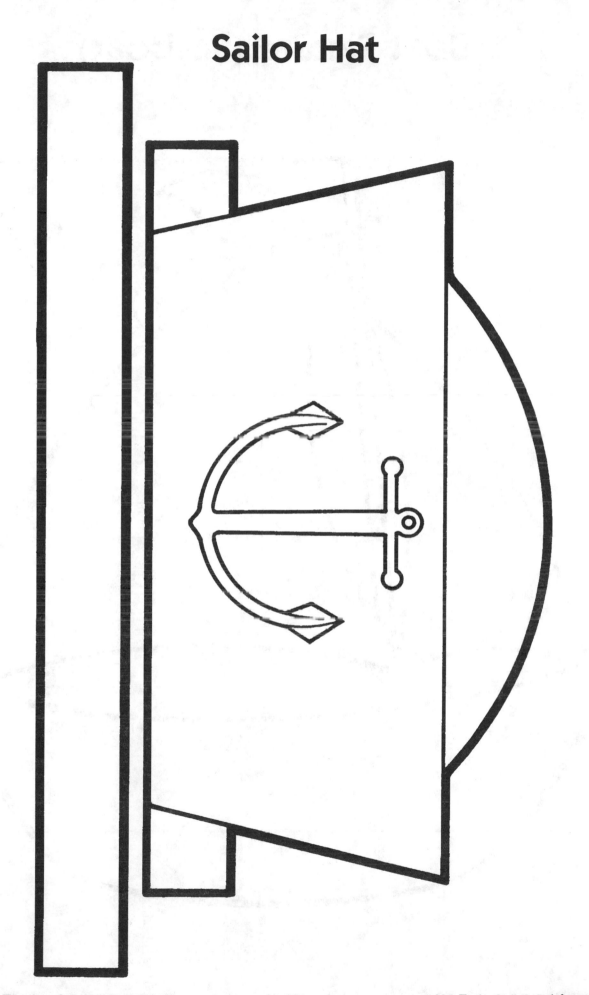

Boat Picture (Sailboat)

Boat Picture (Ship)

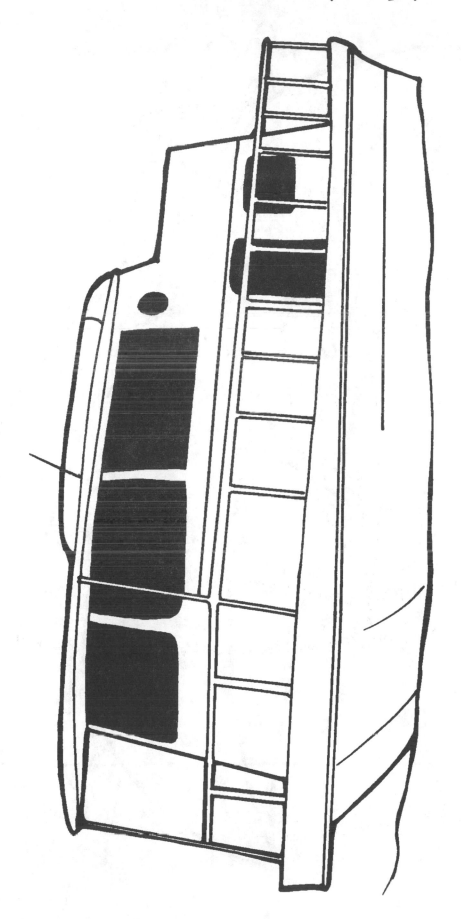

Boat Picture (Canoe)

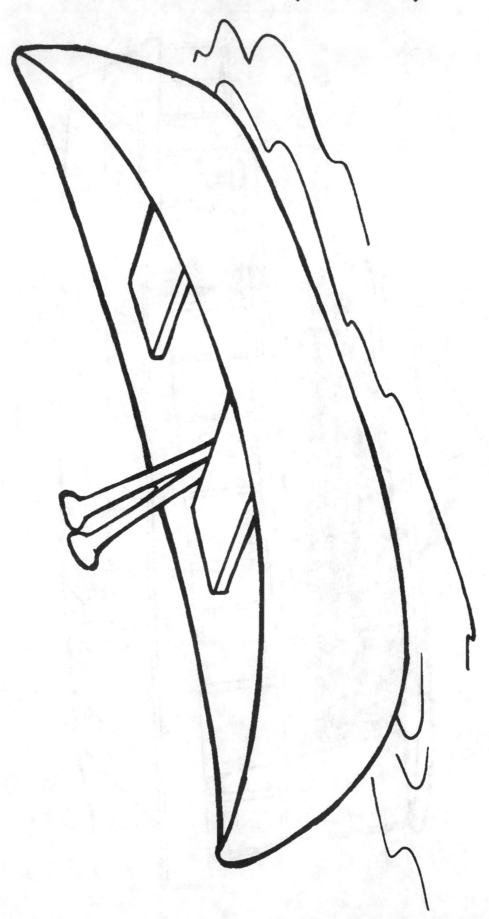

184

Sailor Ribbon Award

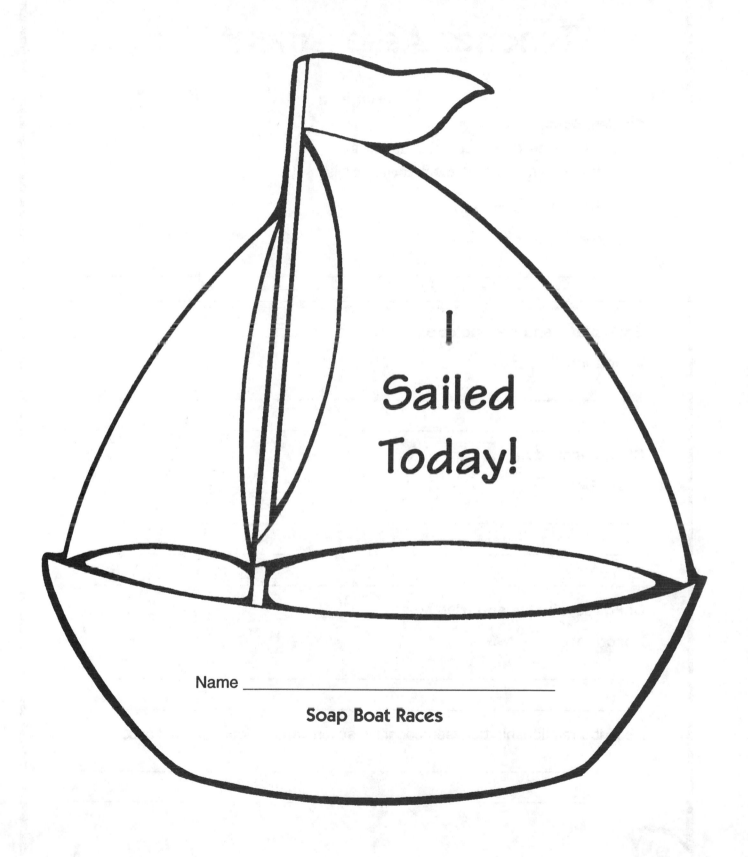

I
Sailed
Today!

Name _____

Soap Boat Races

Teacher Assessment Tool

Cognitive

Problem Solving

Observe child in soap sailboat activity.

Observe and note problem solving skills.

Child identifies problem.

Describe:

_____

_____

Child plans and tries solution.

Describe:

_____

_____

Child succeeds.

Describe:

_____

_____

_____

Child reevaluates and tries again.

Describe:

_____

_____

Describe relationship between cognitive actions and emotional reactions.

_____

_____

Child Self-Assessment

What Happened Yesterday?

Have individual children use a tape recorder to talk about what happened yesterday and how they felt about it. Transcribe conversation here and your observations about your taped conversation. Date and keep tape in child's portfolio for later review or other taped additions.

Taped:

What Happened Yesterday?

Response:

_____

_____

_____

_____

_____

Teacher Observations:

_____

_____

_____

_____

_____

Teacher Evaluation:

_____

_____

_____

_____

_____

Parent Assess-at-Home Form

Talk with your child about the sailboat activity he or she did at school.

Encourage your child to talk by asking open-ended questions, that is those that require an answer other than yes or no, and listen quietly for their response.

Write your observations here:

Did he or she like the activity?

_____

_____

What did he or she stress the most?

_____

_____

Did he or she mention interactions with other children?

_____

_____

What happened with the boat?

_____

_____

How did he or she feel about themselves in the situation?

_____

_____

Was anything unusual or especially interesting mentioned?

_____

_____

If I Met a Dinosaur

Dramatic Play and Storytelling

Dinosaur Puppets

Preparation Time: one hour

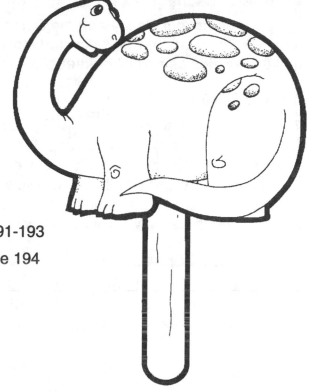

Developmental Connection:

This literature-based, developmentally appropriate activity highlights dramatic play, storytelling, and language skills.

What You Need:

- *Danny and the Dinosaur* by Syd Hoff
- dinosaur and children stick puppets, pages 191-193
- dinosaur-shaped story and picture paper, page 194

Assessment Materials:

Teacher Assessment Tool

Child Self-Assessment Tool

Parent Assessment Tool

What to Do:

This activity allows children to explore language, storytelling, and dramatic play through hearing stories, making their own dramatic plays using puppets, and dictating stories.

To prepare for this activity, make copies of the puppets for your puppet theater, color and laminate them, and glue to craft sticks or tongue depressors. You will probably want to have one set or several sets for your puppet center and at least one, not laminated, for children to color and use to write dictated stories on.

Begin this activity by reading *Danny and the Dinosaur* during circle time. You may want to read it several times over several days. Remember, children love to hear stories over and over again. Then show children the puppets of the little girl, little boy, and dinosaur and tell them they can make up their own stories about when they pretend to meet a dinosaur and use the puppets to act them out.

Also use the dinosaur master for children to dictate stories about what they would do if they had a dinosaur for a friend for the day. Or use the master of the dinosaur to create art projects in your art center.

Self-Directed Teaching Focus

Leave a variety of puppets around the puppet center for children to engage in self-directed play. Make extra copies of the puppet masters for the art center and provide art materials for children to make their own puppets.

If I Met a Dinosaur *(cont.)*

Directed Teaching Focus

Let children act out *Danny and the Dinosaur,* using the puppets while you read it during circle time. Write down children's dictated stories about the day they met a dinosaur. Keep the dictated stories as part of children's portfolios.

What to Say

Today I am going to read you a really wonderful book that I think you will all like a lot. It is called *Danny and the Dinosaur* and it is about this little boy who meets a dinosaur. Listen while I read it. (Read story.) Now let's go look at our puppet theater. I have added three new puppets for us to use—a dinosaur, a little boy, and a little girl. Now we can all pretend to meet a dinosaur and make up puppet shows about meeting a dinosaur. If you would like to tell me your stories, I will write them down for you!

Assessment Connection

The teacher can use the emotional/checklists while observing students during dramatic play. Children can self-assess by drawing expressions on the outlines of the dinosaur and child. Parents can assess at home by keeping a week-long log of their child's emotional responses.

Dinosaur Puppet Master

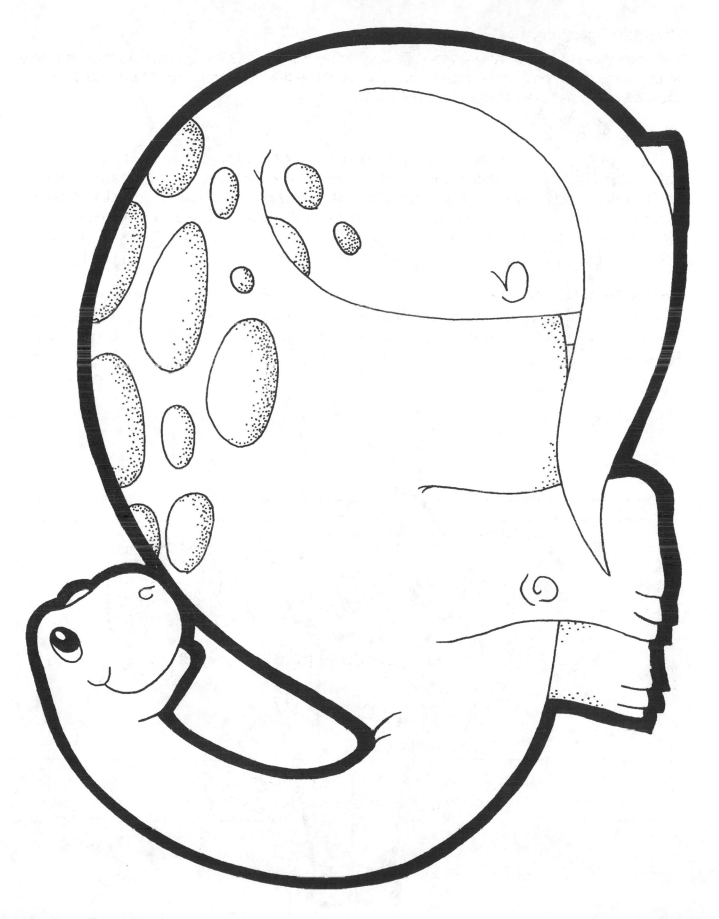

Puppet Master—Girl

Puppet Master—Boy

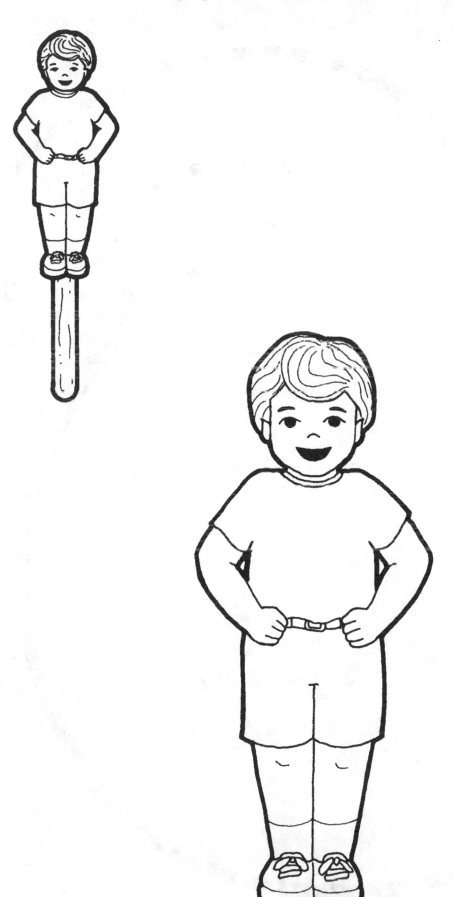

Dinosaur-Shaped Story Paper

Teacher's Assessment Tool

Watching Dramatic Play—Emotional

Child's Self-Awareness and Self-Concept

Child's Name _____

Date _____

Time _____

What emotions does this child display during this activity?

_____   _____

_____   _____

_____   _____

What emotions does the child pretend to have or make his characters have?

_____   _____

_____   _____

_____   _____

How do you think the child is feeling during this activity?

_____   _____

_____   _____

_____   _____

What leads you to believe this?

_____   _____

_____   _____

_____   _____

How is this different from or the same as normal behavior?

_____   _____

_____   _____

_____   _____

Child's Self-Assessment

Teacher reads:

Look at the picture of the dinosaur and the child. Draw their faces to show how they feel.

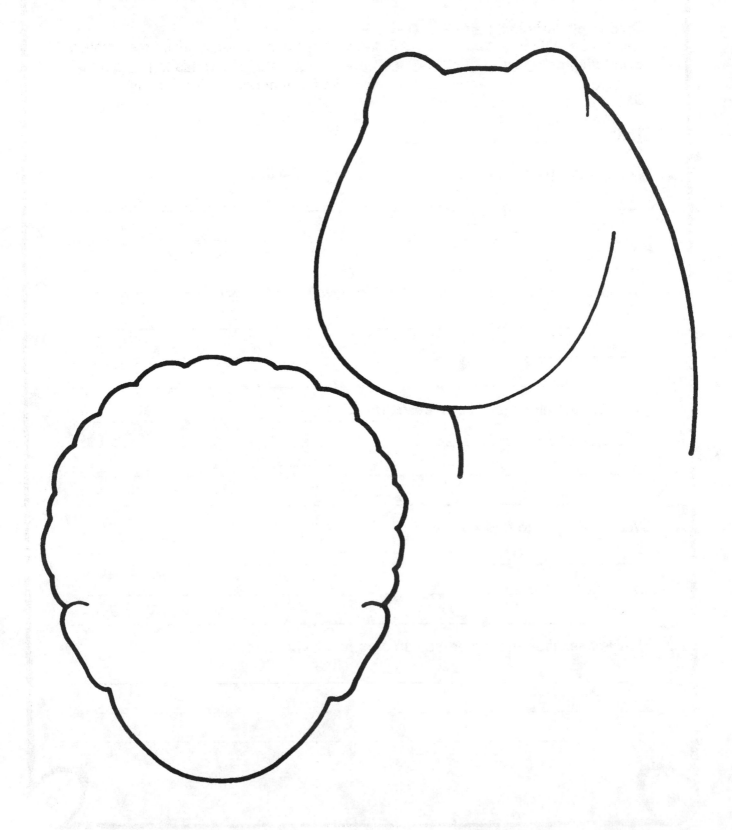

Parent Assess-at-Home Tool

Emotional Development

How did you feel about that?

Keep a casual log of your child's emotional reactions over a week's time. Notice what makes your child glad, sad, frustrated, angry, etc. Bring this log to your next parent-teacher meeting to compare with the teacher's observations.

Monday

Situation: _____

Emotional Response:

_____   _____

_____   _____

Tuesday

Situation: _____

Emotional Response:

_____   _____

_____   _____

Wednesday

Situation: _____

Emotional Response:

_____   _____

_____   _____

Thursday

Situation: _____

Emotional Response:

_____   _____

_____   _____

Friday

Situation: _____

Emotional Response:

_____   _____

_____   _____

Year-Round Birthday Party

Preparation Time: 3-4 hours

Developmental Connection:

In this activity, three, four, and five-year-olds have the opportunity to practice their socialization and self-esteem skills while using oral language skills and becoming aware of letter symbols and their meanings at a pre-reading level. Kindergartners will have the opportunity to further connect verbal and written language.

What You Need:

- bulletin board space
- 12 pieces of colored poster board
- name tag candles, one for each student (see master on page 200)
- birthday party supplies (optional)
- a birthday story (See page 201 for a variety of story selections and brief synopses.)

Assessment Materials:

Teacher Assessment Tool

Child Self-Assessment Tool

Parent Assess-at-Home Tool

What to Do:

In this activity, children have the fun of learning which month their birthday is in and seeing how their own birthdays fit into all the other birthdays in the class. This activity can become as much of a ritual or daily part of your school's activity as you wish. (It is an easy way to remember birthdays and have regular celebrations, as well as give every student his or her own special moment to be the center of attention.)

Begin by reading a birthday party story to your group of children during circle time. Or you may wish to have students view "Barney's Birthday," which is an excellent introduction to birthday parties and fun, or both. You may wish to have preset the party bulletin board over a weekend so children can come in the morning and get the full impact of the giant cake. Next, tell children that everyone in the class will get a chance to celebrate his or her own birthday.

Have parent helpers or aides help children find out when their birthdays are and where on the birthday calendar they fall. (You may already have a calendar and children may be aware of it.) This is an excellent time as well to let them look at the regular classroom calendar and talk about it.

After children each have a name tag, let them have the fun, with the help of a parent volunteer or aide, of finding the places where their own candles go and putting them up on the bulletin board.

Decide how you will celebrate each student's birthday and create a birthday ritual so that students can look forward to their own and each other's birthdays.

Year-Round Birthday Party *(cont.)*

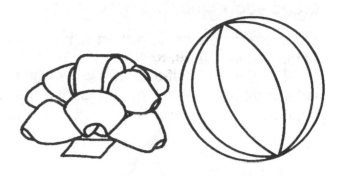

Self-Directed Teaching Focus

Create a self-directed Birthday Present Center for children to make birthday present drawings for one another. Use a piece of colored paper for the actual present box. Have children draw what is inside. Leave a large bowl of 10-cent bows for children to put on their "packages." (Most children love to decorate presents with bows.) Leave space on the bulletin board for children to hang their new present drawings. You may even wish for each birthday child to take home a number of present drawings as part of his or her special day.

Directed Teaching Focus

Have children tell about their favorite birthday experiences as part of sharing or circle time. Have children check the birthday calendar daily to see whose birthday is coming up.

What to Say

Today I am going to read you an enjoyable book about birthdays. *(Read a selected book.)* Now, let's all talk about our birthdays. *(Give children time to relate their birthday experiences as well as past parties and dates, etc.)* Now let's all look at the enjoyable bulletin board we are going to use to tell us when our birthdays are. Each one of us will put up your own birthday candle to remind us all when we should have a party. Then we will have a special day for the people having birthdays! What do you think would be fun for us to do for the birthday boy or girl? Let's all watch "Barney's Birthday" and get some ideas. *(Children view this or any other related video.)*

We are all going to get to make present pictures and put bows on them and then I will leave the bows and present paper right here so we can do it every day if we want to!

Use the birthday calendar to make children aware of the passing months. At the beginning of each month, talk about the holidays that happen during the month and plan special days to celebrate. Or talk about the seasonal changes, etc. Let children use old calendar pages to practice their counting skills or number recognition.

Have children dictate stories about their present pictures and write their stories right on the picture itself. Top them with real bows and mount them on the bulletin board.

Birthday Party Activity

Name Tag Candles

Cover the candle flame portion with non-toxic glue. Sprinkle with gold glitter. Write the child's name in bold, black marker.

Birthdays

Bibliography

Clifford's Birthday Party by Norman Bridwell (Scholastic, 1991)

In *Clifford's Birthday Party*, Emily Elizabeth has a party for the big red dog. Clifford enjoys playing with his friends. His biggest birthday treat comes when the cake is cut—and out pop his family. This delightful book is one of a series featuring the adventures of Clifford and his pals.

Happy Birthday, Dear Duck by Eve Bunting (Clarion Books, 1988)

In this rhyming story, Duck and his friends live in the desert. For his birthday, Duck receives gifts relating to swimming, which seem impractical in this setting. The final guest, Tortoise, arrives late with the most important gift—a plastic pool. The animals have a great time enjoying the water.

Minnie's Yom Kippur Birthday by Marilyn Singer (Harper & Row, 1989)

When Minnie learns that her fifth birthday falls on Yom Kippur, she wonders what will become of the traditional party, cake, and gifts. Not quite sure what is meant by "day of atonement," she can only speculate about what will happen based on her dad's brief explanation. Told in Minnie's own words, this story offers an entertaining introduction not only to the observance of Yom Kippur but to temple practices in general.

Mr. Rabbit and the Lovey Present by Charlotte Zolotow (Harper Trophy, 1977)

A little girl finds Mr. Rabbit in the forest and asks him to help her. It is the little girl's mother's birthday and the girl does not know what to get for her. They both agree that it is a good idea to get her something that she likes. Many choices are presented. Emeralds and sapphires cost too much and she can not give her lakes or stars, but her mother would love pears and grapes. Now all the little girl needs is a basket and she has a lovely birthday gift for her mother.

The Secret Birthday Message by Eric Carle (Harper & Row, 1972)

Tim finds a coded message under his pillow, which reveals the path to his birthday gift. He follows the directions and is rewarded with a puppy. The pages of this book have cut-out shapes which add to the children's interest. Having children try some crack-the-code activities adds to this book.

Happy Birthday Moon by Frank Asch (Simon and Schuster, 1988)

This adorable story features a happy little bear who befriends the moon and decides to get his friend the moon a birthday gift. Each conversation with the moon comes back to him in a happy echo reply, and this makes both the bear and the moon have a great deal in common, including their own wishes in birthday gifts. The story ends with a gift exchange and both the bear and his friend the moon know the joy of giving and receiving.

Bulletin Board Directions

What You Need:
- poster board or construction paper for birthday cake sections
- bulletin board letters for months and titles
- candle name tags, page 200, for each child
- square pieces of colored construction paper for "packages"
- ready-made bows with stick-on strips
- glitter
- scissors
- staple gun
- non-toxic glue

What to Do:
This project will take several hours and can easily be put together in an afternoon to make a great impression the following day.

1. Decide what size you would like the birthday cake section of your bulletin board to be. Make 12 "slices" of cake as seen in the picture. The birthday cake is actually an aerial view. Mount these pieces in a circle. You may wish to use different colors or all the same, whatever you feel would work best for you.

2. Next, create the letters for each month to fit around the edges of the cake. Start with January and go across the top of the cake and then switch letters to the easiest to read position. See the example picture.

3. Prepare candle name tags. You may wish to let children glue and glitter or simply prepare the tags yourself to save time.

4. Create a Present Center so children can make their simple presents. Place a bowl of ready-made 10-cent bows out for children to decorate packages. (After-Christmas sales are an excellent time to stock up on extra bows.)

5. Let children put their own candles on the cake with the assistance of an aide or helper.

6. Enjoy your birthday calendar all year!

Happy Birthday!

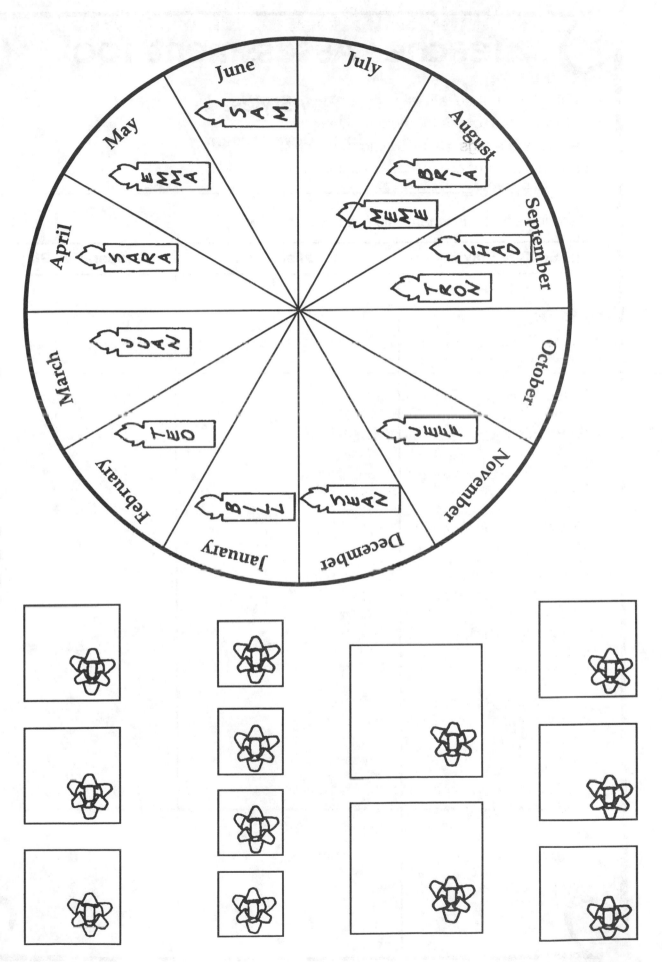

Teacher Assessment Tool

Play Styles

Social Development

Child's Name_____ **Date**_____

Describe situations where this child . . .

Solitary Plays	Parallel Plays	Cooperative Plays

Child Self-Assessment

Year Round Birthday

Child makes one or two "birthday candle wishes" and tells the teacher who writes the wish on candle(s). The child's name can be written on the flame and the candle(s) cut out to add to the bulletin board display or to take home.

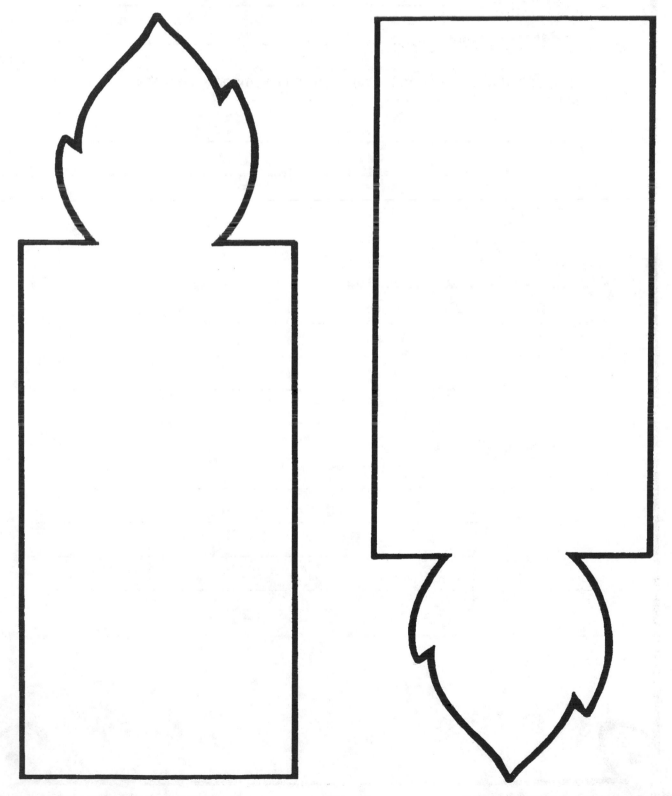

Parent Assessment Tool

Empathy/Social Development

Child's Name _____

Parent's Name _____

Describe a situation where your child cared for someone other than himself/herself.

_____
_____
_____
_____

What were his/her reactions emotionally?

_____
_____
_____
_____

How did you support his/her reactions?

_____
_____
_____
_____

Checklist for Traditional Assessment

Check off those items that you recognize as part of your current assessment.

Traditional assessment . . .

- ❑ 1. uses sit down tests.

- ❑ 2. depends on tests using pencils, papers, and worksheets.

- ❑ 3. depends on written material.

- ❑ 4. requires children to work independently.

- ❑ 5. requires specific guidelines.

- ❑ 6. is matched by specific curriculum.

- ❑ 7. is formal.

- ❑ 8. is graded.

- ❑ 9. is used for statistical research.

- ❑ 10. is used at times throughout a child's education and in life.

- ❑ 11. requires certain "discipline rules."

- ❑ 12. requires an orderly and quiet environment.

- ❑ 13. is written language intensive.

- ❑ 14. is written number intensive.

- ❑ 15. is often state or federally mandated.

- ❑ 16. is something communities are interested in.

- ❑ 17. attempts to meet specific goals for children based on predetermined norms.

- ❑ 18. is concrete.

- ❑ 19. is used for comparisons of students.

- ❑ 20. is used for comparisons of programs and teachers.

Traditional Assessment

What Is It?

Traditional assessment is the kind of assessment we knew when we were in school. It consists of a variety of standardized tests. Often, they are the kinds of tests where one sits quietly and is tested on a preplanned set of things which should have been learned by all students. Sometimes they are tests designed to let someone somewhere know if a student, like all the other kindergartners across the nation, knows whatever it was they thought each student should know.

There are very important examples of traditional assessment that still exist today and are vital parts of students' lives. SAT's are a form of traditional assessment and all high school seniors must have the necessary skills to be able to take this test if they are college bound.

School and Life

There are many times in life when being able to be assessed and do well in a traditional sense will benefit the children in your early childhood classroom. While this is certainly only one small way of assessing today, it still has its place.

Good Reasons

Very young children generally do not respond well to standardized tests and, while many school districts mandate their use, there are also many reasons why they must be used with caution both when giving them to a young child and when using their results as a source of accurate evaluation.

However, as there will be many instances in many districts when children will be subject to this form of testing or tracking in their early childhood careers and since there will be times when such testing is important (intervention for a variety of learning problems, for example), traditional assessment has been provided as a part of this book and certainly an option for testing a child—with a few considerations.

Traditional Assessment Sampler

In this section you will see a broad range of traditional assessment samples with corresponding curricula. Besides achievement tests and readiness tests there are also examples of developmental screening tests and diagnostic tests. Even if your program does not have to use any of these methods, it is valuable to be versed in each of these kinds of assessments when parents or the community have questions.

Traditional Assessment *(cont.)*

Sit Down Tests

The traditional test is a sit-down test. Children sit at desks and are given pre-written tests that determine specific outcomes. Young children work with an adult helper to complete a given set of questions.

Pencils, Papers, and Worksheets

Everyday assessment in classrooms is done by work that requires children to use worksheets and share what they know by answering true and false or multiple-choice questions or circling the correct response, or marking an X.

Written Material

The basis for traditional assessment is any material that is written. Tests are written, distributed, completed, and scored.

Children Are Required to Work Independently

Children are assessed individually. Children do not work cooperatively or in group situations to be observed or in any way evaluated. Individual responses and scores are used to determine statistical outcomes and grades.

Requires Specific Guidelines

Standardized testing tests for specific things. The kinds of standardized tests that are used today are attempting to deliver information about specific and decided-upon criteria.

Is Matched by Specific Curriculum

Often teachers teach to a test. That means they teach the curriculum needed to produce a set of required test results.

Is Formal

Usually standardized testing is formal. There is a certain behavior expected and required of children to produce in an environment where the test is administered.

Is Graded

Traditional assessment produces grades, usually letter or percentage grades.

Is Used for Statistical Research

Traditional assessment or testing is useful for statisticians or people trying to find norms. Statistics can be useful in determining generalities.

Is Used at Times Throughout a Child's Education and in Life

There are unavoidable times when a child will at some point in his or her education sit down and using a pencil or a pen be required to complete a test alone. This is not a bad thing as long as it is not the only way this child is ever assessed. Later in life the ability to work independently and complete something that is being assessed like a job application will prove a useful skill.

Requires Certain Discipline Rules

In traditional assessment settings children are required to sit quietly and listen and then complete a test. They do not move around the room, but take part in whole-class testings by listening to the teacher give instructions and then completing the test as they are asked to.

Traditional Assessment *(cont.)*

Requires an Orderly and Quiet Environment

Traditional testing is done in silence except for the test giver's talking or sometimes asking questions, and the occasional question a child might ask after being called on and given permission to do so.

Is Written Language Intensive

Traditional testing relies on written language. Students are handed a test and are asked to read the directions and answer the questions. Or they are asked questions orally and asked to mark down their answers on paper.

Is Written Number Intensive

Mathematical tests are number intensive, requiring children to work problems and find solutions or answer multiple choice questions using a piece of scratch paper to work the problems to verify their results.

Is Often State or Federally Mandated

At the primary level (as well as later on) school districts are required to give a variety of state and federally mandated tests. This varies from state to state and more slightly from district to district.

Is Something Communities Are Interested In

There are quite a number of traditionally minded people in the United States who value what they feel are traditional educational styles. Traditional testing is part of a traditional education to many people.

Attempts to Meet Specific Goals for Children Based on Predetermined Norms

Testing is the basis for research that produces more testing based on what the results have shown to be "norms." These "norms" are the specific goals that a child or group of children are determined to be ready to meet based on statistical research.

Is Concrete

The nature of traditional testing is that there are right and wrong answers. They do not include an assessment of the problem-solving process, but only the arrived at answer which is then marked either correct or incorrect.

Is Used for Comparison of Students

Testing is a way of comparing students in a classroom in a school or in a community, or even nationally or internationally. It is possible to look at the averages of reading scores from schools in one state and compare the averages of reading scores from children in another state and make some statistical observations about what is an average, a below average, and an above average response based on a designated sample.

Is Used for Comparisons of Programs and Teachers

States use testing as part of their program and budget mandating. Statistics are the way that people prove they need money for their group or need special programs for their group at the state and federal level. Traditionally in this country we trust numbers. A numerical justification for a program is acceptable to many people, in fact, preferable.

Traditional Academic Checklist

Child's Name _____ Child's Age _____

Teacher _____

Writing (Readiness)

_____ Knows that the marks in books, on papers, and on signs represent and can be translated into speech.

_____ Enjoys dictating stories that are written down by the teacher or another classroom helper.

_____ Forms the letters of the alphabet in a variety of media: crayon, pencil, paint, clay, etc.

_____ Writes his/her own name.

Reading (Readiness)

_____ Identifies and names the letters of the alphabet: likes to sing the alphabet song.

_____ Identifies and says the sounds associated with the letters of the alphabet: names something that starts with each letter.

_____ Identifies by sight and names words in his/her environment: e.g., STOP on a stop sign, his/her own name on a cubby, etc.

_____ Enjoys "reading" books by telling a story while looking at the pictures.

Math (Readiness)

_____ Identifies and names the numerals from 1 to 10.

_____ Counts ten objects; gives the number for a set of objects; e.g., 6 blocks, 2 bikes.

_____ Forms the numerals from 1 to 10 using a variety of media: crayon, pencil, paint, clay, etc.

Social Studies (Socialization/Self-Esteem)

_____ Feels good about himself/herself as a person and about his/her own achievements in school.

_____ Recognizes that other children want to feel good too.

_____ Knows what private property is even if he/she does not always manage to respect the property of others.

_____ Understands the concept of sharing (both things and ideas) even though he/she may not choose to share.

_____ Understands that there are rules even though he/she may not always observe them.

Science (Curiosity/Observation/Discovery)

_____ Sees the world as an amazing place, full of interesting things to find out about.

_____ Looks and listens—spontaneously or as the result of directed activity—in order to find out about things.

_____ Communicates with enthusiasm and some degree of accuracy what he/she finds out by observing things.

ABC Mouse

ABC Mouse House

ABC Mouse Story

Preparation Time: The preparation time in this activity will be determined by how intensive and how long you would like the activity to be. This can range from several hours, to several hours a week for a number of weeks.

Academic Connection:

This activity highlights the concepts of reading readiness and letter recognition.

What You Need:

- one shoe box for each participating child
- mouse master on page 220
- one letter item for each letter master
- one copy of each letter master for each child, pages 224-249
- parents helping at home kit, see page 253
- book master text pages 221-250
- book cover picture, page 219
- book cover letter strip, page 218
- ABC letter master blank, page 250
- Mouse Book directions, page 215
- Mouse House directions, page 214
- ABC object directions, page 216
- Shoe Box House Cover, page 217

Assessment Materials:

Teacher Assessment— Reading Readiness Checklist

Child Self-Assessment—Draw a Face

Parent Assessment—Parent Assess-at-Home Form

What To Do:

This activity will give children exposure to the alphabet, becoming familiar with letters and, their names, objects, and pictures that begin with a letter. (Additionally, if you wish, children will be read to and have the chance to write letters. However, you may easily change the focus from academic to developmental; see page 215.) There are many ways to use this activity. Feel free to use all of the aspects of this activity or just one or two; it is up to you.

Begin this activity by getting a shoe box for each child. Use the Mouse House master on page 217 to make a Mouse House Box for each child; see directions page 214. Then, print as many copies of the ABC Mouse Book as you would like; one for each child is best. They are easy to staple and laminate and can be colored by children or pre-colored and laminated by you. You may wish to make one master copy for you to read at circle time. This one will last longer if it is colored and laminated before you start to use it.

ABC Mouse (cont.)

Begin by reading this story to children at circle time and explain that they will all have a copy of the book of their very own to take home as well as their own ABC Mouse House in which to gather ABC objects. Have several in-room copies of the ABC book laminated and copied for children to use during self-directed time. (For several dollars, printers will bind a copy of a book which will be sturdy and looks professional.)

Make a large ABC Mouse House for use with the story in your center or classroom. Simply find a larger box and print and laminate larger copies of the mouse house, the mouse, and the objects. Let children use this with the story.

Self-Directed Teaching Focus

Leave an ABC Mouse Center set up to use during self-directed times. The mouse house and the laminated objects can be taken out and put back in, each time a child does this, he will have exposure to letters and objects that begin with each letter, as well as an opportunity for self-directed storytelling and dramatic play. The ABC Mouse has as many uses as your children's imaginations!

Directed Teaching Focus

Have children take turns at circle time finding the right letters to go with each object and adding them to the mouse house during the story. Begin by placing all the laminated ABC objects face up in the middle of the circle. Ask different children to find a letter and the matching object and put it in the house with the mouse.

What to Say

Today we are going to meet a new classroom friend! His name is the ABC Mouse. Let's all take a look at his house and then I will read a really interesting ABC story about him. Let's put the ABC house in the center of the circle and talk about all of these objects we have here. *(Model the activity, reading the ABC Mouse Story and putting in the ABC objects as you go along.)* Now let's read it again and find the ABC objects together and put them in! We are going to leave the ABC Mouse and his house and all his ABC objects in his own special center so we can play with him whenever we want to! And everyone will get to take home a little mouse and storybook!

Focus on Assessment

Use the reading readiness assessment observation forms to make notes about a children's reading readiness. Send the parent observation forms home for parents to complete after reading the story to their children and as feedback for you about their children's progress and the value of this activity for each individual child. Have children self-assess by using the Draw My Face assessment tool. Have children draw their own faces after using the activity. Simply say, "Draw how you feel. Now, draw your face here."

Making the Mouse House and ABC Mouse

Shoe Box House (And Larger Center Mouse House)

What You Need:

- one large box with cover for classroom, (large gift box size will do, just make sure that the mouse and the objects fit comfortably inside the box with the lid closed)
- one shoe box with lid for each mouse house you are making
- one copied mouse house master page 217 for each mouse you are making
- glue
- colored markers
- laminating paper (clear contact paper)
- scissors

What You Do:

Copy and color the mouse house master and glue to the top of the lid of the mouse house box. Make sure to label each shoe box house with child's name for easy identification. You may wish to have children draw or color their own mouse house pictures and then laminate these and glue them to the top of their shoe box house, or do this ahead of time.

Mouse

What You Need:

- mouse master, one for each house you are making
- colored markers
- glue
- laminating paper (clear contact paper)
- scissors

 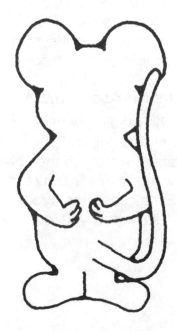

What You Do:

Copy mouse and color his front and back, then cut out and glue front and back together. Then laminate mouse and trim his edges. He is now ready to live in his house!

Making the Mouse Books

With Letter Strips

What You Need:

- book master pages 218-250, one complete set for each book you are making
- coloring supplies
- laminating materials (optional)
- binding materials

What You Do:

To make a mouse book with letter strips, just use the masters on pages 218-250 as they are. Color them or allow children to color them and then laminate. Bind the books by stapling, putting in binders, or binding at a printer. How detailed you want to be is up to you.

Also, if you want children to be able to use the letter strip section, copy extra copies of the book that are disposable and not laminated so children can use these to write and draw in.

Without Letter Strip

What You Need:

- book master pages 218-250, one complete set for each book you are making
- coloring supplies
- laminating materials (optional)
- binding materials

What You Do:

Simply cut the masters to remove the letter strips and discard. The cover on page 219 has been designed to fit the book without the letter strip. Color and laminate the books and bind whatever way works best for you. Send these home with children as part of your Helping-at-Home Kit.

ABC Objects

Depending on your preference you can make the objects with the letters attached or separated. Here are directions for both.

Attached Letters

What You Need:

- copies for each set of objects for each house (the objects are made from the actual illustrations of the master book)
- colored markers
- scissors
- laminating paper (clear contact paper)

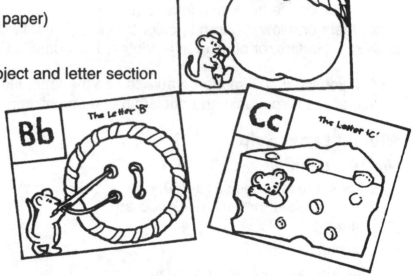

What You Do:

Just cut, color, and laminate each object and letter section like the illustrations shown.

Add to mouse house!

Detached Letters

What You Need:

- copies for each set of objects for each house (the objects are made from the actual illustrations of the master book)
- colored markers
- scissors
- laminating paper (clear contact paper)

What You Do:

Simply cut apart the letters and objects and laminate separately. These can be used for matching games as well as in your mouse house game!

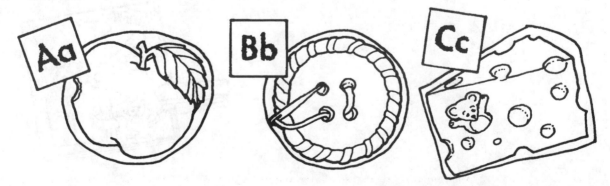

Shoe Box House Cover

This house belongs to

Name

The ABC MOUSE

Book Cover/Picture

Cut off the letter strip on each master to create a developmentally appropriate ABC book. This cover is designed to fit the book without the letter strips.

ABC Mouse

Copy, color, and glue mouse front and back together. Laminate. Put one mouse in each shoe box Mouse House.

ABC Mouse House

I am a little mouse
In an ABC house,
Can you guess what I have for each letter?

First, I'll start with "A"
And go all the way to "Z"
and then we'll know the Alphabet better!

221 #465 Early Childhood Assessment

ABC Mouse House

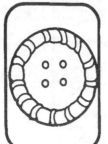

I am a little mouse,
In an ABC house,
Can you guess what I have for each letter?

First, I'll start with "A"
And go all the way to "Z"
and then we'll know the Alphabet better!

Aa — I like to eat APPLES as you can see,
Tell me what's next, what starts with...

Bb — It's a BUTTON and I'll sew it on
As easy as you please!
Now, tell me what's next, what starts with...

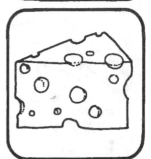

Cc — CHEESE for dinner tastes yummy to me!
Now, what do I have here that starts with...

Dd — DUCKIE'S my friend, He's cute, you'll agree!
Now, I wonder what starts with...

Ee — "E" is for ELEPHANT, a big house guest!
Now, can you tell me what starts with...

Ff — "F" is for FLOWER, a bouquet for me!
Now, can you tell me what starts with...

Gg — "G" is for GRAPES, they taste so great!
Now can you tell me what starts with...

Hh — "H" is for HELICOPTER, flying way up high!
Now, can you tell me what starts with...

Ii — When I talk about myself, "I" is what I say!
Now, please tell me what starts with...

Jj — "J" is for JACKS, have you ever played?
Now, let's guess what starts with...

Kk — "K" is for KID, you are one, I can tell!
Now, let's guess what starts with...

ABC Mouse House *(cont.)*

Ll — "L" is for LEPRECHAUN, he is pretend!
Now, tell me what's next, what starts with...

Mm — "M" is for MOMMY, my very best friend!
Now, can you tell me what starts with...

Nn — "N" is for NUMBERS, which ones do you know?
Now, can you tell me what starts with...

Oo — "O" is for ORANGE, as sweet as can be!
Now, can you tell me what starts with...

Pp — "P" is for PIE, so tasty, it's true!
Now, can you tell me what starts with...

Qq — "Q" is for QUEEN, in her castle, so far!
Now, can you tell me what starts with...

Rr — "R" is for RABBIT, in which hat, can you guess?
Now, please tell me what starts with...

Ss — "S" is for SNAKE as harmless as can be!
Now, let's guess what starts with...

Tt — "T" is for TAIL, I have one, do you?
Can you tell me what starts with...

Uu — "U" is for UMBRELLA, I'm as dry as can be!
Can you tell me what starts with...

Vv — "V" is for VACUUM, when I clean I have lots to do!
Now, let's guess what starts with...

Ww —Sam the WHALE and I wear bow ties for our necks!
Can you guess what starts with...

Xx — "X" is for X-RAY, the doctor sees what's inside!
Tell me what's next, what starts with...

Yy — "Y" is for YELLOW, the color of the sun!
Guess one more letter, you are almost done!

Zz — "Z" is for ZOOM, see the letters whiz by!
I knew you'd learn your alphabet if you tried!

Aa

The Letter "A"

I like to eat apples, as you can see!

apple

Tell me what's next what starts with...

Bb

The Letter "B"

It's a button and I'll sew it on as easy as you please!

button

Now, tell me what's next, what starts with ...

Cc

The Letter "C"

Cheese for dinner tastes yummy to me!

cheese

Now, what do I have here that starts with..

Dd

The Letter "D"

Duckie's my friend, he's cute, you'll agree!

Now, I wonder what starts with ...

Ee

The Letter "E"

"E" is for elephant, a big house guest!

elephant

Now, can you tell me what starts with...

Ff

The Letter "F"

"F" is for flower, a bouquet for me!

flower

Now, can you tell me what starts with...

Gg

The Letter "G"

"G" is for grapes, they taste so great!

grapes

Now, can you guess what starts with...

Hh

The Letter "H"

"H" is for helicopter, flying way up high!

helicopter

Now, can you tell me what starts with...

Ii

The Letter "I"

When I talk about myself, "I" is what I say!

I

Now, please tell me what starts with...

Jj

The Letter "J"

"J" is for jacks, have you ever played?

jacks

Now, let's guess what starts with...

Kk

The Letter "K"

"K" is for kid, you are one, I can tell!

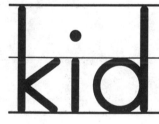

Now, lets guess what starts with...

Ll

The Letter "L"

"L" is for leprechaun, he is pretend!

leprechaun

Tell me what's next, what starts with ...

Mm

The Letter "M"

"M" is for Mommy, my very best friend!

mommy

Now, can you tell me what starts with...

Nn

The Letter "N"

"N" is for numbers, which ones do you know?

numbers

Now, can you tell me what starts with...

Oo

The Letter "O"

"O" is for orange, as sweet as can be!

orange

Now, can you tell me what starts with...

Pp

The Letter "P"

"P" is for pie, so tasty, it's true!

pie

Now, can you tell me what starts with...

Qq

The Letter "Q"

"Q" is for queen in her castle so far!

queen

Now, can you tell me what starts with...

Rr

The Letter "R"

"R" is for rabbit, in which hat, can you guess?

rabbit

Now, please tell me what starts with...

Ss

The Letter "S"

"S" is for snake as harmless as can be!

snake

Now, let's guess what starts with...

Tt

The Letter "T"

"T" is for tail, I have one, do you?

tail

Can you tell me what starts with..

Uu

The Letter "U"

"U" is for umbrella, I'm dry as can be!

umbrella

Can you tell me what starts with...

Vv

The Letter "V"

"V" is for vacuum, when I clean I have lots to do!

vacuum

Now, let's guess what starts with...

Ww

The Letter "W"

Sam the whale and I wear bow ties for our necks!

whale

Can you guess what starts with...

The Letter "X"

"X" is for X-ray, the doctor sees what's inside!

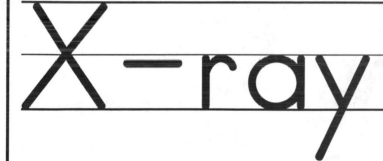

Tell me what's next, what starts with ...

Yy

The Letter "Y"

"Y" is for yellow, the color of the sun!

yellow

Guess one more letter, you are almost done!

Zz

The Letter "Z"

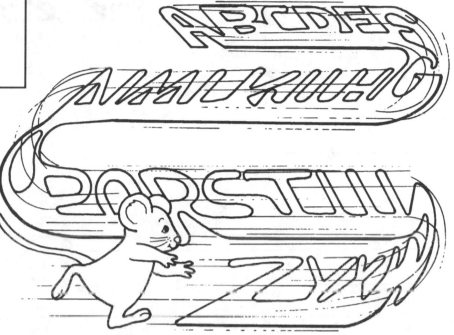

"Z" is for zoom, see the letters whiz by!

zoom

I knew you'd learn the alphabet if you tried!

ABC Letter Master Blank

The Letter " "

Tell me what's next. What starts with...

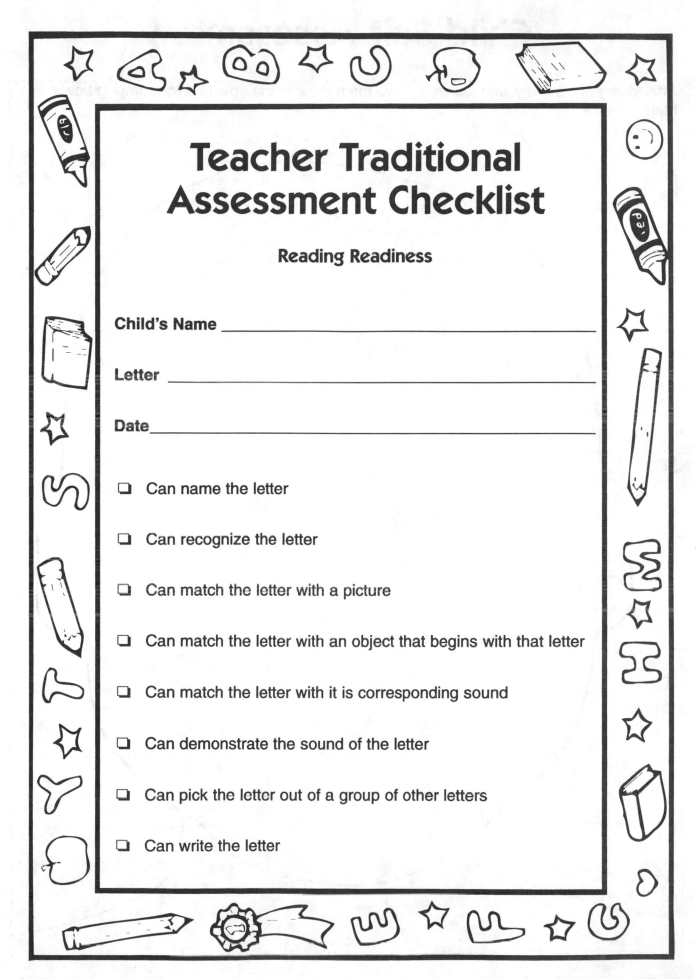

Teacher Traditional Assessment Checklist

Reading Readiness

Child's Name _____

Letter _____

Date _____

- ❑ Can name the letter

- ❑ Can recognize the letter

- ❑ Can match the letter with a picture

- ❑ Can match the letter with an object that begins with that letter

- ❑ Can match the letter with it is corresponding sound

- ❑ Can demonstrate the sound of the letter

- ❑ Can pick the letter out of a group of other letters

- ❑ Can write the letter

Child Self-Assessment

After doing this activity with children, have them draw in their own faces, showing how they feel.

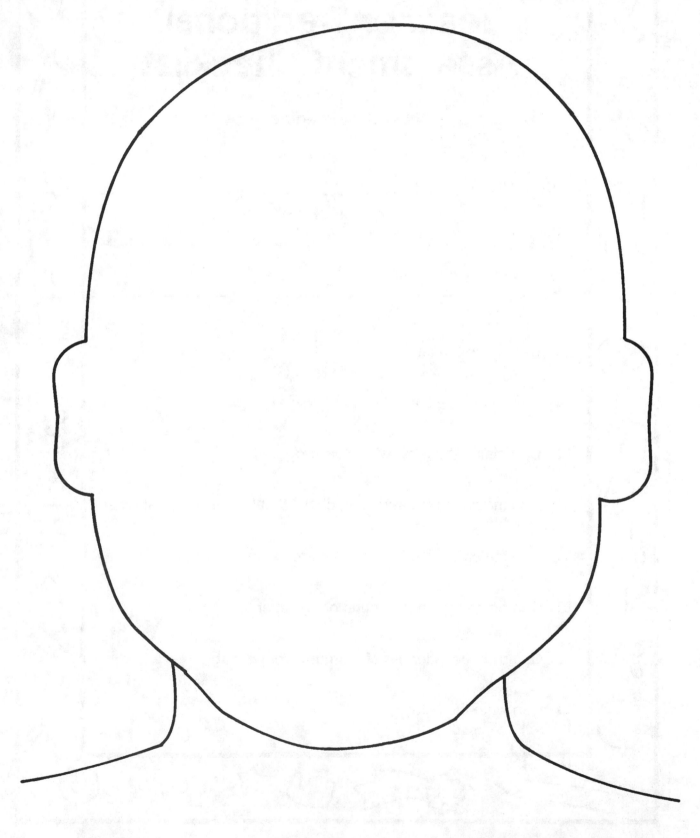

Parents Helping-at-Home

ABC Mouse House

Dear Parent(s),

As part of our "Reading-at-Home" focus, we have created an "ABC Mouse House" for you and your child to use at home. The mouse house has a laminated mouse and laminated ABC objects that can be taken out and replaced in the mouse house. Use this mouse house with the book *ABC Mouse*, or use alone to reinforce letter recognition and pre-reading skills.

Several ways to use the ABC mouse house to reinforce what your child is doing follow:

- Let your child use the mouse house and match the letters to the letters in the mouse book.
- Find objects in your house that start with letters and add these to your child's mouse house.
- Talk about letters and point them out in other books, on signs, and on food packages, etc.
- Let your child play with the mouse house in whatever way he/she likes.

Feel free to contact me regarding this activity, the book, or any other questions you might have about reading to your child. Remember reading to your child will help him or her begin the process of understanding language and eventually to begin reading. It is a wonderful way to promote family togetherness!

Sincerely,

_____
for

_____
school

Parents Helping-at-Home

Book Letter

Dear Parent(s),

As part of our "Reading-at-Home" focus, we have enclosed in this Helping-at-Home Kit a lovely, reusable book called "The ABC Mouse." Please read this to your child and let him or her look at it. Then use the assessing at home form for your own feedback.

Remember to make reading to your child a positive experience by

- having fun while reading.
- answering questions about words and pictures.
- spending some regular time reading everyday, even if it is only five minutes.
- giving your child access to a number of age appropriate books.

Do not pressure your child about knowing his/her letters or make any expectations about when he or she should learn them.

Feel free to contact me regarding this book or any other questions you might have about reading to your child. Remember, reading to your child will help him or her begin the process of understanding language and eventually reading. It is a wonderful way to promote family togetherness!

Sincerely,

_____

for

_____

school

Parent Assess-At-Home Form

Each time you read this alphabet storybook with your child, make a note of your child's reactions and progress.

Date _____

Reactions:

_____

_____

Progress:

_____

_____

Date _____

Reactions:

_____

_____

Progress:

_____

_____

Date _____

Reactions:

_____

_____

Progress:

_____

_____

Number Puzzles

Preparation Time: several hours

Academic Connection:

This activity highlights number recognition and pre-mathematics skills.

What You Need:

- math number puzzle, page 258
- laminating materials
- colored copy paper
- scissors
- shirt box with cover for each number puzzle set made
- number puzzle box cover, page 259
- making number puzzle directions, page 260

Assessment Materials:

Teacher Assessment — Math Readiness

Child Self-Assessment — "I Know My Numbers" Star Sheet

Parent Assessment — Parent Assessment at Home Form, Numbers

What to Do:

This activity will give children exposure to numbers from one to twenty, counting, number recognition, and one-to-one correspondence. Before beginning this activity, set aside an afternoon to prepare the number puzzles. See directions on page 260. After you have made the number puzzle sets, introduce them to your children and model matching the numbers and counting to twenty with individuals or in groups.

Children can then use the number puzzle to count, or to match the number on the puzzle piece to the number board. You can also have children find objects representing whatever number you are counting up to on a certain day, or play a number-a-day game in which you find groups of things to represent each number in your classroom. There are a variety of ways you can use these number sets, from leaving them around at a number center to working with individual students learning and matching numbers.

Use number puzzles as part of a Parents' Helping-at-Home Kit so children will have their own copy of this puzzle to take home and extend the activity and the concepts into their learning at home time with their parents.

Number Puzzles *(cont.)*

Self-Directed Teaching Focus

Use this number puzzle as part of your regular set of puzzles. Let children put it together as they want to. Let them ask about numbers and for your assistance rather than volunteering this information. That way they can discover numbers at their own pace. Additionally, as the number sections are all in different colors, they will have exposure to patterns as well as numbers and colors.

Directed Teaching Focus

Work with individual children naming numbers and having them count with you or count during circle time to twenty every day, having children hold up the number as they speak it. Work with individual children to see what numbers they know and get a sense about their number recognition and counting skills.

What To Say

Today we have a new puzzle to try. It is a number puzzle. Let's take a look at it. Now let's see if we can say all the numbers and count together! *(Model counting to 20 then let children try with you a variety of times.)* Watch! As I say the number, I will find the piece of the puzzle that fits. *(Place puzzle pieces face side up and number board on floor. Then count and place numbers as you go).* Now, who wants to try it with me? etc.

Focus on Assessment

Use the traditional assessment form to determine math readiness. Send home the number puzzle along with the Parent Assessing-at-Home form so children and parents can use the puzzle together and parents can complete their at-home assessment form to give you feedback. Have children self-assess using the number blank completion form. Let children add their own stars when they know a number for a traditional academic twist on self assessment.

Number Puzzle

1	2	3	4	5
6	7	8	9	10
11	12	13	14	15
16	17	18	19	20

Number Puzzle Box

Number Puzzle

_____

Making a Number Puzzle

What You Need:

- number master, two copies for each number puzzle set
- coloring supplies, markers or paint
- laminating materials
- scissors
- shirt box with lid for each puzzle
- cover master page 259, one for each puzzle

What to Do:

1. Decide how large you would like to make the puzzle game. Remember, the younger the child who will be using it, the larger it should be. Also remember the board section must fit in the shirt box, so measure the shirt box or take it with you when you make the copies.

2. Next, color the squares on both the board and the cut-apart numbers the same color for each number but with a variety of different colors so the board is multi-colored.

3. Laminate the pieces as well as the board, and you have a reusable manipulative math puzzle for preschoolers!

Teacher Traditional Assessment Checklist

Math Readiness

Child's Name _____

Number _____

Date _____

- ❏ Can name the number

- ❏ Can recognize the number

- ❏ Can match the number with a picture of correct quantity

- ❏ Can match the number with object(s)

- ❏ Knows what number comes before and after the number

- ❏ Can count up to the number

- ❏ Can pick the number out of a group of other numbers

- ❏ Can write the number

Child Self-Assessment

I know these numbers:

1	2	3	4	5
6	7	8	9	10
11	12	13	14	15
16	17	18	19	20

Parent Assess-at-Home Form

Each time you use the number puzzle with your child, make a note of your child's reactions and progress.

Date _____

Reactions:

_____

_____

Progress: (Circle number counted to)

1   2   3   4   5   6   7   8   9   10   11   12   13   14   15   16   17   18   19   20

Date _____

Reactions:

_____

_____

Progress: (Circle number counted to)

1   2   3   4   5   6   7   8   9   10   11   12   13   14   15   16   17   18   19   20

Date _____

Reactions:

_____

_____

Progress: (Circle number counted to)

1   2   3   4   5   6   7   8   9   10   11   12   13   14   15   16   17   18   19   20

My Name Treasure Box

Name Hunt
Preparation Time: several hours

Academic Connection:
This activity highlights letter recognition and language skills and makes children familiar with their own first names.

What You Need:
- name master, page 267
- name and picture box cover, page 266
- Polaroid camera or regular camera (have film developed as soon as possible)
- large black marker
- pencil boxes or cigar boxes that will fit into children's cubbies

Maria

Assessment Materials:
Teacher Assessment
Child's Self-Assessment
Parent Assessment

What to Do:
This activity is designed to give children exposure to their own first names and connect their own names to their pictures in a "Name Hunt Game." The object of the game is to find and put their own names and pictures on treasure chests that they may use and keep in their cubbies to store their "treasures."

Begin this activity by taking a picture of each child with a Polaroid camera or regular camera. After developing the pictures, write each child's name on a name strip. (See page 267.) Glue the pictures to the name strips and place these around the room in plain sight. Then, tell children they will be looking for their own pictures and when they find them they will also see their names and get prizes. This can go on all day or for several days or, with the help of aides, take only a short amount of time.

Children will then find their pictures and see with their pictures their own names written out. Spend individual time with children, talking about their names and seeing if they know the letters in their names. Say the letters in children's names for them when they find their pictures and then give them their own treasure chests for their very own treasures. Place a small treasure inside, like stickers or crayons or whatever is appropriate for your age group of children.

My Name Treasure Box *(cont.)*

Explain to children that their treasure chests will have their names and pictures on them. Help children glue their name and picture strips on their treasure chests, using their names again and once again pointing out the letters, etc.

Explain that it is good to be able to spell one's name because then you can tell which things belong to you. Point out their names spelled for them other places, on their portfolios or on a roll sheet or some other place that will seem useful to them.

Self-Directed Teaching Focus

Leave name strip forms around so children who are interested can try to write their own names. Let children use treasure chests to store their treasures in and keep in their cubbies or a designated area.

Directed Teaching Focus

At circle time have children bring treasures from home to share and to keep in their boxes. Let them also say the letters in their names and compare the ways their names look by looking at the name strips on their boxes. Use the same strip with a picture on their cubbies and have children locate their cubbies by matching their names and pictures on the cubbies to their names and pictures on the boxes.

What to Say

Today we are going on a treasure hunt. We are going to find our names and pictures. Remember the other day I used my camera to take pictures of everyone? Well, now I have put your picture on a strip of paper with your name, like this. Let's all find our pictures and our names, and then everyone will get a special treasure prize!

(Model spelling of children's names with them and assist them in gluing their names and pictures on their treasure chests.)

Focus on Assessment

Use the teacher assessment form to assess each child's name recognition. Use the self-assessment form for children to self-assess. Send home the Parent Assess-at-Home Form so parents can give you feedback on this name-recognition skill.

Treasure Box and Picture

My Treasure Box

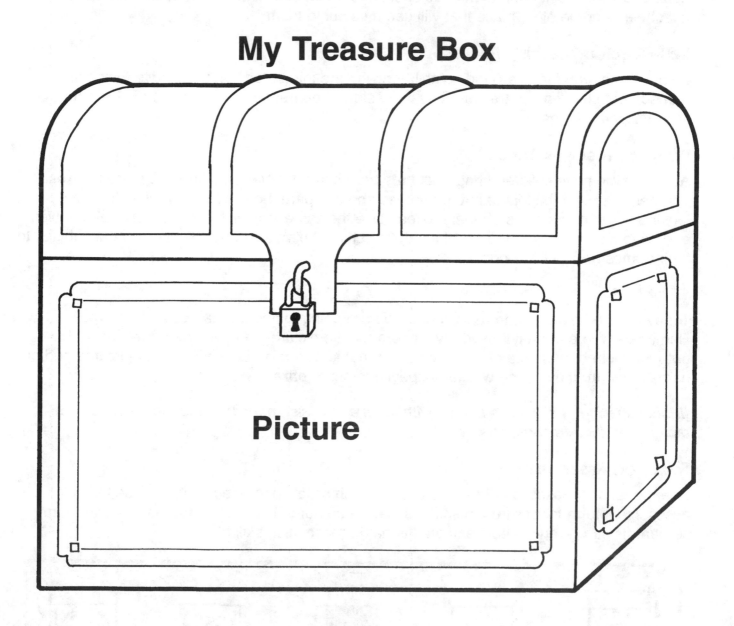

Picture

Name Blank Strips

Teacher Assessment Tool

My Name Treasure Box

Name Hunt

Child's Name _____

Date _____

Teacher _____

❏ Recognizes letters from name on lists and charts

❏ Recognizes name on letters and charts

❏ Names letters in name

    ❏ Some

    ❏ All

❏ Writes letters in name

    ❏ Some

    ❏ All

Name Sample—Date

_____

- -

_____

Name Sample—Date

_____

- -

_____

Child's Self-Assessment

Write the child's name below. Ask the child to draw a picture of how the name makes him or her feel.

Parent Assess-at-Home Form

Ask your child where he/she would like you to write his/her name at home. List the places below:_____

_____

Does your child enjoy seeing his/her name written in various places?

_____

_____

_____

_____

_____

Does he/she notice and recognize the written name?

_____

_____

Have your child practice writing his/her name below.

_____

- -

_____

Checklist for Portfolio Assessment

Check off those items that you recognize as part of your current assessment.

Portfolio assessment . . .

- ❑ 1. creates a concrete place to store evidence of child's learning experiences.
- ❑ 2. allows students to look at their progress.
- ❑ 3. allows teachers to look at children's progress.
- ❑ 4. gives parents something tangible by which to judge the progress of their children.
- ❑ 5. encourages a child's sense of responsibility.
- ❑ 6. requires time and commitment of the teacher.
- ❑ 7. allows evaluation of progress over real time.
- ❑ 8. gives children control of their learning process.
- ❑ 9. builds self-esteem.
- ❑ 10. is part of authentic assessment.
- ❑ 11. gives the teacher concrete evidence to justify grades.
- ❑ 12. helps children develop thinking and evaluating skills.
- ❑ 13. helps children develop judgment.
- ❑ 14. demands knowledge of how children learn.
- ❑ 15. can be made to look "showcase" for public relations reasons.
- ❑ 16. is more subjective than traditional assessment.
- ❑ 17. is a useful tool for future curriculum planning.
- ❑ 18. provides a historical record.
- ❑ 19. provides a place to store teacher evaluations, anecdotal records, etc.
- ❑ 20. can be as simple or as complex as desired.

Portfolio Assessment

What Is It?

Portfolios are a place as well as a method. They are a place to store children's work as well as a way of assessing their progress. Portfolios allow teacher and students to look over a period of time at what a child has done and see the changes in development that have happened in real time.

A Place

A portfolio can be as simple as a shoe box, or as decorative as a mini doll house (page 281-284). The main thing a portfolio is, is that it is the place where a child and a teacher store a child's work and also observations about the work itself. The main thing a portfolio should be is durable and manageable for the child. They will not work if it cannot be opened or used by a child, because in this kind of assessment the child is totally involved.

You can make portfolios out of shirt boxes, files folders, or pieces of construction paper. Before beginning to make portfolios, you will need to decide what kinds of things will be stored in them to best determine shape and size.

A Method

Portfolios focus on the progress and development of the individual child. It is a very personal history and record of a child's development that is ever changing. Portfolios require constant attention by both the teacher and the child, and they encourage children to take personal responsibility for their own learning experiences. Even very young children can be responsible for putting samples of their work inside their portfolios and putting their portfolios away or taking them out. Additionally, very young children can begin to look at their work and notice how it is changing at a very early age. Children are very interested in their own progress.

Tangible Records

One of the great things about a portfolio system in your classroom is that it gives you actual tangible material to show anyone who wants to see it. It is a living record that can be used for parent meetings anytime and is a clear representation of what their children are doing and where they are developmentally.

Additionally, portfolios can be used in conjunction with any other kind of assessment. They lend themselves naturally to anything else you are doing in your classroom.

Creates a Concrete Storage Place

You can touch a portfolio. You can take everything out and spread it on a table. You can look at day one, two, and three to see what has happened. You can hold things inside a portfolio and remember the day you did the work or remember the day your student did something based on a written observation form. Portfolios are tangible.

Portfolio Assessment *(cont.)*

Allows Children to Look at Their Own Progress

Children involved in portfolio assessment become responsible for their learning very early. Very young children become aware of what they are doing and what they did before. It gives children a concept of time and lets them begin to learn to think. Children become responsible for themselves in a way that fosters their own sense of accomplishment.

Allows Children to Look at Children's Progress

A portfolio gives you as a teacher instant access to documentation about a child and a place to store it. They are a great way to organize the learning and assessment process because they are a kind of filing system as well as a process.

Gives Parents a Tangible Record

Many times it is important for parents to see what their children have been doing. In a classroom that encourages self-directed learning, sometimes there are not as many tangible records of progress. A portfolio lets you have the best of both worlds. It allows you to have records of progress without having those records be a string of impersonal grades that are often meaningless. It lets the assessment process become real.

Encourages Child's Sense of Responsibility

Children take pride in keeping their portfolios in order and helping with the process. Children have the feeling that something is "theirs," which is a good feeling for any of us. They can share it with you or with their parents; portfolios bring people together.

Requires the Time and Commitment of the Teacher

Portfolios take time and commitment and regular work. It is important to use the portfolio on a regular basis and date anecdotal record forms and other observation and reflection forms so you have a constant record without gaps.

Allows Evaluation of Progress Over Real Time

A portfolio is a type of assessment that allows a teacher to look at the progress of a child over a period of real time. This provides the kind of real time example of progress that is missing from a one-time standardized test and one of the reasons that portfolios are such a useful type of assessment.

Gives Children Control of Their Learning Process

When children become part of the portfolio assessment process, they become increasingly responsible for their learning experiences. Not only do they feel more ownership over their learning experiences, but they can begin the process of assessing themselves, which is the most useful tool they can have in improving their own performances. Children who are an active part of their own portfolio process become interested in their own development, and they can look at where they have come from, as well.

Portfolio Assessment (cont.)

Builds Self-Esteem

The process of seeing from where one has come is the reason portfolios are useful to make the owners feel good about themselves. When children look at all of their completed stories, pictures, and other examples of work, they can see how, over time, they have become more proficient at each. Also, the act of seeing all of the wonderful things you have done right there before you in an organized and attractive package makes anyone who has ever had a portfolio feel fantastic about the accomplishment. Portfolios can be used to encourage children's sense of mastery and self-respect.

Is Part of Authentic Assessment

Portfolios are authentic because they are real examples of real-life activity in the classroom. A portfolio cannot be faked or contrived for an occasion. Nor can you demonstrate real time instantly. One has to collect samples to see progress over real time.

Gives Teachers Concrete Evidence to Justify Assessment Decisions

When you use portfolio assessment in your classroom, a lot of your "sales pitch" is not necessary. It simply takes the strain out of being the assessor and lets the tool do the assessment for you. It is far easier to recommend a certain action for a child to a parent based on concrete evidence staring them in the eyes, than it is to say "I think Johnny should..." Portfolios can serve to eliminate bias in many cases, and create real reasons that are meaningful both to you and the parents of a child.

Helps Children Develop Thinking and Evaluations Skills

When children are confronted with their own portfolios, they have to think about them. It is interesting to them because it is like picking up a story book and finding out it is about you! Nothing is more interesting to people than their own stories. Portfolios by their very nature give children reasons to think about their performances and their work. Teachers can guide children into a variety of thinking and learning skills through using a portfolio. In fact, the act of using a portfolio is part of a learning experience for children as well as a tool for evaluating past learning experiences.

Helps Children Develop Judgment

Judgment is not a bad word. Everyone on earth needs to develop a sense of good judgment. A portfolio is an excellent way for children to develop noncritical judgment skills. Portfolios are grey rather than black and white in context; therefore, children are required to use their ability to make sound judgments more readily than if they were simply comparing one test to another test. Even very little children can begin simple judgments and evaluations.

Demands Knowledge of How Children Learn

In order to be able to use a portfolio to create an accurate assessment tool, a teacher must have a basic understanding about how children learn so they will have some parameters upon which to base the contributions of the portfolio, as well as know what to save.

Portfolio Assessment *(cont.)*

Can Be Made to Look "Showcase" for Public Relations Reasons

Portfolios look good. Many people like to use them in their classrooms because they are so neat and orderly. But they can also be made into art projects in themselves. Because of this, they can be very useful to make your classroom or center look special and look like a lot of time and effort went into making them.

Is More Subjective Than Traditional Assessment

Portfolio assessment is by nature subjective; that is, it deals with the specifics as they relate to an individual child. In a portfolio we are more interested in a child's "race against himself" than a race against his peers.

Is a Useful Tool for Future Curriculum Planning

Portfolios are excellent sources for teachers and teams to evaluate and plan their new curriculum or alter their existing curriculum. It is possible with portfolios to compare a variety of children's contributions to their portfolios for the same activity and get a sense about how valuable the activity itself was. It is a historical record about each activity's success when looked at with a variety of other portfolios at once.

Provides a Historical Record

Portfolios are historical records. They can be copied and saved over years to look back on and use for reflection. Using a portfolio system over time will allow you to see your growth as a teacher, your development theoretically, what trends are in and out, and other valuable information from which you can over time begin to detect patterns.

Provides a Place for Storage

Portfolios are actual places. You can touch them; you can take them out; you can put them back. They are containers. Finally, they are a place to put everything so when you need it, it is there. They do, however, require work. Besides storing children's work examples, portfolios can store all your children's evaluation and observation forms as well as records of your parent interactions.

Can Be As Simple or Complex As Desired

You can make portfolios as simple or as complicated as you wish. It is really up to you and the time and resources you find yourself constrained by. Some teachers use plastic storage boxes (which are nice but can be costly). Other teachers use cardboard shirt boxes, (which can be free if you save them after a holiday). Some teachers use pieces of cardboard stapled together, large manila envelopes, or shoe boxes. Some teachers have brightly colored, attractive portfolio doll houses or other novelties. It is simply up to you.

Self-Portrait Art

Preparation Time: one hour

Developmental Connection:
This activity highlights artistic and spatial ability while giving teachers a reference to look at and assess cognitive development and motor skill development over real time.

What You Need:
- coloring materials
- art and painting materials
- large marking pens
- small self-portrait masters, page 278
- large sheets of butcher paper, one for each child
- Polaroid or regular camera
- doll portfolios directions and patterns, pages 281-284

Assessment Materials:
Teacher Assessment — Picture History Form
Child Self-Assessment — See Me Grow Self-Assessment
Parent Assessment — Completed Portfolio

What to Do:

This activity highlights children's developing artistic and cognitive abilities and self-concepts and allows teachers to gain an idea of their development over real time by doing this art activity at several intervals during a year. Children create a self-portrait in one of several mediums of their choice and then do it again after a specified length of time. Teachers then can compare and use these samples for a real-time observation.

To prepare for this activity, collect art supplies and one large sheet of butcher paper as well as a small self-portrait master for each child. It is a good idea to have extra butcher paper and self-portrait blanks on hand so children can begin again if they want to.

Begin this activity by telling children they are going to get to make life-size pictures of themselves. With your aides or parent volunteers, have several adults help children to lie down on a large sheet of butcher paper on the floor and trace around them with a large marker. Then provide children with a lot of different art supplies to make themselves in any way they would like to. After children have finished, you might wish to have them place their pictures all in a row and see if they can guess who is represented by each picture.

Then using a self-developing or regular camera, take two pictures for each child, one with them beside their pictures or holding their self-portraits and one of just the portfolio picture. (These you will be able to store in the portfolio along with the original art, if you wish.)

Self-Portrait Art

Self-Directed Teaching Focus

Place lots of small self-portrait blanks in your art center and explain to children that they can make new pictures of themselves whenever they want to. Continue this activity by writing children's dictated stories about themselves on their pictures and storing them in portfolios.

You can also make easy stick puppets out of children's smaller self-portraits so they can have puppets of themselves for dramatic play. This lends itself to all sorts of personal discovery and many opportunities for you to observe children's development while observing dramatic play.

Directed Teaching Focus

Have children bring their small pictures of themselves to sharing time and tell about themselves. You can have children share about their pictures or tell one thing about themselves that they like, that they are proud about, one thing they remember most, or whatever topic you think is appropriate. This will enhance verbal skills in a sharing or circle environment.

What to Say

Today we are going to make life-size pictures of ourselves. We are going to trace ourselves on a large piece of paper and then draw and color our pictures so they look like us! We can also make smaller pictures of ourselves. Let's try it!

Focus on Assessment

Use the photograph history form to take pictures of children's art self-portraits. You may find this easier to look at and store than a large, life-size picture. Make sure to take pictures again when they do the activity later in the year and add this picture to the form to show development over time. Have children glue or paste their own picture on their See me Grow forms. Then put them up on a bulletin board and let them add to it with other pictures. Talk with them about their own growth. Parents will be able to assess their child's growth over time by looking at the completed portfolios.

Self Portrait Paper Dolls

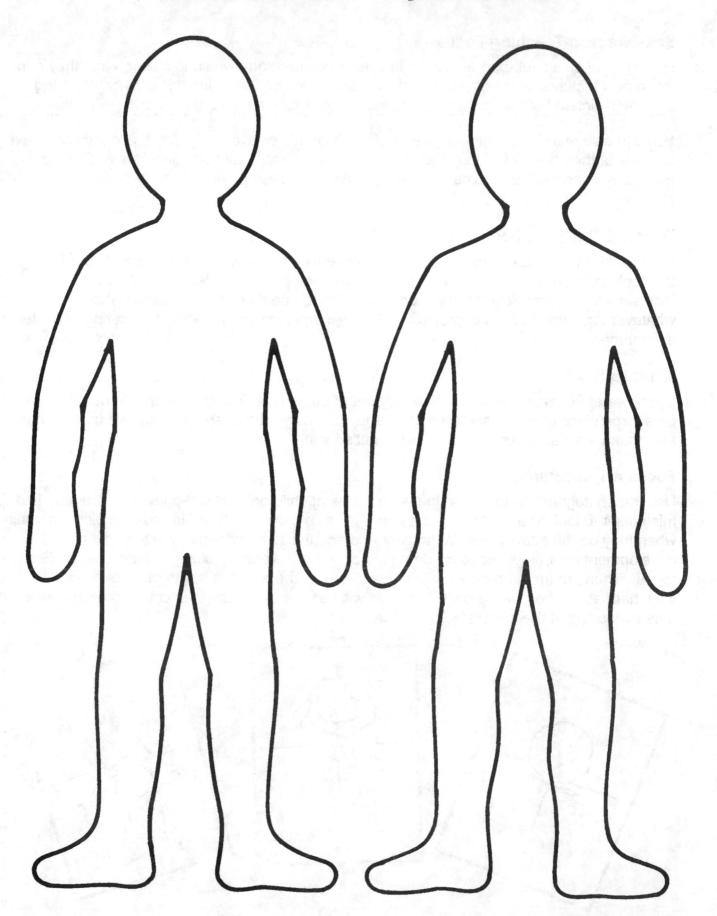

Teacher Assessment

Compare photographs of student's self-portraits over time.

Child's Name _____

Date _____ _____ _____ _____ _____	
Date _____ _____ _____ _____ _____	
Date _____ _____ _____ _____ _____	

Child's Self-Assessment

See Me Grow

Write child's dictated reactions to pictures here.

Child's Name _____

Date _____ _____ _____ _____ _____	
Date _____ _____ _____ _____ _____	
Date _____ _____ _____ _____ _____	

Doll House Portfolios

What You Need:

- doll house patterns (pages 282-284)
- poster board
- glue
- tape
- stapler
- markers

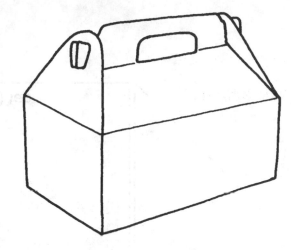

Directions:

1. Copy each pattern piece, enlarging to desired size. (A 233% enlargement of this pattern will make it work well. Copy stores have the ability to do this if your school cannot make the enlargement for you.) Reproduce pattern on page 283 twice.

2. Place the cut pieces of patterns #1-4 from left to right. Tape or glue tabs underneath Fold 1, Fold 2, and Fold 3.

3. Measure pattern and place on large sheet of bendable thin-weight poster board. Tape pattern to board. Trace entire pattern.

4. Fold poster board along folds and insert Tabs A into Slot A, Tabs B into Slot B.

5. Glue or tape Tab 4 on Glue Tab 4.

6. Attach name tag on either end.

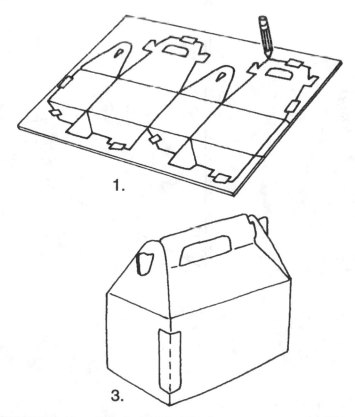

1.

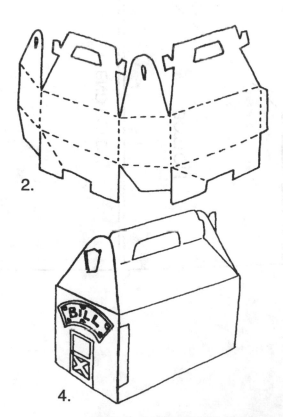

2.

3.

4.

Doll House Portfolio Pattern

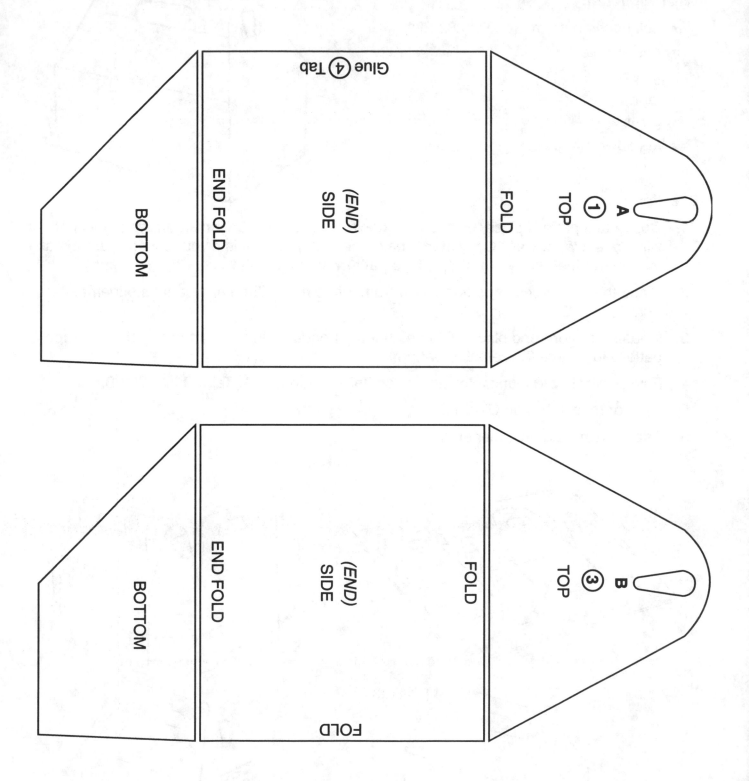

Doll House Portfolio Pattern *(cont.)*

Make two copies.

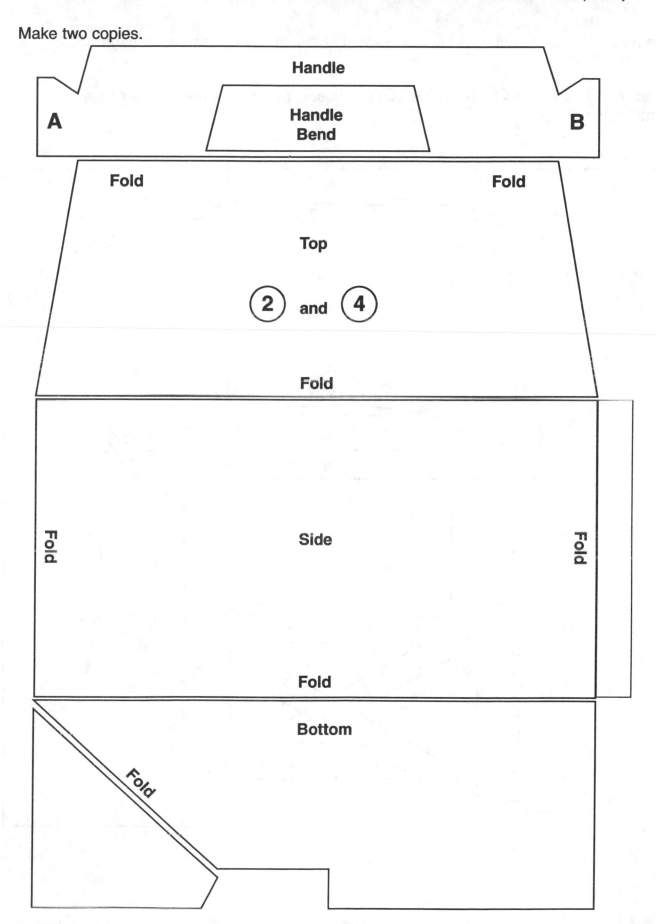

Handle

A

Handle Bend

B

Fold

Fold

Top

② and ④

Fold

Fold

Side

Fold

Fold

Fold

Bottom

Fold

Doll House Portfolio Pattern *(cont.)*

This master is sized to fit a 233% enlargement of the doll house master on pages 282 and 283.

Note: Make two copies for each portfolio doll house; mount on either side for easy identification.

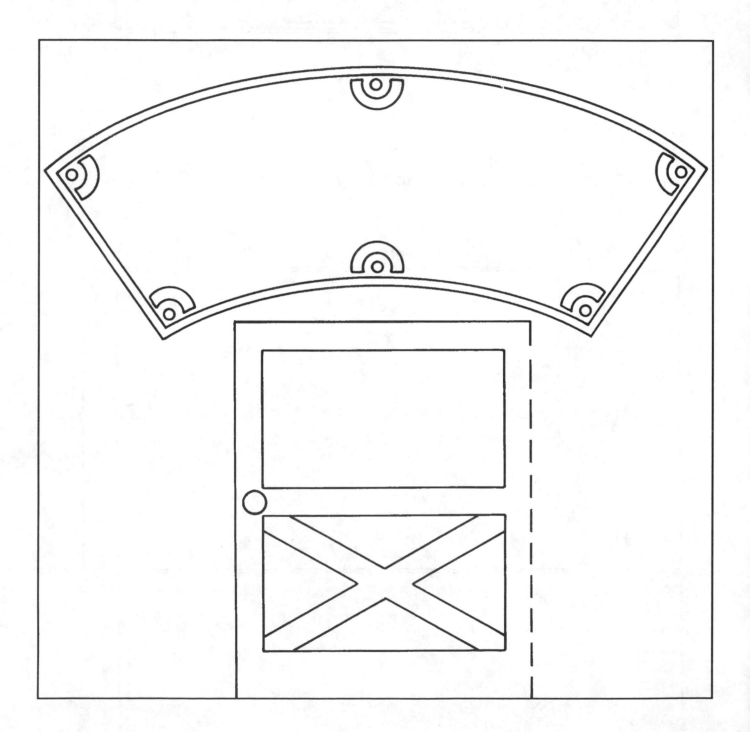

"I Can Do It" Chart and Collage Portfolio

Preparation Time: two hours

Developmental Connection

This activity enhances children's self-concept and self-esteem through real activities and accomplishments that you can keep a record of over real time for portfolios. A variety of developmental areas are enhanced over real time including physical, emotional, cognitive, and social.

What You Need:

"I Can Do It" poem, page 287

"I Can Do It" chart, page 288

"I Can Do It" pictures, pages 289-290

"I Can Do It" award, page 291

"I Can Do It" bulletin board

"I Can Do It" Collage Portfolios directions, page 292

Assessment Materials:

Teacher Assessment — Checklist

Children Self-Assess — Make Your Own Award Blanks

Parent Assessment — Completed Portfolio

What to Do:

This activity allows children to build and enhance their skills in a variety of developmental areas, based on their own decision to do so over real time. This activity, while there are assessments provided for it, also acts as its own assessment. Children complete tasks that they choose from pictures, add those to their own "I Can Do It" charts, and then give themselves awards.

To prepare for this activity, make enlarged copies of the "I Can Do It" chart and activities (masters on pages 289-290). Then cut apart the activities. (You might wish to copy these onto different colored papers because it will make the charts more colorful and interesting. Then, make an "I Can Do It" bulletin board where children can see what their achievements are every day, and have the fun of adding more pictures of activities they have mastered whenever they want.

Begin this activity by reading the poem "I Can Do It." Then tell children they are going to add pictures of what they can do to their own charts on the bulletin board whenever they want to. Each time a child completes an activity, date the activity picture, add it to his chart, and then let him make his own award. Create an award center using the award master pages and lots of glitter and special art materials.

"I Can Do It" Chart and Collage Portfolio (cont.)

Self-Directed Teaching Focus

This activity lends itself to self-direction. Children decide what they are going to do, when they are going to do it, and then do it themselves. Review the activities on the activity cards and make sure that the cards you have available for children to choose from are activities that are possible in your classroom or center. Leave the award and activity center available for children to use during self-directed time.

Directed Teaching Focus

Work with individual children every day discussing which activities they would like to try and then show you, so you can date their activity card and give them to them. Have children share at the end of the day at circle time what activities they did.

What To Say

I am going to read you a poem called "I Can Do It." Let's all listen. *(Read poem and talk with children about the things they can do or want to do or are in the process of learning to do. Then show the bulletin board to children and the "I Can Do It" chart and cards.)* Now we are going to do new things everyday and, when we do, we will add pictures of what we do to the board so we can look at it! Also, after you do something you are happy with, you can make yourself your very own ribbon or award or good job note to take home and share with your parents!

Focus on Assessment

Use the various developmental checklists while you observe different children completing a wide range of activities every day. The span of these activities lends itself to every developmental area. Children are assessing themselves by the process of deciding to make their own awards based on their achievements. Remember to store charts and copies of children's awards in portfolios. Parents will be able to assess their children's growth over time by looking at the completed portfolios.

I Can Do It

by

Grace Jasmine

There are many things that I can do,
Although I'm not so tall,
I can run, and hop, and jump, and skip,
I know how to throw a ball,

I can almost tie my shoes,
I can button up my clothes,
I am learning new things every day,
And what do you suppose?

My Daddy, he once told me,
That he has to learn things too,
And you know what's very funny?
Once, he couldn't tie his shoes!

I Can Do It Chart

Name _____

I am going to try to	Date Started	I tried	I can do it!
I am going to try to	Date Started	I tried	I can do it!
I am going to try to	Date Started	I tried	I can do it!

I Can Do It Chart Activities

hop

run

jump

tie shoes

ride bike

swing

count to 10

count to 20

say my ABC's

whistle

wink

snap fingers

I Can Do It Chart Activities *(cont.)*

sing a song	make a dance	play an instrument
clean up	paint a picture	draw a _____
build with blocks	color a picture	cut out a picture
share with a friend	help a friend	write my name

Child Self-Assessment

Make Your Own Award

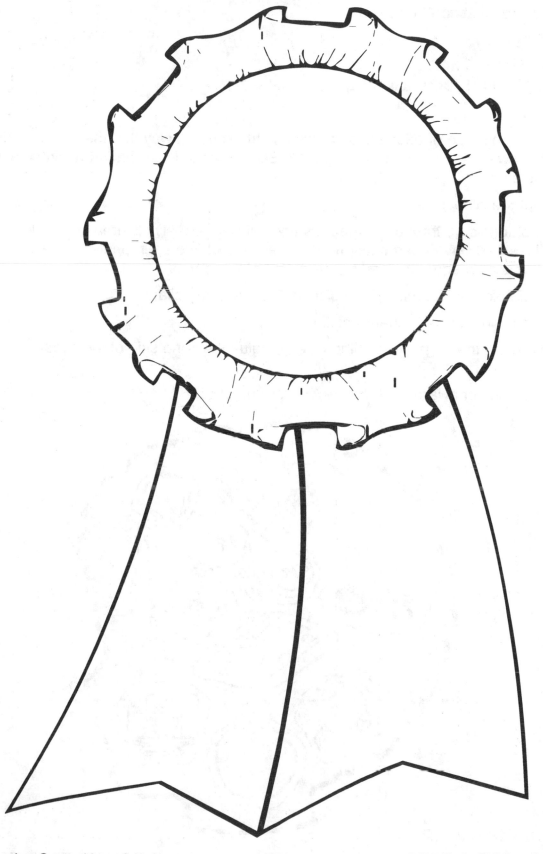

"I Can Do It" Collage Portfolios

What You Need:

- silhouette of each child
- magazines that can be cut up
- scissors
- glue sticks
- large sheets of construction paper

Directions:

1. Draw a silhouette of each child. Shine a light in such a way that the child's profile casts a shadow on a piece of drawing paper. Sketch around the shadow, including simple details such as a pony tail or signature cowlick.

2. Cut out the silhouette.

3. Have students go through magazines and cut out (or tear) pictures of people doing the activities they have been mastering. If they cannot find appropriate pictures, they can use the activity squares used for the "I Can Do It" charts.

4. Glue the pictures on the cut-out silhouette, making a collage.

5. Fold the construction paper in half.

6. Trim around the edge of the silhouette and glue it on one side of the construction paper folder.

7. Store copies of awards in the new Activity Portfolios!

Block Builders

Preparation Time: one hour

Developmental Connection:

This activity enhances children's physical skills including large and small motor, social skills, and cognitive and spatial development.

What You Need:

- video camera

- video tapes, one for each child, to be used at various times through year

- instant or regular camera

- blocks, all kinds

- Television Screen Portfolios, directions page 297

Assessment Materials:

Teacher Assessment   Video Observation Form
Child Self-Assessment — How Many Stars?
Parent Assessment — Completed Portfolio

What To Do:

This activity lets children learn about sizes while having many physical experiences building block structures.

To prepare for this activity, you will need a video camera and blank video tapes for each child which will be stored in their portfolios to create an observation of their development over real time.

Label each of the videos on the outside with labels and enclose in each video tape box an information log sheet, so you can keep a log of where observations begin and what number they are tracked to for easy viewing, especially when showing this video to others.

To begin this activity, have children talk with you during circle time about the idea of sizes: big and small, short and tall. Think of some ways around your center you can demonstrate big and small and short and tall to students easily. Then ask children to build only big block houses that day, as big as they can make them. (Children love to be filmed and may tend to "ham it up" until they are used to having the camera running. So set up a video camera in the block area and tape during the entire day if possible.) You can film one child at a time or groups of children playing together. You will have to try this technique of using video in your classroom or facility several times to see how it will best work for you.

Let children tell you if they are going to make a big block house or a small block house every day. Keep a instant or regular camera handy to take pictures of their favorite structures for the bulletin board.

Block Builders (cont.)

Self-Directed Teaching Focus

Keep your block center available to children during all active playtime and use it as a general observation point to gauge children's physical and social development.

Directed Teaching Focus

Have a tall day. Have children try to make tall block structures. Have a contest to see who can make the tallest one and give prizes. Do the same for short, small, etc.

What To Say

Today we are going to talk about sizes. Look at this bulletin board. I have put pictures from magazines here of things that are little. Can we find something little here. Let's all look around the room and get something little to look at. *(You will need to demonstrate these concepts based on the level of the children.)* Now today, let's all make small block houses. This can be "small house day." Let's think about making block houses for mice. That will be fun. Let's try it! *(And so on with tall, short, etc.)*

Focus on Assessment

Use the video assessment form to keep track of the development you see when you tape the children at play. Keep these videos in your children's individual portfolios. Have children pick their best block houses and tell why they like them. Have them describe this to you while they are being taped. Have students use the "How Many Stars?" form to rate their performances when they view the tapes. Or take a picture of a child's best block structure and have him or her dictate stories to you about why it is their favorite. Parents will be able to assess their children's growth over time by looking at the completed portfolios which will contain the video tapes and/or photos.

Video
Observation Form

Child's Name _____

First Video Date _____

Date Viewed _____

Observations

_____

_____

_____

Action Steps

_____

_____

Second Video Date _____

Date Viewed _____

Observations and Comparisons

_____

_____

_____

Parent Viewing Dates _____

Parent Observation Notes

_____

_____

Student Self-Assessment Form

How Many Stars?

Child's Name _____

First Video Date _____

Date Viewed _____

Rate your performance. How many stars? Draw them here.

Second Video Date _____

Date Viewed _____

Rate your performance. How many stars? Draw them here.

Television Screen Portfolios

What You Need:
- shirt box for each child
- black construction paper the same size as the top of the box lid
- scissors
- glue sticks
- pictures of popular cartoon characters

Directions:
1. Use the black construction paper to make a frame that looks like the border around the picture tube on a television set.

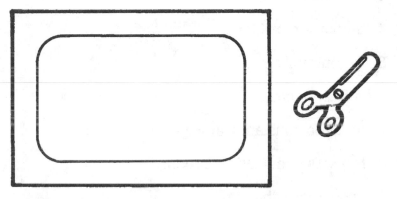

2. Glue the border to the top of the box.

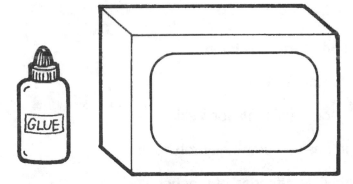

3. Glue pictures of cartoon characters inside the border.

Checklist for Alternative Assessment

Check off those items that you recognize as part of your current assessment.

Alternative assessment . . .

❑   1. encourages team creativity.

❑   2. encourages ideas.

❑   3. is trend setting.

❑   4. empowers children.

❑   5. is nontraditional.

❑   6. is high energy.

❑   7. requires constant learning.

❑   8. requires community support.

❑   9. encourages the arts.

❑ 10. values the individual.

❑ 11. requires teamwork.

❑ 12. requires conflict management.

❑ 13. requires communication.

❑ 14. requires good public relations skills.

❑ 15. requires intensive community relations.

❑ 16. requires flexible attitudes of teacher.

❑ 17. requires cooperation of students.

❑ 18. requires cooperation of parents.

❑ 19. is sometimes disorderly, and sometimes noisy.

❑ 20. requires assessment in context of specific intelligence.

Alternative Assessment

What Is It?

Alternative assessment as we use the term in this book is whatever is up and coming. This book will highlight two specific kinds of assessment (and curriculum development). This section will highlight the recent work of Howard Gardner and his theory of Multiple Intelligences (MI), as well as ideas of emergent curriculum and anti-bias curriculum as they relate to assessment.

Gardner states the belief throughout his work that there are many different ways of being intelligent, that the standardized IQ tests leave many people and many different kinds of intelligences undiscovered. He has set up a way of looking at a variety of intelligences that lends itself totally to the idea of developmentally appropriate learning and assessment.

Different Kinds of Intelligence

The different kinds of intelligence that we will look at in this section are the following:

- linguistic intelligence
- logical/mathematical intelligence
- spatial intelligence
- musical intelligence
- bodily-kinesthetic intelligence
- intrapersonal intelligence
- interpersonal intelligence

Cutting Edge Learning and Assessment

Alternative assessment, wherever one finds it, is a new way of looking at things. It is exciting and opens up new possibilities for children in a positive way. Gardner's work lends itself to developmentally appropriate practices because it highlights and supports the individual strengths of the child.

In this section current and new assessments are explored.

Alternative Assessment *(cont.)*

Encourages Team Creativity

In any alternative environment of assessment, teachers are able to use their creativity. This kind of assessment and nontraditional ideas in general allow a creative environment in your program for you as well as your children.

Encourage Ideas

When something is new and exciting, it naturally generates more thinking and more ideas. Just as Gardner's work looks at and celebrates the differences among people, this kind of non-traditional environment encourages one to take a new look at curriculum and assessment.

Trend Setting

Anything that is new is also trend setting. Be aware that with this new label comes excitement and often fear. Starting new ideas and programs requires that you get everyone excited about their value. Be prepared to generate excitement and commitment and persuade those that think they are not a good idea.

Empowers Children

Empowering children is what good and fearless educators want to do. Not everyone agrees that empowering children is the right thing to do, however. Empowered people, including children, literally have power; they cannot be led as easily, and they are often opinionated. But later, they will have the kind of coping skills they will need to get along happily and productively in the world.

Nontraditional

If your team uses alternative methods of learning and assessment, be prepared for the traditional people around you to feel threatened and perhaps even mock your efforts. You may want to provide yourself with research that supports your ideas so you will feel more secure about implementing them.

High Energy

New ways of doing things require energy. Changing ideas is a vital and exciting process. It is important to keep yourself and your life well balanced when you begin an exciting and, perhaps, controversial program or approach.

Alternative Assessment *(cont.)*

Requires Constant Learning

Alternative assessment is what is new and up and coming in early childhood, and being aware of the newest discoveries and theories requires a constant commitment to learning. Teachers who want to be aware of what is going on are constantly taking classes, attending workshops, in-services, and seminars. Also, they are reading anything and everything related to early childhood education.

Requires Community Support

When you are attempting a new assessment program based on new ideas at your school, you need to have the support of the people around you. First, you must have the support of your team and then you must gain the support of your parents. Since parents are part of the community, well-pleased parents who like and understand your assessment program talk to other parents and generate good feelings about what you are trying to do. Naturally, the reverse is possible, so it is important to constantly be communicating when you are doing alternative assessment at your school.

Encourages the Arts

Alternative assessment encourages children's self-expression and also their artistic expression. As a form of developmentally appropriate assessment, the creativity of the individual child is respected and enhanced in alternative assessment.

Values the Individual

The individual child and what he or she is that is unique and how he or she learn and what he or she excel at is the focus of alternative assessment. It could be said that in alternative assessment every child has his or her own time to be a genius at something. Alternative assessment is based on the belief that everyone has gifts. It is our job as teachers assessing children to help them determine those gifts and expand them.

Requires Teamwork

Alternative assessment cannot function without a closely working team. This is an area where teachers all need support from their peers as well as their director and, conversely, a director needs the support of his or her staff. Without a united team, you will not have the strength to bring new and unusual ideas into practice regarding assessing children and the curriculum choices your assessments are dependent upon.

Requires Conflict Management

Alternative assessment is about new ideas. However, where there are new ideas, there are conflicts— that is part of the process. Conflict management embraces conflict. Conflict is part of new and exciting things and learning how to deal with a variety of different ideas and different children is part of the goal of learning how to assess for multiple intelligences. We are embracing differences, a new and forward-thinking way to be.

Alternative Assessment *(cont.)*

Requires Communication

Communication is the way that people manage conflicts and prevent them too. Alternative assessment requires communication because it is a new and vital and ever-changing thing. You can quite literally not know what is going on with a child if you are not kept aware of all of the different observations made by teammates. Communication is very important to team members (and to parents) all the time.

Requires Good Public Relations Skills

Alternative assessment requires that you be able to talk to the various "publics" you deal with simply because it is new and people need to understand it. You can think of it not as public relations, if you do not like that term, but rather as sharing information, because sharing information about something new and valuable is really all it is.

Requires Intensive Community Relations

Alternative assessment can be labeled as wrong because it is new. Think of all the great innovations and inventions over time and how people reacted to them. People are naturally afraid of what they do not know or understand, and parents are worried about their children. That is their right, after all. If you are met with negativity, do not look at it as a reason to disband your program but as a sign you have not given everyone involved enough information.

Requires Flexible Attitudes of the Teacher

If you thought you were a flexible early childhood teacher you have not seen anything yet. You will change gears at least seven times a day. But not to worry! You can focus on whatever you want in early childhood assessment and set up a program that will make it easy to organize.

Requires Cooperation of the Children

Alternative assessment requires that children be part of the process of their own discipline. This approach to assessment is one where children are asked to self-assess, therefore, children begin to be more responsible for their own learning and interests at a very early age.

Requires Cooperation of the Parents

To use alternative assessment, whatever kind it might be, requires the cooperation as well as the consensus of the parents. It is absolutely necessary to have parents feeling that their children are benefiting by your program on every level including the assessment portion. Using a variety of methods of parent communication and education will make this aspect of your alternative assessment program easy to manage.

Alternative Assessment *(cont.)*

Is Greatly Aided by the Participation of Parents

When using multiple intelligences as a way of assessing and building the multifaceted curriculum, extra hands and minds are always helpful. This kind of assessment is a vital, changing process and it is fun and exciting for parents to become involved.

Sometimes Disorderly and Sometimes Loud

If you have seven children experiencing seven different areas of their intelligence at once be prepared for the happy sounds of learning! There is going to be the noise of discovery in any classroom that allows children to develop appropriately because they will not be uniformity of thought or action. But there will be children being the best they can be and that is exciting!

Requires Assessment in the Context of Specific Intelligences

Alternative assessment requires that you assess what is going on. In other words the type of assessment must be in alignment with the kind of instructional theory. You have to have a good grasp of the idea behind multiple intelligences in order to assess for it properly, but the good news is, that it is a simple, easy theory that makes instant sense.

My Own Storybook

Linguistic Intelligence
Preparation Time: several hours

Multiple Intelligences Connection
This activity highlights the area of linguistic intelligence. That is a child's ability with language at whatever level he or she is developmentally ready to use it.

What You Need:
- storybook masters, pages 306-317
- laminating materials (It is possible to buy sheets of clear contact paper that will work for this.)
- yardstick or ruler
- poster board
- scissors
- glue
- strips of Velcro, two for each master
- colored markers

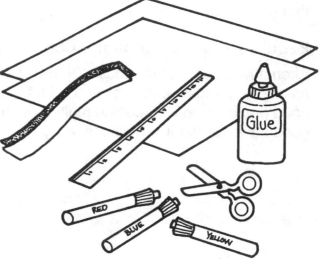

Assessment Materials
Teacher Assessment — Observation Log

Child Self-Assessment — Successful Use of Book

Parent Assessment — Observation Log

What To Do:
This activity will give children an opportunity to explore and enhance their linguistic intelligence in both a self-directed and directed manner. To begin, set aside an afternoon or evening to create the pull-apart book.

The idea is to create a reusable book, or several reusable books, that a child can pull apart and put back together anyway he or she wants to. Notice that on the masters for the book there is room for a teacher to write, but the main idea behind the book is for children to tell their own story and combine the masters in any way they want to over and over again, creating their own stories that they can either tell someone or write by themselves.

After making copies of the masters, color each one with marking pens, colored pencils, or crayons and cut a piece of poster board that is the exact same size as the master to mount the picture on. You will need to decide if you want to have a picture on each side or not. If you choose to have a picture on each side of the page like a regular storybook, simply glue a picture to each side of the poster board. Repeat this for each master. Next laminate each of the storybook pages and glue a strip of Velcro to each side of each page and on only one side of the cover pieces. You can make the cover out of two pieces or one large cover piece that is folded in the middle.

My Own Storybook (cont.)

You might want to make several of these for use in your classroom, so that more than one child can use them for solitary playing purposes.

Now, introduce the book to individual children or introduce it during story time or circle time by telling a story and explaining that this is a special book that can tell any story you want it to and modeling the activity. This book has as many possibilities for your children as they have ideas.

Self-Directed Teaching Focus

Leave several complete sets of the My Own Storybook available for children to use whenever they would like to. Also, copy a number of story masters so children can color them and make stories to take home for their parents. Let children know that they can make a story whenever they want to and provide plenty of blank paper as well so children can make up entirely different stories by combining their own pictures and telling a story about them. (Simply staple the story together and send home with the child.)

Directed Teaching Focus

Make the My Own Storybook part of a storytelling experience. Have children who would like to share a story do so, either during circle time or any other time you want to. Also be ready to listen to children tell their own stories to you individually. Ask them to tell you a story. Or once again use the book to tell your own story whenever you would like to as well.

What To Say

Today we have something new to do. How many of you love to hear stories? I know you all do! Let me show you this new special book and the way it works. Let's all look at all these pretty pages and talk about what we see on them. Aren't these neat? What is this? (*Point to the dog.*) Right. Let's look at all of the pages and then I will show you something that is fun. I am going to put these pages together any way I want and then I'll tell you a story that I make up. (*Demonstrate process.*) We can change these pictures any way we want and tell a new story. (*Teacher demonstrates.*) Now these are going to be in our book center, so anytime we feel like making up a story we can. I am also going to put some copies in our art center so you can make up stories to take home. You do not have to use these pictures. You can try a bunch of your own pictures and make a story too.

Focus on Assessment

There are many excellent ways to assess this activity for linguistic intelligence. First, try the Linguistic Intelligence Observation Log Form on page 318. It is also possible to use a tape recorder and follow up with the conversation log form on pages 319–320. If you prefer, try the alternative assessment checklist form on page 298 and, finally, save all of these assessments of linguistic intelligence in each child's portfolio to follow up with portfolio assessment. Parents can also use the log form at home. Student self-assessment is accomplished through participation in the activity—successful use of the book to tell a story.

MY OWN STORYBOOK

My Own Storybook (cont.)

Glue Velcro here

My Own Storybook (cont.)

Glue Velcro here

My Own Storybook (cont.)

Glue Velcro here

#465 Early Childhood Assessment

My Own Storybook (cont.)

Glue Velcro here

My Own Storybook (cont.)

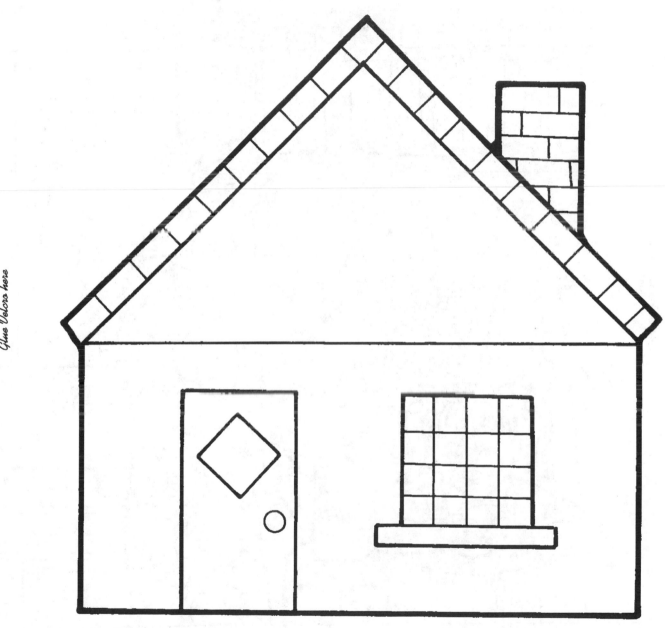

Glue Velcro here

My Own Storybook (cont.)

Glue Velcro here

My Own Storybook (cont.)

Glue Velcro here

My Own Storybook (cont.)

Glue Velcro here

My Own Storybook (cont.)

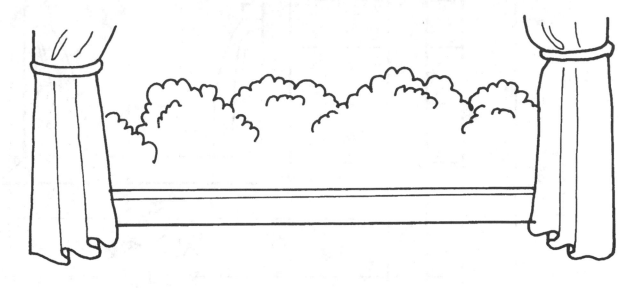

My Own Storybook *(cont.)*

Glue Velcro here

and...
they lived happily
ever after.

The
End

Glue Velcro here

Linguistic Intelligence Observation Log Form

—For the Teacher—

Child's Name _____

Use this log on a daily basis to keep notes about the kind of linguistic experiences this child is having every day. Remember, with a log, you can make these notes at the end of the day or anytime. It does not have to be while the experience is happening. Compare and discuss this log at your next meeting with this child's parent(s).

> **Linguistic**
> Linguistic Intelligence is about:
> - words
> - language
> - speaking
> - reading
> - listening to stories
> - dictating stories
> - writing stories

Day _____

_____

_____

_____

_____

_____

Day _____

_____

_____

_____

_____

_____

Linguistic Intelligence Observation Log Form

—For the Parent—

Child's Name _____

Use this log on a daily basis to keep notes about the kind of linguistic experiences your child is having every day. Remember with a log, you can make these notes at the end of the day or anytime. It does not have to be while the experience is happening. Bring this log with you to your next parent/teacher meeting to discuss.

Linguistic

Linguistic Intelligence is about:
- words
- language
- speaking
- reading
- listening to stories
- dictating stories
- writing stories

Day _____

_____

_____

_____

_____

_____

Day _____

_____

_____

_____

_____

_____

Log Form *(cont.)*

Child's Name _____

Day _____

_____

_____

_____

_____

Day _____

_____

_____

_____

_____

_____

Day _____

_____

_____

_____

_____

Day _____

_____

_____

_____

The All About Me Photo Album

Interpersonal Intelligence

Preparation Time: one to two hours (on going activity)

Multiple Intelligence Connection

This activity highlights the area of intrapersonal intelligence. That is the child's self-knowledge and the ability to demonstrate it at whatever level is currently appropriate developmentally.

What You Need:

- photo albums for each child participating. (The easier it is to put a picture in and take it out the better.)

- extra removable photo album pages

- letter to parent(s), page 323

- parent photographs

- Polaroid or regular camera

Assessment Materials

Teacher Assessment — Observation Log

Child Self-Assessment — Successful Use of Book

Parent Assessment — Observation Log

What to Do:

This activity will give children an opportunity to explore and enhance their intrapersonal intelligence. That is the way they feel about themselves and their own self-knowledge. Begin by reading the story "All About Me" on pages 328-338 at story or circle time. This story will set the stage for modeling the activity.

The activity is a simple one and easy to use in a self-directed or directed manner. Each child will be making and enjoying his or her own photo album of pictures of themselves doing a variety of different things in different situations and with people they care about. (See the parent letter on page 323 about requesting photographs.)

Any picture children like of themselves will work for this activity; however, these different areas will provide a large and varied group of pictures for the child to explore a variety of the different parts of intrapersonal intelligence:

- baby pictures

- pictures that show children's emotions

- pictures that show people or things important to individual children

- pictures that show children doing something

- pictures that a child particularly likes

The All About Me Photo Album *(cont.)*

Simply give children access to their own pictures and a photo album that the pictures can be added to and removed from. Younger children will need assistance putting in the pictures and arranging them, and older children may not. It really depends upon the child. The activity is modeled in the story, but you will need to model it again. This is a good time to use parent volunteers or aides.

Self-Directed Teaching Focus

The idea of intrapersonal intelligence is that it is based in a self-directed idea. It is about the self and, therefore, should be directed by the individual child. While it is possible for a child to tell about his or her photo album, just having the opportunity to have one and look at it is enough to have an intrapersonal experience. Create a photo album center where each child can have a group of his or her pictures to arrange and rearrange. There is no right or wrong way to arrange a photo album; just like adults, children will want to add and subtract and play with it. Make a Polaroid or regular camera available and let children know they can request a pictures to be taken of anything important they want to include in their photo albums.

Directed Teaching Focus

Sit with a child or group of children at circle time and let them share their own books. This should be voluntary. Also spend time with individual children letting them dictate descriptions about each of their photographs, and add these to the photo albums. Let children "read" their photo albums to you, explaining who everyone is and telling the story about their experiences to you.

What to Say

Today we are all going to have fun doing something that is just for us. How many of you have a photo album at home where your mom or dad or maybe your grandmother keeps pictures of you and the whole family? I am going to read you a story called, "The Photo Album That Was All About Me." After we hear the story, we will all get to make our own photo albums. *(Read the story and model the activity. It is very useful to make your own photo album and let children see it. It builds an example of an intrapersonal task that you can have on hand.)*

Focus on Assessment

There are many ways to assess this activity for intrapersonal intelligence. However, it is important not to violate the personal quality of the child's experience. Probably the least intrusive method is the use of the observation log on page 343. Parents can also use the log form on page 342 at home. Student self-assessment is accomplished through participation in the activity—making and enjoying having a personal photo album.

All About Me Parent Letter

Dear Parent(s),

As part of our Multiple Intelligences enhancement program, your child will have the opportunity to explore his/her Intrapersonal Intelligence.

Intrapersonal Intelligence is the knowledge of the self. Everything from how we feel about life on a day-to-day basis to our dreams and hopes, our memories, our feelings, our sense of self-respect and our self-confidence and self-worth.

All of the children will be making personal photo albums, full of pictures of themselves. This will give them the opportunity to reflect about themselves, think about their past experiences and who they are and what they think and feel about themselves. The children will all need to have a number of photographs for their photo albums. We will also be taking photographs at school in case some parents are unable to send in pictures for this activity. **Please Note:** This photo album will be yours to keep after your child is finished with it. They are wonderful for the children to have as keepsakes.

The kinds of pictures that would be useful include the following:
- baby pictures
- pictures that show your child's emotions
- pictures that show people or things important to your child
- pictures that show your child doing something
- pictures that your child likes

We *will be / will not be* providing the photo album.

We are excited about giving the children an opportunity to explore this very important part of their intelligence.

Please feel free to call me at anytime regarding questions you might have or observations you have made at home. Remember, we love to have you take part and you are welcome here as an observer or a participant anytime. Simply let me know how you would like to get involved.

Sincerely,

_____
For

_____
School

Intrapersonal Intelligence Observation Log Form

—For the Teacher—

Child's Name _____

Use this log on a daily basis to keep notes about the kind of intrapersonal experiences this child is having every day. Remember with a log, you can make these notes at the end of the day or anytime. It does not have to be while the experience is happening. Compare and discuss this log at your next meeting with this child's parent(s).

> **Intrapersonal**
> Intrapersonal Intelligence is about the following:
> - self-knowledge
> - thinking about past experiences
> - thinking about personal feelings
> - self-esteem
> - self-awareness
> - self-respect

Day _____

_____

_____

_____

_____

_____

Day _____

_____

_____

_____

_____

_____

Intrapersonal Intelligence Observation Log Form

—For the Parent—

Child's Name _____

Use this log on a daily basis to keep notes about the kind of intrapersonal experiences your child is having every day. Remember with a log, you can make these notes at the end of the day or any time. It does not have to be while the experience is happening. Bring this log with you to your next parent/teacher meeting to discuss.

Intrapersonal

Intrapersonal Intelligence is about the following:

- self-knowledge
- thinking about past experiences
- thinking about personal feelings
- self-esteem
- self-awareness
- self-respect

Day _____

_____

_____

_____

_____

_____

Day _____

_____

_____

_____

_____

_____

Log Form *(cont.)*

Child's Name _____

Day _____

_____
_____
_____
_____
_____

Day _____

_____
_____
_____
_____
_____
_____

Day _____

_____
_____
_____
_____
_____

Day _____

_____
_____
_____

Photo Album

Picture Goes Here

All About Me:

_____

_____

_____

All About Me

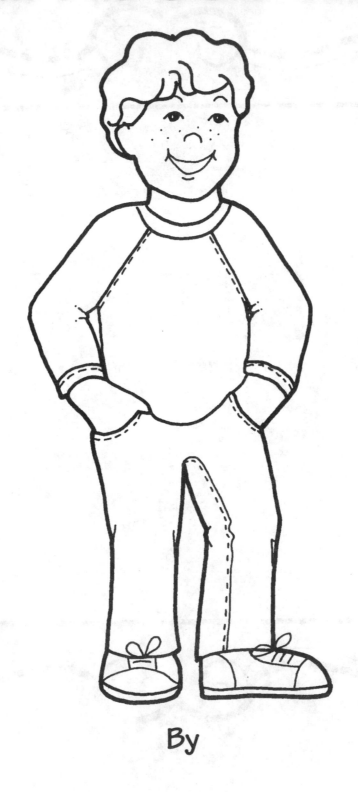

By

_____

328

All About Me

By

_____

The Photo Album
That Was All About Me

Once there was a photo album that was all about me.

My mother found a shoe box full of many pictures.

I bet there were one million pictures.

There might have been a billion pictures.

My mother helped me count the pictures that were all about me.

She said there were ten.

The Photo Album
That Was All About Me

Page 2

We looked at them together, and my mother laughed and laughed.

There was a picture of me when I was a little tiny baby.

I was very cute.

 #465 Early Childhood Assessment

The Photo Album
That Was All About Me

There was a picture of me when I was
learning to walk.
It must have been hard to learn to walk.
I don't know if I remember.
Do you?

332

The Photo Album
That Was All About Me

Page 4

There were pictures of me and people I love.
I am lucky to have such nice people love me.
Can you think of people who love you?

         #465 Early Childhood Assessment

The Photo Album
That Was All About Me

There was a picture of me in a costume.
I was dressed like a bunny.
I looked silly.
Have you ever dressed up in a costume?

334

The Photo Album
That Was All About Me

There were pictures of a party.
Have you ever been to a party?

The Photo Album
That Was All About Me

Then there was a picture of me, and I was crying.

My mom said I was afraid of something.

Have you ever been afraid of something?

The Photo Album
That Was All About Me

But the very best picture
is this one.
I like the way I'm smiling.
Have you ever seen a picture of you that made you
very happy?

The Photo Album
That Was All About Me

My mother gave me an old photo
album.

She told me it was just for me.

So I put all these pictures in it.

And whenever I feel like it,

I look at it

and I smile.

The End

Everyone Is Special

Interpersonal Intelligence
Preparation Time: two hours

Multiple Intelligence Connection
This activity highlights the area of interpersonal intelligence; that is, it is about the child's understanding of others and their feelings and the ability to interact with and understand others.

What You Need:
- story *Benny's Wheels*, pages 346-358
- special people mural picture, page 359
- alphabet letter masters, pages 360-368 (to create bulletin board letters for this and other activities)

Assessment Materials
Teacher Assessment Form
Child Self-Assessment Form
Parent Assessment Form

What to Do:
This activity will give children the opportunity to explore and enhance their interpersonal intelligence. That is their ability to understand other people, interact with them, and understand how they feel, etc. Through this activity children will become aware of the specialness of others through a variety of means. They will make a mural called Special People Mural including people of all shapes, sizes, and ablities.

To begin this activity read the story on pages 346-358, *Benny's Wheels*. This story will also double as pictures for the Special People Mural of people in all different shapes, sizes, genders, ages, cultures, and abilities. You can use these for the mural or there are a variety of other ways you can add pictures to your mural, and it can be an ongoing process for your children.

After reading *Benny's Wheels* during circle time, use circle time to talk with children about the different kinds of people they know. Remember to use reinforcing language and treat each child's input as equally important. (This activity addresses the issues of multiculturalism, anti-bias, and full inclusion.)

Everyone Is Special *(cont.)*

Next explain to children that they will be taking part in making a special people mural. Before circle time set up the basics of the mural bulletin board (see page 359 for example).

Use the pages of pictures in *Benny's Wheels* for pictures of all sorts of special people that may be hard to find other places. Then supply children with old magazines, newspapers, art supplies, and blank paper so they can add to the mural.

Self-Directed Teaching Focus

Make an Everyone is Special center filled with magazines, newspaper pictures, and art supplies to let children find their own pictures or make them for the bulletin board whenever they would like to.

Directed Teaching Focus

Read *Benny's Wheels* several times at circle time as children love to hear stories more than once. Select other stories about special people and let children choose special people books from your existing library for circle time reading.

What to Say

Today I am going to read a wonderful story about a special person and his friend. Listen while I read the story and then we will talk about it. *(Let children share what they know about all sorts of special people and their personal experiences.)* Now let's look at this. I made a place for us to put pictures of special people so we can look at them all and see just how many different ways there are of being special. As Benny says in the story, everyone is special. *(At this point have children help you put copies of the illustrations from the story on the mural to demonstrate.)* Now we can all make or find pictures to add to the mural.

Focus on Assessment

There are many excellent ways to assess this activity for interpersonal intelligence. First, try the Interpersonal Intelligence Observation Log Form on page 342. If you prefer, try the alternative assessment checklist form on page 298 and, finally, save all of these assessments of interpersonal intelligence in each child's portfolio to follow up with portfolio assessment. Parents can also use the log form on page 342 at home. Students can use a sharing cube on page 345 for a self-assessment activity.

Interpersonal Intelligence

Parent Letter

Dear Parent(s),

As part of our Multiple Intelligences enhancement program, the children will have the opportunity to explore their Interpersonal Intelligence.

Interpersonal Intelligence is the understanding of others and their feelings and the ability to interact with others and understand them—everything from learning to play with other children and working in groups to understanding and appreciating other cultures and having sensitivity for people that are different from them.

Your child will be taking part in making an Everyone Is Special Mural and will hear a story called *Denny's Wheels*. Children will be gathering pictures of all kinds of special people. We will be using old newspapers and magazines and drawing and painting in our classroom to add to our mural. As part of the process you can also help your child collect some Special People Pictures and send them along to add to our mural.

We are excited about giving your child an opportunity to explore this very important part of his/her intelligence.

Please feel free to call me at anytime regarding questions you might have or observations you have made at home. Remember, we love to have you take part and you are welcome here as an observer or a participant at anytime. Simply let me know how you would like to get involved.

Sincerely,

_____

for

_____

School

Interpersonal Intelligence Observation Log Form

—For the Parent—

Child's Name _____

Use this log on a daily basis to keep notes about what kind of interpersonal experiences your child is having every day. Remember with a log, you can make these notes at the end of the day or anytime. It does not have to be while the experience is happening. Bring this log with you to your next parent/teacher meeting to discuss.

> ### Interpersonal Intelligence
> Interpersonal Intelligence is about the following:
> - interacting with other children
> - sharing
> - playing in groups
> - caring about others' feelings
> - cooperative play
> - teamwork
> - interacting with adults

Day _____

_____

_____

_____

_____

_____

Day _____

_____

_____

_____

_____

_____

Interpersonal Intelligence
Observation Log Form

—For the Teacher—

Child's Name _____

Use this log on a daily basis to keep notes about what kind of interpersonal experiences this child is having every day. Remember with a log, you can make these notes at the end of the day or anytime. It does not have to be while the experience is happening. Compare and discuss this log at your next meeting with this child's parent(s).

Interpersonal Intelligence

Interpersonal Intelligence is about the following:
- interacting with other children
- sharing
- playing in groups
- caring about others' feelings
- cooperative play
- teamwork
- interacting with adults

Day _____

_____

_____

_____

_____

_____

Day _____

_____

_____

_____

_____

_____

Log Form *(cont.)*

Child's Name _____

Day _____

_____

_____

_____

_____

Day _____

_____

_____

_____

_____

Day _____

_____

_____

_____

_____

Day _____

_____

_____

_____

Child's Self-Assessment—Sharing Cube

What to Do:

To prepare for this activity, enlarge the pictures of the sharing cube faces on this page, color, and glue the sharing-cube faces to a square box to use during oral sharing at circle time. The sharing cube will create a directed sharing atmosphere *(you may choose to have children share about whatever they would like)*. The sharing cube may be used intermittently as a way of changing topics or as a way to create a topical theme based on what is happening in your children's lives, moods, etc. For example, if the children are upset about a world or local event or an event in a classmate's life, use the sharing cube to give children an opportunity to express their feelings and to enhance their ability to come to terms with real-life situations.

Benny's Wheels

by

Grace Jasmine

Benny's Wheels (cont.)

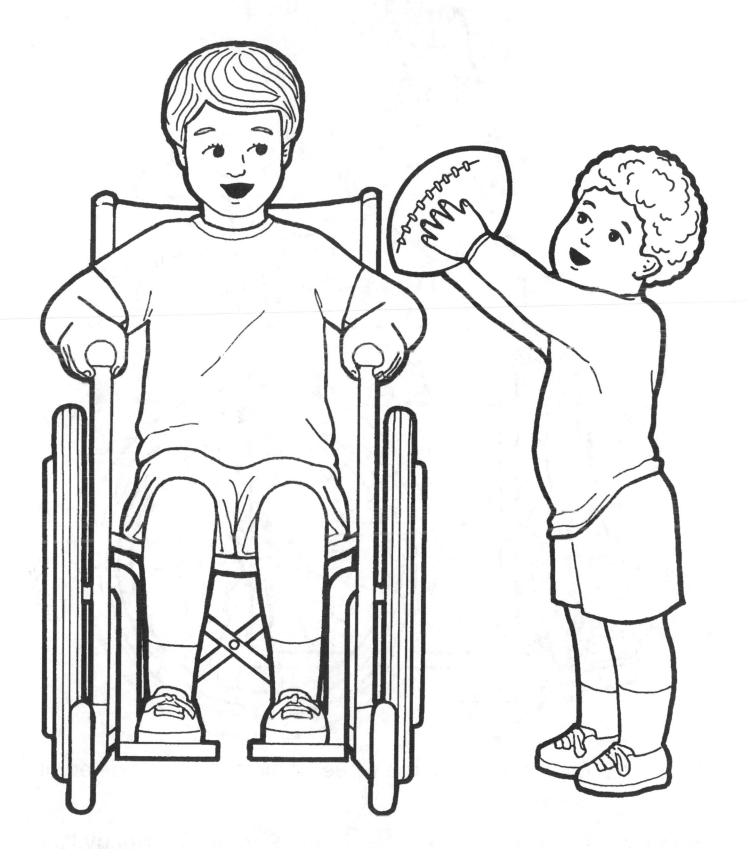

I have a friend named Benny. Benny has wheels.

#465 Early Childhood Assessment

Benny's Wheels (cont.)

Some people think being in a wheel chair makes you different. Benny says it's true.

Some people walk; some people ride. Sometimes Benny lets me ride too!

Benny's Wheels (cont.)

Benny says we all have things that make us different.

Benny's Wheels (cont.)

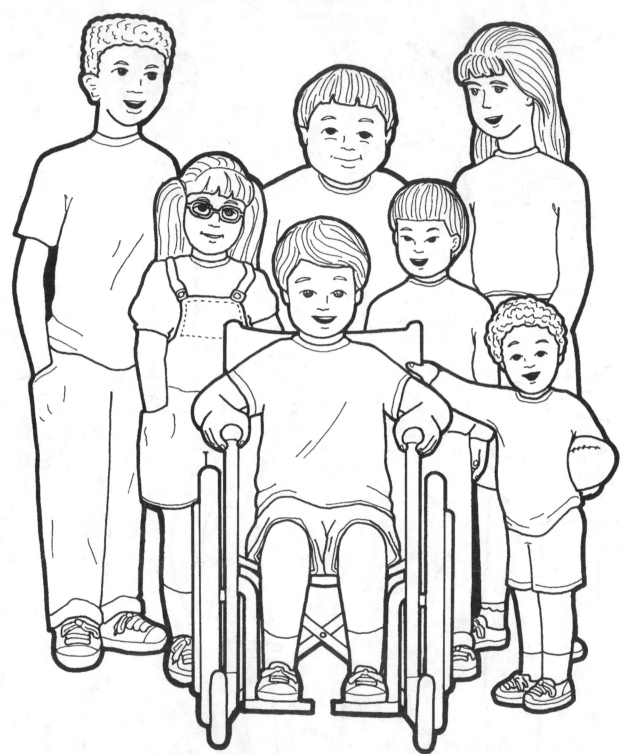

We look different.
Some people are big, and some are small.
Some are short, and some are tall.
Some people have brown eyes, and some people
have green eyes or blue eyes or hazel eyes.

Benny's Wheels (cont.)

We talk in different languages.

English, Spanish, Russian, Italian, Vietnamese, French, German, Polish, Japanese, Chinese, and Arabic are just some of the many languages.

There are many, many different ways to talk.

Benny's Wheels *(cont.)*

Some people talk using their hands.

Benny's Wheels (cont.)

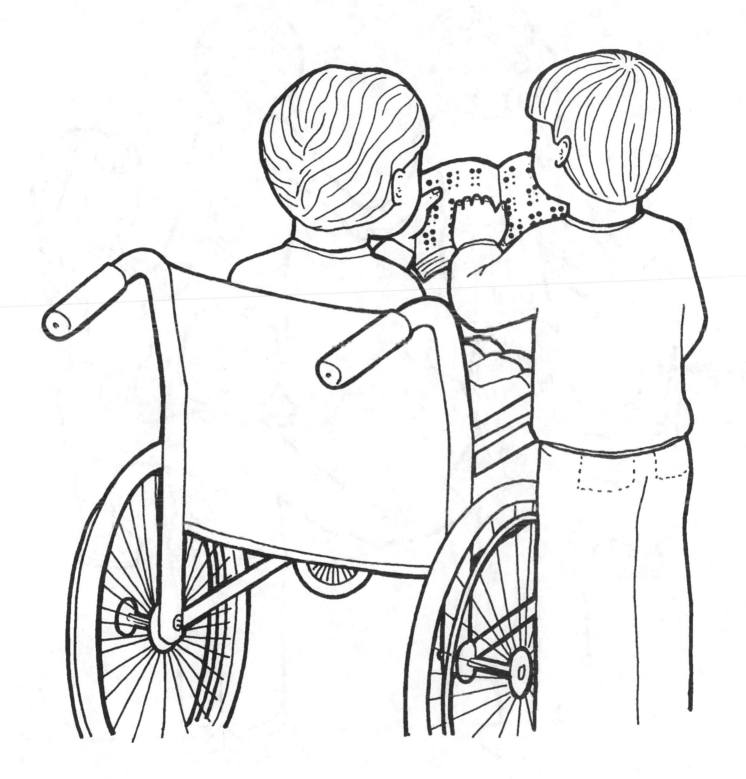

Some people read Braille.

Benny's Wheels (cont.)

Benny says the important thing is that we find a way to talk to each other, no matter what it is.

Benny's Wheels (cont.)

Benny says, "We are a rainbow of color and a salad bowl of differences."

Benny talks in pictures—when he says something I can almost see it!

Benny's Wheels (cont.)

Benny says our differences make us special and that we are all special.

Benny's Wheels (cont.)

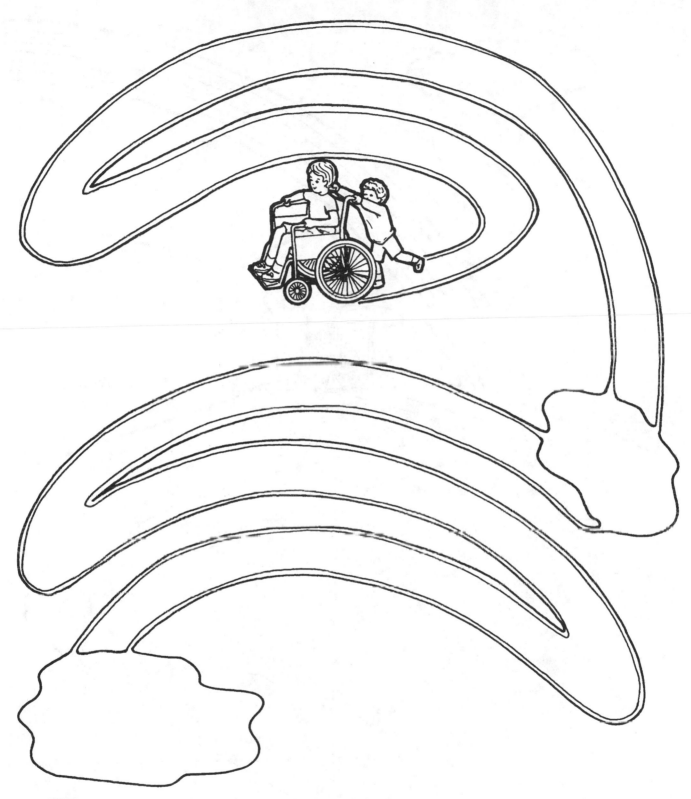

After it rains Benny and I make rainbows.

First, we go through a puddle, and then we paint with the wheels of Benny's wheel chair on the cement.

Benny's Wheels *(cont.)*

Wouldn't you hate a world without rainbows?

Special People Mural Picture

Bulletin Board Alphabet and Numbers

Bulletin Board Alphabet and Numbers

(cont.)

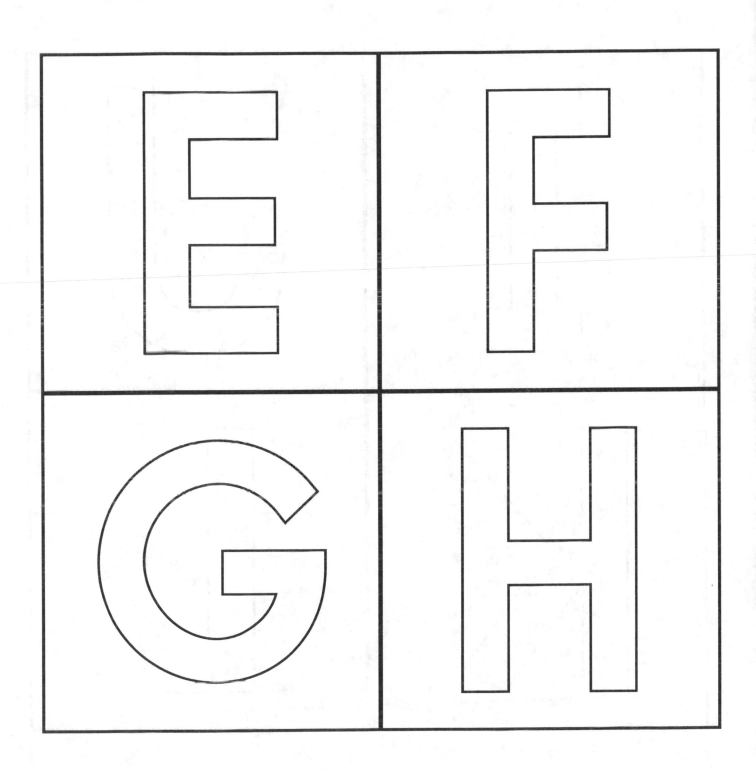

 #465 Early Childhood Assessment

Bulletin Board Alphabet and Numbers

(cont.)

Bulletin Board Alphabet and Numbers

(cont.)

Bulletin Board Alphabet and Numbers
(cont.)

364

Bulletin Board Alphabet and Numbers

(cont.)

Bulletin Board Alphabet and Numbers
(cont.)

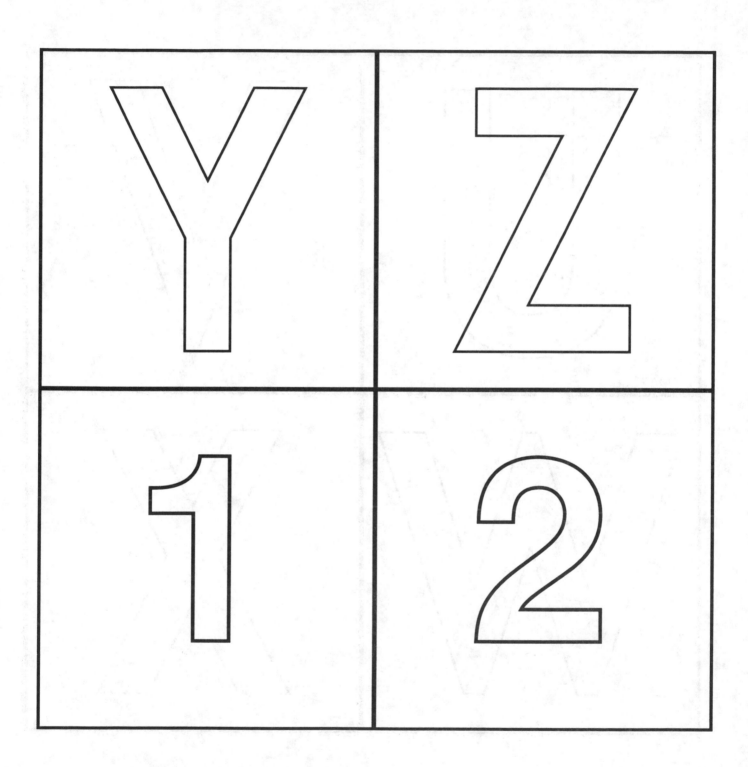

Bulletin Board Alphabet and Numbers
(cont.)

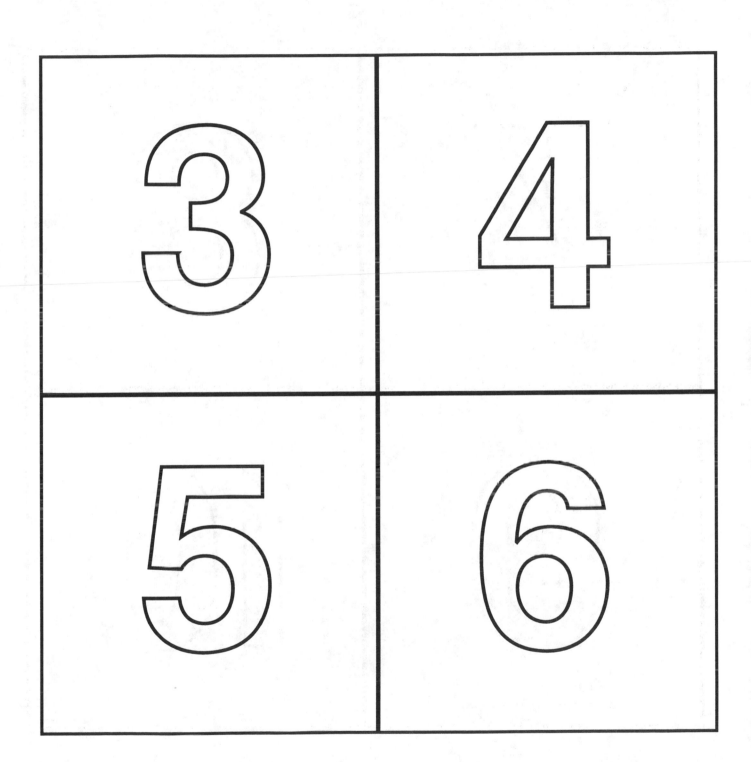

Bulletin Board Alphabet and Numbers

(cont.)

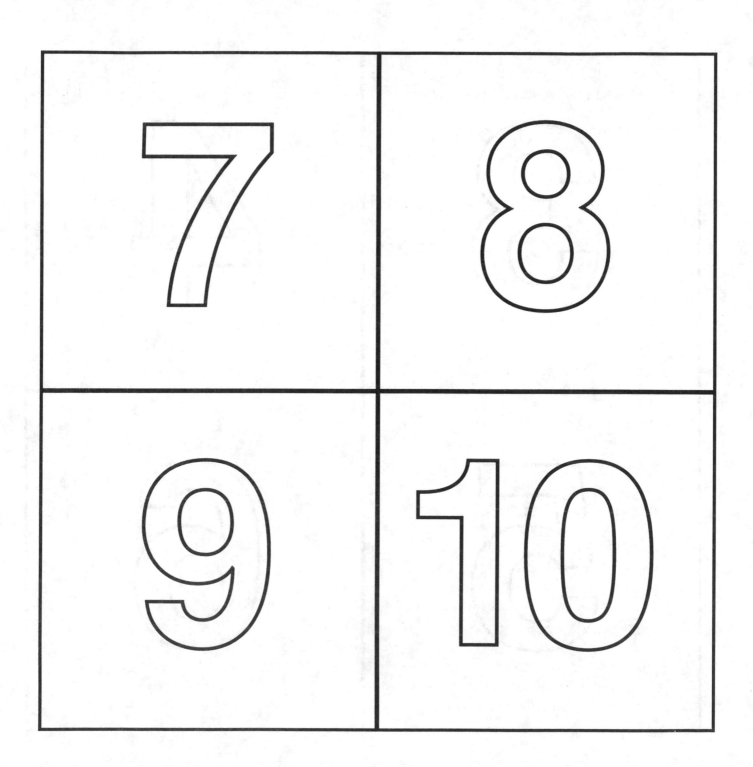

Soap Bubble Party

Bodily-Kinesthetic Intelligence

Preparation Time: several hours over the course of several weeks

Multiple Intelligence Connection:

This activity highlights the area of Bodily-Kinesthetic Intelligence. That is the intelligence of the body, movement, and physical activity, including the hands.

What You Need:

- parent soap bubble party invitation, page 371
- parent request letter, page 372
- personalized soap bubble wrapper master, page 373
- one bottle of bubbles for each participating child.
- large bottle of bubble liquid for making large bubbles (nontoxic no-tear baby shampoo also works and can be bought in large quantities)
- music you can move to *(You can play tapes or even have someone play the piano if you have one.)*
- bubble-making tools—Make sure to include some of the larger bubble makers; these make great bubbles and even a three-year-old can quickly become very good at this.

Assessment Materials:

Teacher Assessment Forms

Child Self-Assessment Forms

Parent Assessment Forms

What To Do:

This activity will give children the chance to explore and enhance their Bodily-Kinesthetic Intelligence. That is their ability to move physically, to dance, and to use their bodies and hands for a hands-on experience. In this activity children will be taking part in a Soap Bubble Dance Party. This activity can be as easy to do or as complex as you wish. Begin by sending out parent request letters and invitation forms and planning your actual party. You will need to have a large space *(outdoors works very well, but if weather does not permit, you can have a bubble party inside.)* But make sure you have something to cover the floor because bubbles inside can become very slippery and you certainly want to prevent anyone falling or sliding, especially since you want them to be able to move.

Use music to encourage movement when children are blowing bubbles. The large bubble makers are made for large sweeping movements of the arms and body, which is a lot of fun.

Make the party an occasion for parents to take part in the fun. Also, in a situation where children are all doing this kind of activity together, a lot of adults are helpful because there are going to be children of all different skill levels making bubbles.

Soap Bubble Party (cont.)

Serve refreshments. You might ask your parent helpers to bring cookies and juice or whatever else appeals to your children. Or, if it is a hot day, popsicles or frozen yogurt are a nice ending to a soap bubble party. Have a contest to see who can blow the largest bubble. You might even want to give children a new and unused bottle of bubbles to take home after the event. (These are very inexpensive and can be bought in bulk.) Use the personalized wrapper master to cover bubble bottles with your own wrapper that you can add each child's name to for a personalized touch. Have a wonderful time!

Self-Directed Teaching Focus

This activity lends itself to children exploring in a self-directed manner. Set up a regular bubble center in your classroom for use whenever children feel like it. This works very well as an outdoor center.

Directed Teaching Focus

Lead a bubble dance or a Simon Says bubble game. This will give children the opportunity to follow physical instructions which is part of bodily-kinesthetic intelligence.

What to Say

Before the party:

We are going to be having a soap bubble party in a few days, and your parents are going to come and have fun with us. So let's practice so we can be good at blowing bubbles before we have our party. *(Model bubble blowing process and let children try it—just give children a little time to try it so they will still think it is exciting when you hold your party.)*

At the party:

We have a bunch of different ways to blow bubbles here. Let's all blow bubbles together and remember to share the bubble tools and take turns. Then we will do a bubble dance and have refreshments. Then we will see who can blow the largest bubble. Have fun!

Focus on Assessment

There are many excellent ways to assess this activity for bodily-kinesthetic intelligence. First, try the Bodily-Kinesthetic Intelligence Observation Log on page 374. It is also possible to use a tape recorder and follow up with the conversation log form on page 376. Remember to save all of these assessments in each child's portfolio to follow up with portfolio assessment. This is an excellent opportunity for parents to do on-site observations. Let parents use on-site assessment forms to assess the activity as a whole and their own children as they feel like it during the party. Parents can also use the log form at home. Children can self-assess with "How I Feel Buttons" on page 377.

Parent Soap Bubble Party Invitation

Join Your Child's Class

for

A Soap Bubble Dance Party

When: _____

Time: _____

(Be sure to wear comfortable clothes
that you can get messy and send
your child wearing the same!)

R.S.V.P. _____

Soap Bubble Party

Parent Assistance Letter

Dear Parent(s),

As part of our multiple intelligence discovery unit, we are having a Soap Bubble Dance Party! This party will focus on the kind of intelligence that is called Bodily-Kinesthetic, and besides being a valuable developmental experience for your child, it will also be a lot of fun!

Besides your attendance (which will make this experience wonderful for you and your child), we are in need of volunteers to help in the following ways:

Please check any items that you can assist with and return this letter.

- ❑ bubble liquid
- ❑ bubble wands
- ❑ party supplies
- ❑ refreshments

Child's name _____

Parent's name _____

Best time to call: _____

Number: _____

Thank you for your help, and we hope to see you there!

Sincerely,

_____

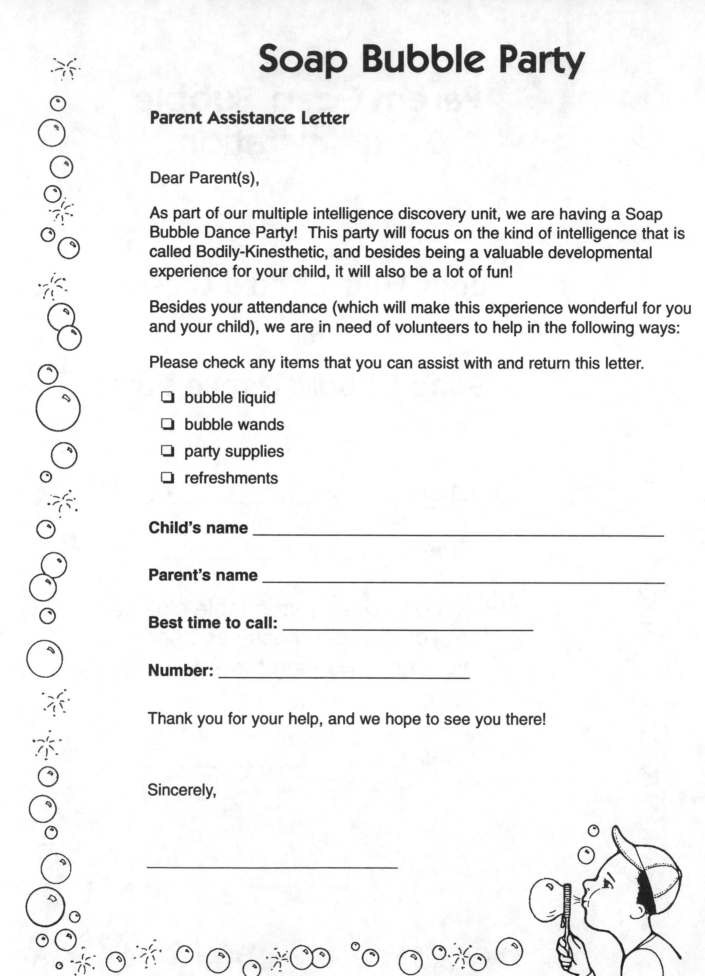

Personalized Soap Bubble Wrapper

Bodily-Kinesthetic Intelligence Observation Log Form

—For the Teacher—

Child's Name _____

Use this log on a daily basis to keep notes about what kind of bodily-kinesthetic experiences this child is having every day. Remember with a log, you can make these notes at the end of the day or anytime. It does not have to be while the experience is happening. Compare and discuss this log at your next meeting with this child's parent(s).

> **Bodily-Kinesthetic Intelligence**
> Bodily-Kinesthetic Intelligence is about . . .
> - anything to do with the physical self
> - movement
> - dance
> - athletics
> - hands-on learning experiences

Day _____

_____

_____

_____

_____

_____

Day _____

_____

_____

_____

_____

Bodily-Kinesthetic Intelligence Observation Log Form

—For the Parent—

Child's Name _____

Use this log on a daily basis to keep notes about what kind of bodily-kinesthetic experiences your child is having every day. Remember with a log, you can make these notes at the end of the day or any time. It does not have to be while the experience is happening. Bring this log with you to your next parent/teacher meeting to discuss.

> **Bodily-Kinesthetic Intelligence**
> Bodily-Kinesthetic Intelligence is about . . .
> - anything to do with the physical self
> - movement
> - dance
> - athletics
> - hands-on learning experiences

Day _____

_____

_____

_____

_____

Day _____

_____

_____

_____

_____

Log Form (cont.)

Child's Name _____

Day ____

_____

_____

_____

_____

Day ____

_____

_____

_____

_____

Day ____

_____

_____

_____

_____

Day ____

_____

_____

_____

How I Feel Buttons

Copy these buttons, color and affix them to contact paper, and then cut out the circles. Put out on a tray a variety of these buttons expressing different emotions on a tray. Have children select the one they want after an activity for self-assessment.

Whisper Sticks

Musical Intelligence
Preparation Time: several hours

Multiple Intelligence Connection:

This activity highlights the area of Musical Intelligence. That is the child's ability to enjoy and listen to music, noises, sound, and rhythm of all kinds, as well as make their own music, sounds, and rhythms.

What You Need:

- "Can You Whisper?" Poem, page 380
- Whisper stick masters (small), page 381
- Whisper stick masters (large), page 382
- empty paper towel and toilet paper rolls to cover for "Whisper Sticks"
- glue or paste
- art materials paint and drawing supplies

Assessment Materials:

Teacher Assessment

Child Self-Assessment

Parent Assessment

What To Do:

This activity will give children the chance to explore and enhance their Musical Intelligence. That is their ability to listen to music and sound as well as reproduce sound, music, and rhythm. In this activity children will be exploring their vocal modulation by learning how to whisper *(which will also prove useful in those rare moments you would like the children in your center or classroom to lower the noise level!)*

To begin this activity read the poem called "Can You Whisper?" Give children time to practice their whisper voices, and then show them the whisper sticks. *(You will need to decide beforehand if you want to pre-make these sticks or have children take part in putting them together.)* See pages 381 and 382 for directions about making Whisper Sticks.

Self-Directed Teaching Focus

Leave a variety of whisper sticks in your musical center. Suggest that children use them, and use them yourself when you are trying to get a child's attention, etc.

Whisper Sticks (cont.)

Directed Teaching Focus

Play Whisper Telephone during circle time. Start by saying a word and have each child whisper it to the next. When the last child hears the word, ask what the word was, etc. This activity will also give you some clues regarding whether or not children are hearing normally. If you have doubts, then you might wish to consider talking to the parents about developmental screening.

What to Say

I am going to read a really nice poem called "Can You Whisper?" Listen as I read the poem, and then we will talk about it. *(Read poem, and introduce and model the whisper sticks.)* Now we are going to try them. Let's all whisper a secret to each other. *(The children try.)* Now let's put these whisper sticks over here in our music center so we can use them whenever we want. Tomorrow we will try whisper sharing. That will be different, and we will be able to see how carefully we can all listen!

Assessment Focus

Use the musical intelligence observation log for both in the classroom and as an at-home assessment for parents. Students can self-assess by discussing how they feel about whispering.

Can You Whisper?

by

Grace Jasmine

Can you whisper? asked the dormouse,

As she tiptoed by,

I don't want to wake my baby cause my baby,

She will cry,

Can you whisper, little children?

Oh, wont you try!

Oh, whisper,

Won't you whisper?

Whisper, please!

Can you whisper? asked the owl,

As he sat in the tree,

Don't you noisy children wake

My family!

Can you whisper, little children?

Oh, won't you try!

Won't you whisper?

Whisper, whisper, whisper,

Please!

Have you ever talked as quiet as a little mouse?

Or as quiet as the silence of a sleepy house?

Have you ever tried to whisper?

It's an easy little trick,

Especially when you have a whisper stick!

Whisper Stick—Large Stick Cover

WHISPER

SHHHH!!

WHISPER

SHHHH!!

#465 Early Childhood Assessment

Directions: Make one copy of the Whisper Stick cover below, cut it out and color it. Glue it to paper towel roll.

Whisper Stick—Small Stick Cover

Directions: Make one copy of the Whisper Stick cover below, cut it out, and color it. Glue it to a toilet paper roll.

WHISPER

SHHHH!!

Musical Intelligence Observation Log Form

—For the Teacher—

Child's Name _____

Use this log on a daily basis to keep notes about what kind of musical experiences your child is having every day. Remember with a log, you can make these notes at the end of the day or anytime. It does not have to be while the experience is happening. Compare and discuss this log at your next meeting with this child's parent(s).

Musical Intelligence

Musical Intelligence is about the following:

- singing
- appreciating music
- hearing rhythms
- melody, tone, and timbre
- playing instruments or hearing them played

Day _____

_____

_____

_____

_____

_____

Day _____

_____

_____

_____

_____

Musical Intelligence Observation Log Form

—For the Parent—

Child's Name _____

Use this log on a daily basis to keep notes about what kind of musical experiences your child is having every day. Remember with a log, you can make these notes at the end of the day or anytime. It does not have to be while the experience is happening. Bring this log with you to your next parent/teacher meeting to discuss.

> ### Musical Intelligence
> Musical Intelligence is about the following:
> - singing
> - appreciating music
> - hearing rhythms
> - melody, tone, and timbre
> - playing instruments or hearing them played

Day _____

_____

_____

_____

_____

_____

Day _____

_____

_____

_____

_____

Log Form <small>(cont.)</small>

Child's Name _____

Day _____

_____
_____
_____
_____
_____

Day _____

_____
_____
_____
_____
_____

Day _____

_____
_____
_____
_____

Day _____

_____
_____
_____

Rainbow Pictures

Spatial Intelligence
Preparation Time: two hours

Multiple Intelligence Connection:
This activity highlights the area of Spatial Intelligence. That is the child's ability to think in pictures and images. Spatial intelligence includes artistic ability, color, being able to organize space, and the ability to visualize, that is, see concepts mentally.

What You Need:
- rainbow master, pages 389–390
- sky master, page 391
- making manipulative rainbow pictures, directions, page 392
- hands-on rainbow ideas

Assessment Materials
Teacher Assessment

Child Self-Assessment

Parent Assessment

What to Do:
This activity will give children a chance to explore and enhance their Spatial Intelligence through exploring rainbows in a variety of artistic ways.   This includes a Velcro or felt rainbow hands-on manipulative set, and a variety of other ways to use rainbows to encourage children to see in pictures, explore colors and organize shapes.

To prepare this activity, see page 392 for directions on making a manipulative rainbow set. You will need to decide if you prefer to use felt (for a felt board manipulative) or if you prefer a Velcro and paper set. This will depend on whether or not you have an available felt board set up in your center or classroom and your personal preference.

Before beginning this activity with your class, set up a rainbow center. Look at the Hands-On Rainbow ideas and pick several that you can provide supplies for to make in your center.

This way children can explore their spatial intelligence naturally and gravitate to the materials that they feel intrigued by.

Pre-make a rainbow manipulative so you can model the rainbow center and give them a sense about rainbows in general at the beginning of the activity.

Begin by talking about rainbows during center time. Ask children if they have ever seen a real rainbow outside after it rained. Then model the activity by showing children the manipulative rainbow you have prepared and letting them touch it and talk about the colors. Then show them the rainbow center and let them create whatever kind of rainbows there are to make using their own preferences and imaginations.

Rainbow Pictures *(cont.)*

Self-Directed Teaching Focus

This activity lends itself to a self-directed format. Keep the rainbow center available for children to use again and again. Encourage children to try different kinds of art materials, and provide new materials in the center occasionally so they can experiment.

Directed Teaching Focus

Have children use the hands-on manipulative rainbow strips and ask them to put the colors of the rainbow together in a certain way. Name the colors in the order they should put them in the rainbow. This will allow you to see how many of the colors they recognize, etc.

What to Say

I want to show everyone something I think is really beautiful. I made a rainbow game we can use in our center. Let's try it. Has anyone here ever seen a real rainbow after it rained? *(Model the rainbow manipulative and answer questions about rainbows for children, etc.)* Now let's go look at something new in our art center. I have made this part of it a rainbow center. And I have added a lot of wonderful art materials to make rainbows. Now we can all make rainbows whenever we would like to and in many different ways. *(Demonstrate the variety of possibilities, etc.)*

Assessment Focus

Use the Spatial Intelligence Observation Log Form to keep a note of individual children's spatial intelligence and interests in this area. Parents can also use this form for an at-home-assessment. Students can self-assess, showing they are happy about what they have learned about rainbows by choosing to wear the rainbows they have made.

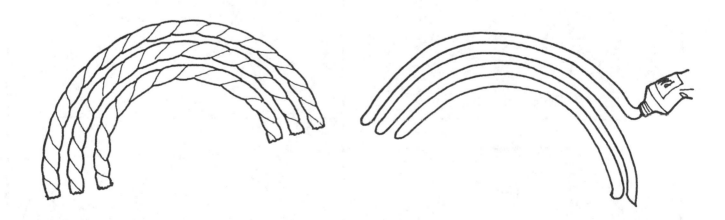

Hands-On Rainbows

Other Ways to Make Rainbows

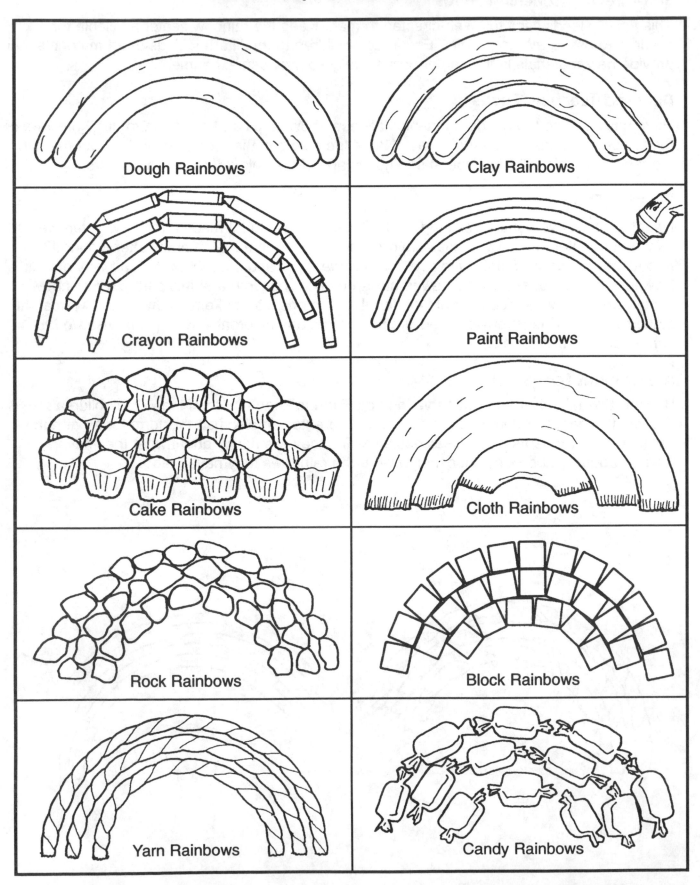

Dough Rainbows

Clay Rainbows

Crayon Rainbows

Paint Rainbows

Cake Rainbows

Cloth Rainbows

Rock Rainbows

Block Rainbows

Yarn Rainbows

Candy Rainbows

Rainbow

Directions: Cut the rainbow from pages 389-390, and piece it together and color it.

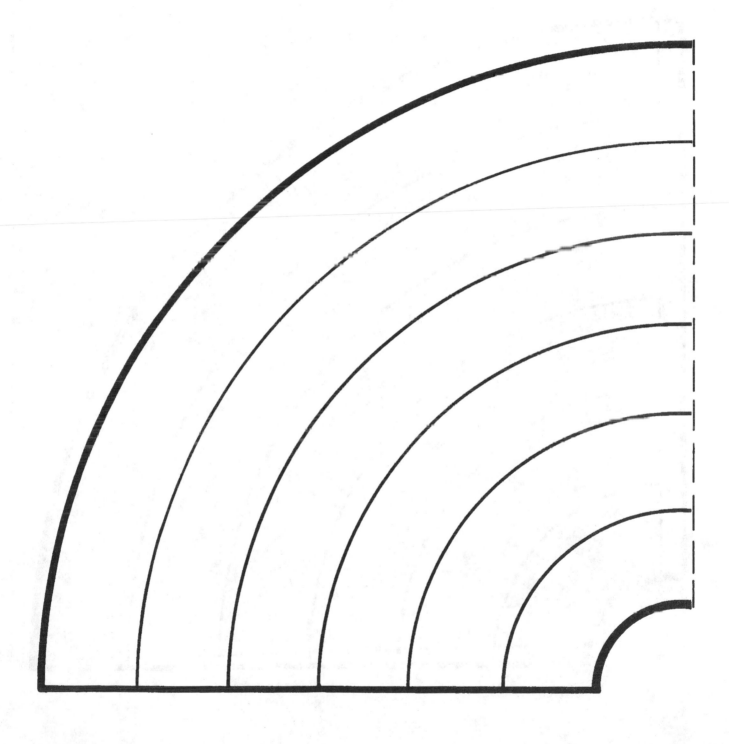

Rainbow *(cont.)*

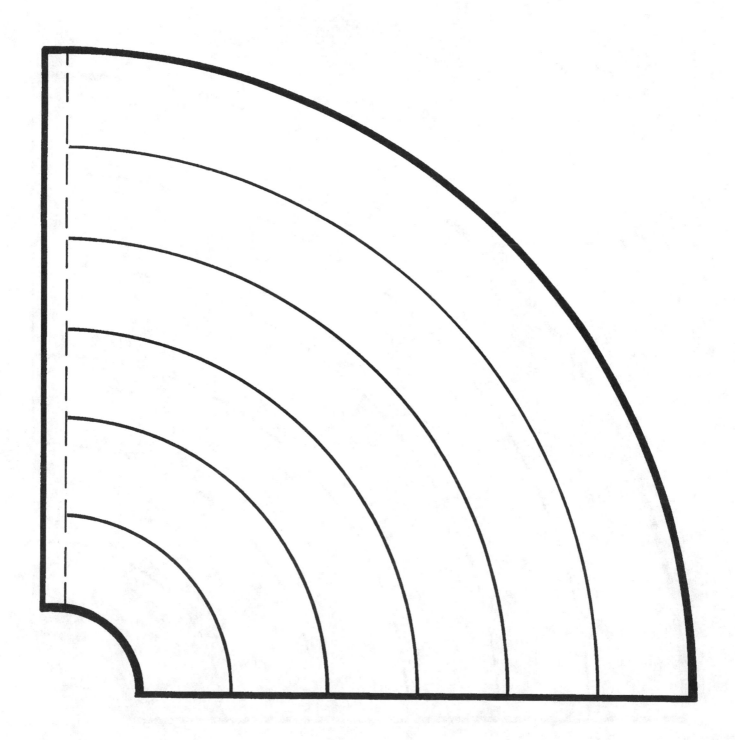

Sky

Directions: Enlarge to poster size using copy machine.

Making a Felt or Velcro Rainbow Set

Velcro

What You Need:

- rainbow master printed on colored paper or colored felt
- laminating materials
- Velcro ® strips
- glue
- good scissors
- easel

What You Do:

1. Color and laminate the entire rainbow and sky masters.
2. Mount the sky master on an easel or heavy cardboard.
3. Cut two pieces of Velcro the same size as the rainbow master.
4. Glue one piece of Velcro to the sky master.
5. Glue one piece of Velcro to each of the rainbow masters.
6. Cut the rainbow masters into color strips.
7. Attach the rainbow color strips to the sky master.

Felt

What You Need:

- colored felt
- glue
- felt board

What You Do:

1. Use the rainbow master as a guide to create several felt rainbows, color strips to be made into rainbows.
2. Make clouds.
3. Use the set to create felt rainbow manipulative scenes.

Spatial Intelligence Observation Log Form

—For the Parent—

Child's Name _____

Use this log on a daily basis to keep notes about what kind of spatial experiences your child is having every day. Remember, with a log, you can make these notes at the end of the day or anytime. It does not have to be while the experience is happening. Bring this log with you to your next parent/teacher meeting to discuss.

> **Spatial Intelligence**
> Spatial Intelligence is about the following:
> - pictures—making them and looking at them
> - art—drawing, painting, coloring, using clay, other art materials
> - color
> - the way things look
> - the way you see things

Day _____

_____

_____

_____

_____

_____

Day _____

_____

_____

_____

_____

_____

Spatial Intelligence Observation Log Form

—For the Teacher—

Child's Name _____

Use this log on a daily basis to keep notes about what kind of spatial experiences your child is having every day. Remember, with a log, you can make these notes at the end of the day or anytime. It does not have to be while the experience is happening. Compare and discuss this log at your next meeting with this child's parents.

Spatial Intelligence

Spatial Intelligence is about the following:

- pictures—making them and looking at them
- art—drawing, painting, coloring, using clay, other art materials
- color
- the way things look
- the way you see things

Day _____

_____

_____

_____

_____

_____

Day _____

_____

_____

_____

_____

_____

Shape Cupcakes

Logical-Mathematical Intelligence
Preparation Time: several hours

Multiple Intelligence Connection

This activity highlights the area of Logical-Mathematical Intelligence. That is a child's ability to use the intelligence of numbers and reasoning. This includes being able to understand mathematical ideas (at a developmentally appropriate level) numbers, shapes, basic logic, classifying, sorting, and other mathematics skills.

What You Need:

- cupcake shape patterns master, page 397
- cupcakes, one for each child participating
- M & M's or other colorful and easy to chew candy
- gummy bears, etc
- plastic containers
- napkins
- paper plates
- (punch optional)

Assessment Materials:

Teacher Assessment
Child Self Assessment
Parent Assessment

What to Do:

This activity will give children an opportunity to explore geometric shapes, their names, sorting, classifying, and basic logic skills while making shape cupcakes and enjoying the edible results!

To prepare for this activity, prepare at least one frosted cupcake for each child. *(It is a good idea to have some extras in case of accidents, upside down cupcakes, etc)*. Decide upon a variety of cupcake toppings that can be used to form shapes on top of cupcakes. There are a variety of alternatives, not all of them candy. You can use:

- alphabets cereal
- gummy bears
- M & M's
- frosting in small frosting tubes

- shapes cut out of fruit roll ups
- jelly beans
- sprinkles
- real fruit candies

Shape Cupcakes (cont.)

Prepare for this activity by inviting a few parent volunteers because this is one where children will need some assistance. Set up a cupcake shape area with access to water, paper towels, etc., and put the shape pictures and the candy materials in small plastic containers or bowls. Have children wear large T-shirts or aprons over their regular clothes, as this can get messy.

Begin this activity by talking with children about shapes. Use the shape master to see which shapes children recognize by names and model the names of the shapes for children. See who in your class can find a round or circle shape, a square shape etc. Then explain to children that they will be making shape cupcakes. Show children the cupcake making area and let children pick materials and make the shapes they want to on their cupcakes. As you are helping, mention the proper shape names to reinforce name and shape recognition. End the activity with a shape cupcake party, and add napkins and punch!

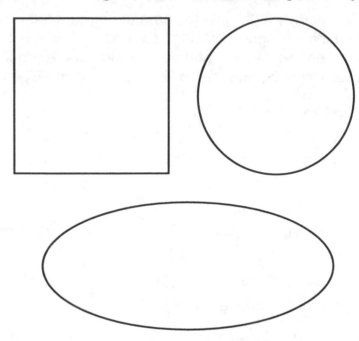

Self-Directed Teaching Focus

Enlarge the shape master on page 397 and add these shapes to your art center. Or, cut out various shapes of colored paper for children to use as drawing paper. Leave these in your art center for logical mathematical exploration.

Directed Teaching Focus

Ask children the names of the shapes daily in circle time. Make a day a "circle day." Give Good Job ribbons to children who can name the most circle shapes in the room.

What To Say

Today we are going to learn about shapes in a very nice way—by making shape cupcakes. Let's look at these shapes and see if we can name them and then I will show you how we will make our cupcakes. Let's all pick out our favorite shapes and use these candy and other small foods to make these shapes on our shape cupcakes. Let's try it!

Assessment Focus

Use the Logical-Mathematical Intelligence Observation Log form for participating parents to take time to observe. Teachers can use this same form. Have students make faces on their cupcakes to show how they feel about the activity.

Cupcake Shapes

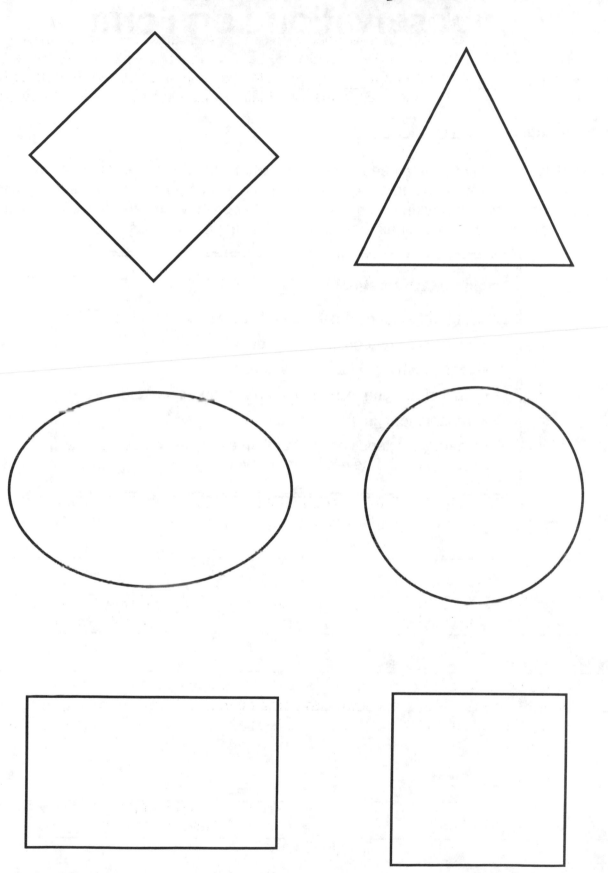

Logical-Mathematical Intelligence Observation Log Form

Child's Name _____

Parent's Name _____

Use this log on a daily basis to keep notes about what kind of logical-mathematical experiences your child is having every day. Remember, with a log, you can make these notes at the end of the day or anytime. It does not have to be while the experience is happening. Bring this log with you to your next parent/teacher meeting to discuss.

Logical-Mathematical Intelligence

Logical-Mathematical Intelligence is about the following:

- numbers, recognition and meaning
- logic, learning what makes sense
- critical thinking skills, being able to understand ideas
- reasoning, figuring things out
- math skills, addition subtraction, etc. (Remember, this is based on the developmental level.)

Day _____

_____

_____

_____

_____

_____

Day _____

_____

_____

_____

Bibliography

Althouse, Rosemary. *The Young Child: Learning with Understanding.* Teachers College Press, 1981.

Bredekamp, Sue and Teresa Rosegrant (Editors). *Reaching Potentials: Appropriate Curriculum and Assessment for Young Children, Volume 1.* National Association for the Education of Young Children, 1992.

Bringuier, Jean-Claude. *Conversations With Jean Piaget.* The University of Chicago Press, 1980.

Brockner, Joel. *Self-Esteem At Work: Research, Theory, and Practice.* Lexington Books, 1988.

Charles, C.M. *Educational Psychology: The Instructional Endeavor.* The C.V. Mosby Company, 1976.

Derman-Sparks, Louise. *Anti-Bias Curriculum: Tools for Empowering Young Children.* National Association for the Education of Young Children, 1991.

Dowling, Colette. *Perfect Women.* Summit Books, 1988.

Fallon, Berlie J. (Editor). *40 Innovative Programs in Early Childhood Education.* Lear Siegler, Inc./Fearon Publishers, 1973.

Fiscus, Edward D. and Colleen J. Mandell. *Developing Individualized Education Programs.* West Publishing Company, 1983.

Fowler, William. *Curriculum and Assessment Guides for Infant and Childcare.* Allyn and Bacon, Inc., 1980.

Genishi, Celia (Editor). *Ways of Assessing Children And Curriculum.* Teachers College Press, 1992.

Goldman, Jacquelin, et al. *Psychological Methods of Child Assessment.* Brunner/Mazel, Publishers, 1983.

Goodnow, Jacqueline. *Children's Drawing.* Open Books, 1977.

Hargis, Charles H. *Curriculum Based Assessment: A Primer.* Charles C. Thomas, 1987.

Holcombe, B.J. and Charmaine Wellington. *Search for Justice.* Stillpoint Publishing, 1992.

Hutchinson, Marcia Germaine. *Transforming Body Image.* The Crossing Press, 1985.

Idol, Lorna with Ann Nevin and Phyllis Paolucci-Whitcomb. *Models of Curriculum-Based Assessment.* Aspen Publishers, Inc., 1986.

Jones, Elizabeth and John Nimmo. *Emergent Curriculum.* National Association for the Education of Young Children, 1994.

Klein, Pnina and Abraham J. Tennenbaum (Editors). *To Be Young and Gifted.* Ablex Publishing Company. Norwood, 1992.

Krampen, Martin. *Children's Drawings: Iconic Coding of the Environment.* Plenum Press, 1991.

Labinowicz, Ed. *The Piaget Primer: Thinking, Learning, Teaching.* Addison-Wesley, 1980.

Bibliography *(cont.)*

Lindberg, Lucile and Rita Swedlow. *Early Childhood Education.* Allyn and Bacon, 1976.

Mack, John E. and Steven L. Ablon. *The Development and Sustenance of Self-Esteem in Childhood.* International Universities Press, Inc., 1983.

Meisels, Samuel J. with Sally Atkins-Burnett. *Developmental Screening In Early Childhood: A Guide, Fourth Edition.* National Association for the Education of Young Children, 1994.

Reynolds, Cecil R. and Julia H. Clark (Editors). *Assessment and Programming for Young Children with Low-Incidence Handicaps.* Plenum Press, 1983.

Shinn, Mark R. (Editor). *Curriculum-Based Measurement: Assessing Special Children.* The Guilford Press, 1989.

Siccone, Frank and Jack Canfield. *101 Ways to Develop Student Self-Esteem and Responsibility, Volume II.* Allyn and Bacon, 1993.

Stafford, Laura and Cherie L. Bayer. *Interaction Between Parents and Children.* Sage Publications, 1993.

Stant, Margaret A. *The Young Child: His Activities and Materials.* Prentice-Hall, 1972.

Steinem, Gloria. *Revolution from Within.* Little, Brown and Company, 1992.

Stipek, D., and S. Recchia and S. McClintic. *Self-Evaluation In Young Children.* University of Chicago Press, 1992.

Tarvis, Carol (Editor). *Every Woman's Emotional Well-Being.* Doubleday & Company, 1986.

Varma, Ved P. (Editor). *Anxiety in Children.* Croom Helm, 1984.

White, Burton L. *The First Three Years of Life.* Prentice-Hall, 1975.

Wiggin, Kate Douglas. *Children's Rights.* Houghton, Mifflin, 1992.

Williams, Harriet G. *Perceptual and Motor Development.* Prentice-Hall, 1983.

Acknowledgements

Rita Jamieson, Director of Step By Step Early Learning Center; Early Childhood Instructor, University of Riverside, Irvine Valley and Orange Coast Colleges, California.

Yvonne Woods, Professor of Child Development, Cerritos College, Norwalk, California.

Dorene Ruse, MA, Director of Linda Vista Child Care Center, Placentia-Yorba Linda Unified School District.

Verla Miller, President of Orange County Child Care Association, Owner and Operator of Va-Va's Little People.

Robert and Debra Miller, Owners and Operators of H.E.L.P. Child Care.

The Orange County Chapter for the Education of Young Children (OCAEYC)

and Daisy Jasmine, Early Child, Age 3.